Literature and Politics
in the Central American Revolutions

D1450999

New Interpretations of Latin America Series
Institute of Latin American Studies
University of Texas at Austin

LITERATURE AND POLITICS
in the CENTRAL AMERICAN REVOLUTIONS

**By John Beverley
and Marc Zimmerman**

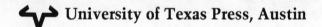 University of Texas Press, Austin

First Edition, 1990

Requests for permission to reproduce material from this work should be sent to:

Permissions
University of Texas Press
P.O. Box 7819
Austin, Texas 78713-7819

 ∞ The paper used in this publication meets the minimum requirements of American National Standard for Information Sciences—Permanence of Paper for Printed Library Materials, ANSI Z39.48–1984.

Library of Congress Cataloging-in-Publication Data

Beverley, John
    Literature and politics in the Central American revolutions / by John Beverley and Marc Zimmerman
      p. cm. — (New Interpretations of Latin America series)
      Includes bibliographical references and index.
    ISBN 0-292-74666-0. — ISBN 0-292-74672-5 (pbk.)
      1. Central American poetry—20th century—History and criticism.
2. Revolutionary poetry, Central America—History and criticism.
3. Politics and literature—Central America. 4. Literature and revolutions.
I. Zimmerman, Marc. II. Title. III. Series.
PQ7472.P7B48   1990
861—dc20   90-12667
                                               CIP

For our mothers:
Edith Pilcher and Dorothy Zimmerman

Contents

Preface

This book began in the intuition shared by its authors that what had been happening in modern Nicaraguan poetry was crucial to the development and eventual victory of the Sandinista Revolution. In our own "postmodern" North American culture, we are long past thinking of something like poetry as mattering much at all in the real world, so how could this be? Our answer is strongly influenced by recent developments in the theory of ideology that highlight the relational and discursively constituted nature of social identity itself. Though we do not share all aspects of their argument, we depend in particular on the insight advanced by Ernesto Laclau and Chantal Mouffe (1985)—itself built on the work of Antonio Gramsci and Louis Althusser—that what we think of as "society" as such is not some essence that is prior to representation but rather the product of struggles over meaning and representation. Such a perspective allows us to consider the ways in which literature, rather than being simply a reflection or epiphenomenon of the social as in the traditional base-superstructure model, is constitutive—in historically and socially specific ways—in some measure of it.

We propose to look at Central American literature as an ideological practice of national liberation struggle, emerging from a complex set of cultural relations and institutions given by tradition and encoding new forms of personal, national, and popular identity. Though we hope our conclusions will have some relevance to Central America as a whole, our focus is on the three countries where major revolutionary movements have emerged since the 1960s: Nicaragua, El Salvador, and Guatemala. A decade after the high tide of 1979–1981, of course, it is clear that the moment of optimism about the possibilities for rapid revolutionary victory and social transformation in these countries has passed (we write these words on the heels of the defeat of the Sandinistas in the Nicaraguan elections of February 1990). Whether this represents a new, postrevolutionary stage in the region's history or simply a recession before the appearance of a new cycle of radicalization is uncertain. It is likely, however, that any renewal of revolutionary activity will take somewhat different forms and involve actors other than the ones we will be concerned with here, and this may well modify our argument in important ways.

We will show that since the end of the nineteenth century a sometimes liberal-radical, sometimes ultrareactionary set of nationalist discourses develops in Central America, which finds its key, if not its only, means of expression in poetry. The reasons why such a tradition has not been recognized as important in the development of revolutionary activity in the region involve on the one hand academically sanctioned notions of art and literature that insist on their separation from politics, and on the other, the persistent prestige in the social sciences of a kind of economic reductionism—dependency theory would be an example—which sees the essential determinants of Latin American countries as their structural location in the world economy and cultural phenomena therefore as at best secondary. While we have no wish to deemphasize the economic or "objective" bases of revolutionary change—we argue in fact that it is the specific structure of socioeconomic dependency in Central America that positions literature as a crucial ideological practice—we share with Laclau and Mouffe a sense that, particularly in situations of large-scale political mobilization like revolutionary movements, the unity of a class or people is fundamentally a *symbolic* unity constructed in discursive practices.

How is this unity produced? Related to this question are the role of literature itself in the generation of an authentic and viable national culture in the face of the residues of colonialism and new forms of cultural imperialism, and the nature and role of sectors of the Central American intelligentsia involved in the formation of political and cultural vanguards in the region. The place that literature occupies in Central American societies is somewhat different from its place in the United States or even some other Latin American countries. To begin with, it is far from being a generalized cultural form. Less than a majority of the population of Nicaragua, El Salvador, and Guatemala is functionally literate; moreover, the distinction between the even smaller minority of persons who actually write and/or read literature and those who do not corresponds to deep class and, especially in the case of Guatemala, ethnic divisions. Literature as a social practice remains in Central America very much bound up with colonial and neocolonial structures of domination and privilege. While we argue that Central American writers have produced in their work a revolutionary or proto-revolutionary articulation of what Gramsci called the "national-popular," they are only heuristically genuinely national or popular voices, given that illiteracy, partial literacy, even the lack of institutionalization of literature itself at both a national and a regional level, are problems the revolutionary movements can begin to deal with effectively in a sense only *after* taking power.

At the same time, it is clear (1) that these movements, like similar ones in the colonial and postcolonial world, have generally involved a union of popular sectors (peasantry, wage workers, rural and urban poor) with a radicalized intelligentsia, drawn partly from formally educated members of these sectors but also from the petty bourgeoisie and bourgeois or oligarchic strata; and (2) that literature, precisely because it is marked as an elite cultural practice closely related to forms of political and bureaucratic power, has been an important means of radicalization of such an intelligentsia. Moreover, the institution of literature itself changes in the course of revolutionary mobilization and in postrevolutionary processes of cultural disalienation and appropriation that involve a transformation in the nature of its dominant forms and concerns, particularly a breakdown or renegotiation of the distinction between elite and popular, European and indigenous cultures on which its status and prestige have rested.

We begin with a discussion of a number of theoretical issues concerning the relation of literature, ideology, and politics in general and their relevance to the structural characteristics of Latin and Central American development. We move on in chapter 2 to sketch the main lines of evolution of Central American literary culture up to the eve of the revolutionary period, with special attention to its role in the formation and radicalization of sectors of the regional intelligentsia. This leads to the core of the book, which is a presentation in chapters 3 to 6 of the evolution of a regional literary system—with distinct national trajectories in Nicaragua, El Salvador, and Guatemala—beginning in the late nineteenth century with Rubén Darío and *modernismo*, passing through the so-called *vanguardista* literary movements of the 1920s and 1930s, and culminating in the writers of the 1960s and 1970s who link their work in literature more or less directly to the building of revolutionary organizations. We highlight the work of the three most significant poets of this third phase—Ernesto Cardenal in Nicaragua, Roque Dalton in El Salvador, and Otto René Castillo in Guatemala—and the coincident movement in women's poetry. We also describe the Nicaraguan poetry workshop project (*poesía de taller*) initiated by Cardenal and recent developments in literature in the context of the evolution of the Guatemalan and Salvadoran revolutionary movements, including an account of the major debates over cultural and literary policy. Finally, we analyze in some detail the *testimonio* (testimonial narrative), which has become the most influential narrative form associated with the Central American revolutions.

We alluded to the fashionable topic of postmodernism in our opening sentences. In our work on this book, we found ourselves thinking time and time again about this concept and its relation to contemporary Central American and Third World cultural production. Though it may be of concern mainly to readers in literary and cultural studies, we need to say a few words about it here. As Fredric Jameson (1984) has pointed out, postmodernism in its most general sense (the term is notoriously subject to imprecision in its uses) is a periodizing concept whose function is to correlate the emergence of new formal features in culture with the technological, economic, and social features of a new, "multinational" stage of capitalism. Clearly, there is a problem in applying a concept that is conceived in relation to the cultural anomie of advanced capitalist consumer societies to social formations such as those of Central America that in a sense have not gone through the phase of "modernity" yet. (A r elated problem is that *modernismo* and *postmodernismo* designate in Latin American Spanish specific early-twentieth-century literary movements that have no relation to what is understood as modernism and postmodernism in English.) Clearly, there is also a correspondence between cultural phenomena identified as postmodernist—North American television and fashion, for example—and the present sensibility and strategies of multinational capitalism, which give some credence to the idea that postmodernism may be a new form of cultural imperialism.

However, we think there is also an important sense in which the forms of cultural resistance represented by the Central American revolutions themselves rise up on a postmodern terrain, understood in a broad sense. The two central, and interrelated, problematics that are usually taken as defining postmodern culture as such are: (1) the collapse of the distinction between elite and popular (or mass) cultures, sometimes expressed as the loss of aesthetic autonomy, and (2) the collapse of the "great narratives" of "Western" progress and enlightenment with which the specifically aesthetic project of Modernist art was associated, a collapse that includes what is often designated as the "crisis of Marxism" (Lyotard 1984). The ideological and political significance of the literature we are concerned with elucidating depends on its ability (1) to function in the historically constituted space that separates elite and popular cultures in the region; and (2) to generate a new postcolonial, noneurocentric narrative of historical space and destiny. If it has been largely Marxist in inspiration, it has also been concerned with redefining an inherited European Marxist tradition to respond to the very different dynamics of Central American society and history. In these senses, we see this literature as coincident with postmodernism, rather than its other.

The general critique of postmodernism by the Latin American left (see, e.g., Yúdice 1985a) tends, we think, to set up a false dichotomy between complex, antirepresentational, value-leveling and predominantly "high-culture" forms of literature (of the sort represented by Borges or the work of the Latin American boom novelists) and simple, lineal, representational, value-affirming, forms of "folk" or popular culture. The first, in this view, is seen as in some sense or other imported or imposed from above, the second as a spontaneous and authentic creation of the people in conditions of underdevelopment and exploitation. Our perspective suggests that, rather than a clear dichotomy between a purely popular culture of resistance and a purely oligarchic and/or neocolonial high culture, Latin American literature in general has involved since its origins in the colonial period a series of shifts and transformations that play off elite and popular cultural forms. We want to posit Central American revolutionary literature as in effect involved in and constructed out of a dialectic of oppressor and oppressed, negotiating between the opposing terms of its dichotomies: literature/oral narrative and song, metropolitan/national, European/Creole, ladino or mestizo/indigenous, elite/popular, urban/rural, and intellectual/manual work. We by no means see this literature as transcending these dichotomies—that would require as we have suggested a series of social and cultural transformations that have as their minimal prior condition the victory of these revolutions in the first place; but we do see this literature as constituting new possibilities of articulating them and, in particular, of defining new paradigms of the relationship between the intelligentsia and popular classes. In this sense, we argue that literature has been in Central America not only a means of politics but also a model for it.

In focusing on poetry, we are choosing to deal with literary expressions within the dominant Spanish-speaking Creole-mestizo cultural tradition of Central America. This tradition is nationally inflected in different ways, but has excluded until fairly recently—and then usually only in the context of the revolutionary movements themselves—other voices: those of the indigenous, non-Spanish-speaking peoples in the region, particularly in Guatemala; of minorities like the English-speaking black population of the Atlantic coast of Nicaragua; of women (the few important Central American women writers prior to the 1960s like Claudia Lars in El Salvador are exceptions that confirm the rule).

While our thesis is that this poetry has been a materially decisive force in the Central American revolutions, it is also important to stress that it is by no means their only significant or important ideological practice. There is, for example, the very rich heritage of Central American indigenous and mestizo oral culture: song—particularly the traditional *corrido* or narrative ballad, but also including new styles of urban popular music and hybrid folk music (what in Latin America is usually designated as *nueva trova*)—street theater, storytelling, *refranes*, myth and superstition, forms of rumor and gossip. There is the complex ideological substratum provided by nineteenth-century Liberalism and Conservatism. There is the field of indigenous and European religious ideologies implicated in both Liberation Theology and Indian resistance movements in the region. There are the innumerable anonymous individual and collective strategies of daily survival and resistance. There is an important sense that remains to be adequately described and theorized—Ché Guevara outlined some of its elements in his account of the guerrilla *foco*—in which the revolutionary organizations themselves are as much cultural as military-political forms, concerned with the articulation of symbols of power, resistance, and domination. To tell the story of all of this would be a much more complex and ambitious task than the one we propose, however.

While we argue that the institution of literature as such and the "national question" become conjuncturally related in the process of Central American development (so that even a nominally apolitical writing can have measurable ideological consequences), and on this basis we include a considerable amount of literary history, our account should not be taken as a general introduction to modern Central American literature. Despite our attention to *testimonio*, we do not provide anything like an adequate account of developments in the novel, short story, and theater.

Costa Ricans and Hondurans will question in particular our decision to limit our focus to Guatemala, Nicaragua, and El Salvador, pointing out that their countries have traditions of proto-revolutionary nationalist writing quite similar to the ones we describe, and that in any case literature functions in Central America on a regional as well as national basis. This is true—the significance of Ernesto Cardenal or Otto René Castillo's poetry is by no means limited to their respective countries, for example; by the same token the great Costa Rican proletarian novel *Mamita Yunai* or the contemporary protest poetry of Honduran Roberto Sosa have been factors in Central American literary culture generally (there is also the question of the relation of Panama to contemporary Central America). But in defense of our choice, we need to insist on the obvious: revolutionary processes involving broad popular participation have developed in Nicaragua, El Salvador, and Guatemala in the last twenty-five years, but not in Honduras or Costa Rica. The reasons for this are complex (see, e.g., Dunkerley 1988 and Vilas 1989 for a current discussion); they certainly cannot be reduced simply to a question of different literary-cultural systems, nor do they exclude the possibility, particularly in the case of Honduras, of eventual revolutionary upsurges.

However, they do make Honduras and Costa Rica less than paradigmatic in terms of the problem of the relation of literature to revolutionary mobilization we want to explore here.

The ideal of Central American unity is an important feature not only of the ideology but also of the long-term strategy of the revolutionary movements in the area, but in general we have not been able to articulate the relationship among international, regional, and nationally specific levels in Central American cultural dynamics—a problem faced in a different way by the revolutionary movements themselves. One sign of this was an indecision on our part as to whether we should speak of a Central American *revolution* or Central American *revolutions*.

Ideologies generally operate at some level as historicisms; that is, they give a sense of shape and meaning to historical experience. In developing our argument, we run the risk of historicism ourselves, of constructing a teleological narrative that reduces the complexity of the social and cultural phenomena we deal with to a perspective peculiar to our own time, or more accurately to our own structure of hopes and convictions. We take this risk, because we believe that the reality of historical becoming—and by extension the validity of our approach—is at least in part a matter of position taking and struggle. We have not been able to separate problems of focus and method from the concrete practice of the revolutionary movements themselves. This is a book *about* ideology, then, but also one situated *in* ideology.

In different degrees, we have both been involved in the cultural practice of the Central American revolutions. However, the main limitation of our study (which is perhaps also the precondition for the kind of theoretical abstraction it involves) is that we write at a considerable distance from the direct cultural producers and from the rich and complex national and regional traditions that they articulate. We expect that they may find much of it overly schematic when not simply misinformed or wrong-headed.

We hope, nevertheless, that what we have done here will be of interest not only to them, but also to Latin American and Central America specialists in the academy and to a broader audience of persons involved in literature and poetry, cultural studies, and political or humanitarian work, particularly in Central American solidarity and human rights organizations and in movements for social justice and change throughout the Americas.

Because of space limitations we have not been able to give much representation or description of the actual poetry or narrative. A number of anthologies and individual works of Central American literature currently available in English are included in the bibliography. Unless otherwise noted, all translations in the book are our own.

We owe a common debt to many people in making this book. Among them are Margaret Randall, Barbara Harlow, Steven White, Sergio Ramírez, Claribel Alegría, Sandy Taylor and Curbstone Press, Ernesto Cardenal, Manlio Argueta, Ileana Rodríguez, George Yúdice, Ivan Uriarte, Hugo Achugar, Todd Jailer, Hernán Vidal and the Ideologies and Literature group at the University of Minnesota, Fred Jameson, the Marxist Literary Group, and Richard Graham at the University of Texas Institute of Latin American Studies for his interest in this project and editorial help with it. The authors were both graduate students in the Department of Literature of the University of California, San Diego, in the late 1960s, an experience to which we owe this collaboration and which has marked its concerns and approach deeply. John Beverley would like to thank in particular the Department of Spanish and Portuguese at Stanford University for allowing him to try out some ideas for this book in a seminar on Central American Revolutionary Literature in the spring of 1986; the Center for Latin American Studies of the University of Pittsburgh for a grant to finish writing it; and the people of the municipality of San Isidro, Pittsburgh's Sister City in Nicaragua, for being "the soul of a heartless world." Marc Zimmerman would like to thank Otto Pizaka and the Latin American Studies Program of the University of Illinois at Chicago for encouraging him to develop a course based on the material in this book; UIC's Circulation Desk and Interlibrary Loan Staff (Kathy Kilian, Michael Williams, and, above all, Janice McFadden) for many services; the Fulbright Program of the Council for the International Exchange of Scholars, and UIC's Office of Social Science Research for financial support; Mario Widel for help with computer problems; Raúl Rojas and Andrea Barrientos for research assistance; and—in the last hours—Yolanda Miranda, Leta Daly, Margo de Ley, Carmen Matute, Amada Cabrera Urizar, Esther Soler, and Max Araújo.

Literature and Politics
in the Central American Revolutions

1. Literature, Ideology, and Hegemony

One of the most difficult challenges any movement for social change faces is how to create an effective counterhegemonic ideology, a vision of how things can and should be different that will, in Lenin's phrase, "grip the masses." If in turn ideology is materialized in cultural activities, including literature and the arts, these may become in certain circumstances a decisive component of political mobilization rather than its mere accompaniment (as in what we might call the cheerleader theory of political art). Are explicitly political forms of literature like protest poems or songs the expression or reflection of a radicalized consciousness that is *already there*, engendered directly by inequality or exploitation in the social and economic arrangements of a society; or is it rather that political consciousness is itself consciously or unconsciously *produced* in the cultural elaboration of sensations, images, myths, visions, and expectations that happens in, among many other places, literature and the arts? It is a truism that the existence of oppressive social conditions is a necessary but not a sufficient cause for the emergence of revolutionary will. Exploitation may be an objective fact of a given set of relations of production, but the way it is experienced existentially has to do with the way human subjects are positioned in ideology.

Literature as an Ideological Practice

We propose to consider some aspects of modern Central American literature as an ideological practice of national liberation struggle. By ideology—to refer to Althusser's well-known definition—we understand the representation of an imaginary relation between the individual and his or her real conditions of existence.[1] We assume that ideologies are not simply images or mental ideas (distorted, inverted, or the like, as Marx suggested in *The German Ideology*); they must be produced in and by practices—philosophical, legal, political, aesthetic, pedagogic, psychosexual—located in concrete social institutions like the family, the school, religious institutions, fashion and custom, the arts, the media. Such practices reflect and engender at the same time the will of individuals and/or social groups to maintain or posit the conditions of their actual or potential domination. The "work" of ideology consists in constituting (Althusser: interpellating) human subjects as such, with coherent gender, ethnic, class, or national identities appropriate to their place in a given social order or, in the case of counterhegemonic ideologies, their place in a possible social order. Ideologies provide human beings with a structure of experience that enables them to recognize themselves in the world, to see the world as in some way created *for* them, to feel they have a place and identity in it.

Ideologies have multiple power functions (of distinction, domination, subordination) that are not reducible to or intelligible in terms of class or group interests alone, although they are the sites in which class or group struggle occurs. Similarly, they are not always circumscribed by modes of production or concrete social formations; they can cut across modes of production and social formations, as in the case of religious ideologies. In particular, ideologies are not reducible to politics or political programs or isms, because their nature is unconscious rather than explicit; their effect is to produce in the subject a sense of things as natural, self-evident, a matter of common sense.[2] Political practices— say of parties, organized groups, or movements—represent specific articulations on the terrain of ideology.

Language is the principal symbolic system through which human beings represent their relation with the norms and projects of a social collectivity. This supposes that the means of ideological interpellation are primarily, though not exclusively, discourse. In all human societies narrative is a basic form of ideology since it serves to organize the randomness of lived experience into a meaningful sequence that appears to have the character of necessity or fate. In those societies where it has developed—because it is far from being a universal cultural form— literature, as a special sort of poetic and narrative discourse, is then an ideological practice par excellence.

The dominant academic approaches to literature, however, have limited the awareness and study of the full consequences of this asser- tion. On a methodological level, we refer in particular to formalism. The root of the formalist approach to art is to be found in Kant's definition of the aesthetic effect as the experience of a "purposiveness without purpose" and his consequent distinction between aesthetic and tele- ological judgment. In wanting to constitute the study of the forms of art as separate academic disciplines, it was thought necessary to define their specific nature as objects of knowledge. In considering literature, formalism distinguishes between "poetic" or literary language and ordinary language. The "aesthetic effect" of literature is held to result from the "estrangement" or "dehabitualization" that a poetic language operates on the normal processes of linguistic representation. A habitualized perception is one molded by its instrumentality within the routines of everyday life. Politics and ideology are seen as forms of social utilitarianism and therefore as extrinsic to the aesthetic experience as such. For formalism—or what has sometimes been called an "intrinsic" approach to literature, centered on the dynamics of the text—aesthetic effect and ideological effect are not simply different, they are in a sense opposed.[3]

We don't want to question the appropriateness of the art/ideology distinction in all contexts. For one thing, it does reflect the ways in which art and literature become independent from religion and court patronage, and the consequent separation of the spheres of science, morality, and culture in the modern world. The aesthetic idealism of Kant and the European Romantics—which Marx and the early socialists shared—was among other things both a recognition of the new commodity status of artworks (which freed them from the restrictions imposed by feudal patronage) and at the same time a reaction against the philistinism and utilitarianism of the emerging capitalist value system. In a more contemporary context, Herbert Marcuse's celebration of the counterculture, based on a formalist aesthetics and an idealist ethics, was an important component of the politics of the New Left in the 1960s. For Marcuse (1978), it was precisely the autonomy of art insisted on by critical formalism that was the locus of its radicalizing and redemptive power, the sense in which, by alienating practical or instrumental reason, it sides with the repressed and challenges domination and exploitation, particularly the rationality of capitalist institutions.

Such a view has been associated with the work of the Frankfurt School in general and has tended to permeate academic work in the sociology of culture. We feel, however, that it has a number of serious limitations as a normative model for both cultural production itself and its representation in cultural studies: for example, a general contempt for mass or popular culture as degraded or fetishized; an excessive reaction against social realism and other forms of message-oriented art, which despite the distortions they undergo in the official art of the Stalinist era in the socialist countries, represent extensive and important movements in modern art; the consequent belief that art can only be a negation of the status quo when it is not being used directly for utilitarian political ends, which in practice limits oppositional art to avant garde art.

There is a different way of conceptualizing the relation of art and ideology that depends on breaking down the disciplinary separation between humanities and social sciences in the study of art and culture, and the fact/value distinction as it operates in the social sciences. If, to recall Althusser's definition, ideology is what constitutes the human subject in relation to the "real" (e.g., of a particular society or historical conjuncture), then the domain of ideology is not simply a worldview or set of (verbal) ideas, but rather the ensemble of signifying practices through which social identities are formed, that is, culture. On the model of the Enlightenment critique of religion, the force of the art/ ideology distinction is in part given by the tendency to confuse ideology as such with a particular ideology that is being contested. If, as classical Marxism maintained, feudal or bourgeois ideologies were forms of false consciousness, in the sense that they misrepresented the real situation of the subject in society (by masking exploitative relations of production), socialism is no less an ideology in that it must also construct an imaginary representation of and for the subject (new forms of personal duty and morality, new senses of history and destiny).

The traditional problematic of ideology in the social sciences, founded in both its positivist and Marxist variants on the epistemological question of distinguishing "true" from "false" forms of consciousness, has been displaced in contemporary cultural studies by the recognition suggested in psychoanalytic theory that truth *for* the subject is something distinct from the truth *of* the subject, given that it entails an act of identification between the self and something external to it.[4] Indeed, the nature of truth itself is, in this perspective, ideologically determined. From the point of view of positive science (*connaissance*), all ideologies involve a structure of misrecognition of reality (*méconnaissance*); on the other hand, collective or individual human agents are conscious of themselves as such (e.g., as subjects of history in the case of social movements) only in and through ideology.

The question then is not whether ideology is present in works of art and literature, or whether—to allude to a commonplace conception— great art transcends ideology (whereas, presumably, bad or mediocre art does not), but rather what ideology or ideologies are present. The social reception of the artwork is precisely one of the places where ideology happens. What formalism wanted to isolate as an autonomous "aesthetic effect" is a way of describing the material incidence of ideology on consciousness.

The ideological effect of a given work of literature is not, however, something immanent in the text or, for that matter, always the same in different circumstances. It depends rather on the way the text is activated by its audience in specific sociohistoric circumstances, which depends in turn on the ideological practices that bear on how literature is read and interpreted in those circumstances (e.g., literary pedagogy and criticism, the formation and transformation of literary canons, the way a given text may be combined with other concerns, as in the common situation where a work of the past is seen as touching on issues in the present). That is why, to take a case we will be looking at in more detail, the poetry of Rubén Darío might be read as reactionary in a given conjuncture (the moment of Nicaraguan vanguardism in the 1930s), while in another (articulated with Sandinista cultural nationalism in the 1960s) it can have progressive or even revolutionary connotations. The question is not the correctness of the interpretation of Darío in each of these cases, but rather the respective uses they make of Darío as an ideological signifier.[5]

An Example: One Hundred Years of Solitude

Where an earlier Marxist literary criticism—the work of Georg Lukács is exemplary in this respect—was bound up with the question of the adequacy of the ways in which different forms of literature represented social reality, the dominant note in contemporary cultural theory has been to stress precisely the illusory character of literature, which is seen on the model of Althusser's account of ideology as a way of producing discursively a sensation or "effect" of the real mediated by desire. Literature is a form of experiencing the real; it confirms or problematizes the relation of its reader or listener with the real.

Most readers will be familiar with Gabriel García Márquez's novel *Cien años de soledad* [One hundred years of solitude] (1967) as a fiction that condenses symbolically a number of features of the history of Colombia in particular and Latin America in general. In the terms we have just outlined, the novel is not so much a representation of the reality of this history (something that would be the object of study of the social sciences) as of those psychic identifications through which this reality has been experienced or, to use the Althusserian term, "lived" (which can include the magical or supernatural states of mind the novel describes).

In other words, what *Cien años* is about is ideology. It presents a new way of experiencing the historical past and potential of Latin America in its yet incomplete or uncertain project of national liberation. In particular, the logic (or illogic) of the novel questions the premises of Liberal historicism as an ideology adequate to Latin American development; it is a deconstruction of the Liberal "century," which extends in Latin America roughly from independence to World War I and its aftermath. This impulse corresponds in turn to the economic, cultural, and organizational crises of traditional elites in Latin America in the context of expanded penetration by multinational capital and the rapid growth of industry and consumer markets experienced after World War II.

For García Márquez the genetic moment of Latin American independence is also a traumatic one. The anabasis that will lead to the foundation of Macondo in the nineteenth century begins at the end of the sixteenth with a narcissistic aversion to history: the great-great-grandmother of the matriarch of the Buendía dynasty flees inland, escaping the attack of Sir Francis Drake on the coastal city of Riohacha. Drake and his pirates suggest in *Cien años* the primitive forms of the emergence of the bourgeois world. Many centuries later, the Anglos will return in the form of the "leaf storm" (*hojarasca*) of the banana plantation. But here, at the edge of Latin America's present as history, the expected apotheosis of the Buendías—who symbolize the nineteenth-century Liberal oligarchy—collapses instead into a sort of historical-cultural black hole.

Under the surface melodrama and fantasy, the basic experiences of Macondo are those of fear, dependency, sterility, repression, and amnesia. The narrative time of the novel turns out to be a pseudotime where a traumatic fixation repeats itself endlessly: Macondo is "a city of mirrors (or mirages)." The apocalyptic ending of the novel, by now a cliché of Latin American boom fiction, creates a sort of semiotic tabula rasa where new ideological inscriptions—representing new class or group forces and projects in Latin America—can be made.

In this sense, *Cien años* coincides with and supplements the account of Latin American political economy and development generated more or less at the same time by dependency theory. What it does not provide, however, is the precise *political* form that these new inscriptions might take, which could range from, for example, modernizing forms of bourgeois nationalism like Christian Democracy, to Peronism and the various modes of Latin American populism, to guerrilla *foco* theory, to Liberation Theology. Given García Márquez's own public position of solidarity with the Cuban Revolution, we may imagine that for him what fills the void at the end of the failed epic of the Buendías is Fidel Castro's epic vision in *The Second Declaration of Havana* of the dispossessed and marginalized masses of Latin America taking center stage in its future history. But this is not something represented in the text; indeed, the apocalypse of Macondo also envelops an earlier stage of Latin American radicalism represented by the banana workers' strike; nor is García Márquez explicitly political—in a propagandistic sense—in any of his novels, short stories, or journalism. His work produces an ideological effect without being explicitly political: several different kinds of politics might be read into it.

Nevertheless, this way of looking at literature assumes the possibility, consciously contrived or not, of a closer correspondence between artistic practices and forms of political domination and mobilization. Like most Latin American literary figures, García Márquez is still very much what

Gramsci called a "traditional intellectual"; although a fellow traveler of the left, he is not directly bound up with a specific social group, political party, or movement, and depends generally on commercial publishing houses—increasingly controlled in Latin America by transnational capital—to get his work to a public.

But there is the rather different question of how to evaluate literature produced in a direct connection to the interests and projects of particular social groups, parties, or movements, literature that has an explicit political "tendency." The usual response—again founded on a formalist ideology of the aesthetic—is that literature suffers by being subordinated to politics of any kind, that even the best progressive literature is dictated by the freely exercised talent and imagination of its author rather than partisan political instrumentalities. We doubt that this is the case as a matter of fact. More important for our purposes here, however, a number of the writers we will be considering—like Roque Dalton, Otto René Castillo, and Leonel Rugama—represent a new type of Latin American intellectual: no longer, like García Márquez, the "fellow traveler" who occupies the relatively privileged social position of the intellectual or *letrado*, but rather a cadre of national liberation struggle movements for whom the intricate cabala of Marxist-Leninist sectarianism and clandestine struggle is as familiar as the world of Parisian surrealism. The problem with such writers is to understand how they consciously stake the artistic success or failure of their work in literature on its effectiveness as a means for building and maintaining a revolutionary movement: how, in other words, they produce a "party literature."

Party Literature?

The concept of party literature comes from Lenin's 1905 essay "Party Literature and Party Organization" (1971), which was subsequently much abused as a justification for party control and censorship of literature during the Stalin period in the Soviet Union. Lenin's main point, nevertheless, merits recalling. He argued that it was possible and desirable for writers to conceive of their work as part of the overall political work of a revolutionary party or movement, and therefore subject, via democratic centralism, to its discipline or guidance.

Lenin was quick to caution that not all literature should be of this type and that a party could not simply dictate to the artist. But he was suggesting for at least some writers a new role model, and a new way of putting their work in relation to collective social processes and organizations, which could be posed against the traditional ideal of the writer or artist as an individual creator and not incidentally an entrepreneur (who might or might not be in accord with the goals of a party or political movement).

We rejoin here the point that revolutionary political consciousness does not derive directly or spontaneously from exploitative economic relations, that it must be in some sense produced. Successful revolutionary movements in this century have generally involved a union of working-class—or to use a more inclusive term, popular—forces with a radicalized intelligentsia, drawn partly from formally educated sections of the working class but also from the petite bourgeoisie and déclassé bourgeois strata, which have become imbued with socialist theory, culture, and organizational forms. But if this is the case—and whatever their originality, the Central American revolutions are certainly no exception to it—then the question of what practices produce a revolutionary or potentially revolutionary intelligentsia becomes a decisive one. What is clear in this respect is that literature, in the form it assumes in modern societies, has been one of those practices, particularly in the sense that the appreciation of literature is closely bound up with the development of subject identity (through the usual processes of identification, projection, and so on we have alluded to above).[6]

Modern literature is historically the product of a prior ideological struggle against feudal culture. Its emergence, generalization, and prestige as a cultural form depend on such factors as its usefulness as a secular surrogate for the oral myths and religious texts and rituals of precapitalist societies, the development of print technology and the emergence of the book as a commodity with the requisite networks of production and distribution, new conceptions of individual rights and citizenship that stress the formative role of literature, and corresponding forms of mass public education that allow for the social production of an extended reading public. All of these factors can be unevenly developed between one nation-state and another, between regions of the same state, between classes, between genders, and between ethnic groups.

But if literature is not formative of the people as such, it is formative of strata that have been and will be decisive in initiating revolutionary ideas and organizations. Students, professionals and technicians, journalists, teachers, seminarians and clergy, artists, social workers, young officers or noncoms—for such members of the middle strata in dependent societies like those of Central America, as well as for sectors of an actual or would-be national bourgeoisie, there is not always an identity of interests with the power bloc represented by the local oligarchies in alliance with foreign interests. In particular, this nonidentity can be articulated through the belief that the dominant bloc has retarded or repressed the full development of a national culture in both its popular and elite forms. The maximum counterhegemonic efficacy is achieved in the characterization of the oligarchy as philistine or uncultured. The aesthetic as such, which in situations of bourgeois normality has a generally affirmative and apolitical character, can function in peripheral social formations to define and stimulate discontent with the status quo and to provide alternative senses of social possibility. The educated classes, which are in Third World societies the primary audience for modern literature, span a series of contradictory sociocultural locations that can be mobilized for, or against, movements for reform or revolution. Precisely because it is a socially privileged cultural form, imbricated in colonial and neocolonial forms of status consciousness, literature can be a matter of passionate concern to these strata, closely bound up with personal self-images and ideals. It is therefore a key place to link private experiences of authenticity and alienation to the awareness of collective situations of social exploitation, injustice, and national underdevelopment.[7]

We will come back to the issue of the particular valence of literature as a cultural form in Central America. What is important for the moment is the idea that literature can be a means of producing the subject position of a radicalized intelligentsia. With the proviso that neither it nor the parties involved are much like those traditionally associated with Leninism, much of the poetry and prose literature we will be dealing with is "party literature" in the sense that its finality *as art* is to activate, mobilize, and maintain revolutionary consciousness and organizations.

Intellectuals, Literature, and the National-Popular

Few if any intellectual groups could contend for hegemony unless, intentionally or by accident of history, their project begins to embody and articulate the aspirations latent in the popular classes, whose exploitation in social formations like those of Central America is predicated precisely on their exclusion from the sort of high culture represented by written literature. Part of what has determined the ebb and flow of the Central American intelligentsia has been its need to adapt to the shifting relations of hegemony of classes and class fractions whose projects, in turn, are represented or authorized ideologically by specific sectors of this intelligentsia. How and to what degree do intellectuals become representative not of their initial social group or class, but of the whole range of popular forces potentially available for a revolutionary project—that is, for the overthrow and transformation of the institutions, including the cultural-artistic, which maintain previous structures of hegemony?

In remarking above on the role of literature in authorizing the identity and activity of intellectuals, we have in mind Gramsci's (1985) well-known discussion of the role of intellectuals in Italian history. To recall simply the main lines of this: For Gramsci, there is no innate distinction between intellectuals and nonintellectuals. Intellectuals are the designated specialists in the production and reproduction of ideas and values for specific social classes or groups, some of which (as well as their linguistic, intellectual, and cultural conventions) are more dominant in a given social formation than others. Intellectuals do this by taking up existing bodies of knowledge and, according to existing divisions of institutional and extrainstitutional intellectual practice, seeking to work these bodies of knowledge in favor of the hegemony of the class or social group whose interests they represent.

For Gramsci, the arena of intellectual work was increasingly important in thinking about the possibilities of revolutionary change in Italy, given on the one hand the peculiarity of Italian history and on the other the rise of fascism, which forced on the European left in a particularly dramatic way the realization that social subjects responded to economic and political forces through the grid of ideological and still deeper cultural patterns, attitudes, and values. The question for Gramsci—sometimes suggested in his slogan of a "long march through the institutions"—was one of the struggle for hegemony in and over the means of intellectual and cultural production. This required in turn the development of groups of intellectuals who would, in the fashion envisioned by Lenin for writers, systematically and consciously devote themselves to the creation of a new culture that would help to bring about a new social and economic order.

Gramsci argued that every relationship of hegemony is necessarily an educational relationship. A given social class or intraclass bloc achieves hegemony when its project can appear as the embodiment of popular and/or national will, what Gramsci called the "national-popular" (sometimes also the "people-nation"). The concept of national-popular is at once a cultural one—associated with progressive forms in literature and the arts—and a political one, designating the possibility of an alliance or bloc of different social agents in a given society around a common program. As David Forgacs has noted (1984), these two apparently distinct senses are in fact related. The concept of national-popular emerges in connection with Gramsci's thoughts about the function and evolution of national literatures in European history since the Renaissance, where he argues that the absence of an Italian popular realist literature, like the serialized novel in France or Britain or the work of Tolstoy in Russia, was a factor in the political disunity of Italy and the partial failure of the democratic Risorgimento in the nineteenth century. This absence stemmed from the separation produced in the

Renaissance between a humanistic intelligentsia and the Italian popular classes. Where in other parts of Europe humanism and the new secular vernacular literature it projected became proto-democratic forms, in Italy, as in Spain and Latin America, they were co-opted under the impulse of the Counter-Reformation by Catholic seignorial ideology. Consequently, in Italy, Gramsci noted, "neither a popular artistic literature nor a local production of 'popular' literature exists because 'writers' and 'people' do not have the same conception of the world." Where "in France the meaning of 'national' already includes a more politically elaborated notion of 'popular' because it is related to the concept of 'sovereignty': national sovereignty and popular sovereignty have, or had, the same value . . . in Italy the 'national' does not coincide with 'popular' because in Italy the intellectuals are distant from the people, i.e. from the 'nation'. They are tied instead to a caste tradition that has never been broken by a strong popular or national political movement from below" (Gramsci 1985: 206–208).[8]

This is to suggest (1) that the relation between the two terms of the concept—national and popular—is one of a moving equilibrium that can shift ideologically one way or another depending on who controls their representation (and how they control it); and (2) that therefore the relation is mediated by the concrete nature of the relation between the intelligentsia and the popular classes in a given society. In the case of Italy, Gramsci argued, the "nation" had been more a legal and rhetorical concept cultivated by the intellectual elites than a genuine cultural experience at the level of popular life: "people" and "nation" in other words were disarticulated.

National-popular thus designates neither a fixed nor an internally homogeneous content, but rather the possibility, which will vary from country to country, or region to region, of producing an alliance of interests and feelings between different social agents. The terrain of the national-popular is formed by the cultural residues and current production of a shared, multidimensional community of experience, belief, and expectation: what Gramsci understood by "common sense." "'Culture' in Gramsci," Forgacs remarks, "is the sphere in which ideologies are diffused and organized, in which hegemony is constructed and can be broken and reconstructed" (1984: 91).

Though its starting point is in Leninism, there is an important sense in which this idea of a hegemonic project built around the articulation of the national-popular is different from the older social democratic concept—which Lenin shared—of "class-alliance" (e.g., in underdeveloped countries to assure the tasks of a bourgeois-democratic stage), cemented and led by the working class and its political vanguard. As Laclau and Mouffe have pointed out, the notion of class alliance presupposes that the vision and interests of each class are already given (by their material location in the relations of production) and are more or less adequately represented ideologically in already existing parties or organizations. It entails an additive political logic in which hegemony consists essentially in political leadership within a class alliance. By contrast, Gramsci's conception of hegemony is articulatory: it does not presuppose that the ideological representations of different class and group interests are given in advance by the relations of production. Hegemony depends on constructing, through a process of intellectual innovation and reform, new forms of cultural-moral leadership at all levels of society. Rather than reflecting an already constituted interest or value, determined in the last instance by the economic relations of production, the practice of hegemony may imply that a social agent like a class modifies its very nature and identity.[9]

Because of the peculiarities of Italian history—what Gramsci called the Southern Question (the influence of the Counter-Reformation, the persistence of *latifundia* and a large peasant population, a relatively small or regionally based industrial working class, weakly developed liberalism and secular culture)—the concept of the national-popular fits very closely the contours of peripheral capitalist social formations. The structure of dependency in agro-export economies such as those of Central America creates not only a proletarian relation of production (and even where proletarianization occurs it may be highly uneven or mediated, e.g., the common case in Central America of poor peasants who also work seasonally as agricultural workers). It creates a whole social mechanism that dominates everyone not in the immediate power bloc of the comprador bourgeoisie. That is why the normal form of Third World revolutionary movements has been the national liberation struggle rather than the struggle for socialism as such.

This is to recall Laclau's (1977) influential revision of Latin American populism as a political form available to different class projects. To transpose Laclau's argument: in a situation like that of Central America in the last half-century or so, if it were not possible to construct discursively a relation in process between class partisanship and a nationalist, anti-imperialist multiclass bloc, there would be no force that could represent and mobilize the struggle of a people (*pueblo*)—which includes social agents with identities unmarked or partially or ambiguously marked by their location in the relations of production, for example, women, children, students, the unemployed and marginal sector, poor farmers—only the sort of "proletarian" vanguard party or sect whose sectoral limitations and dogmatism can stifle the growth of a genuine mass movement.

But populist-nationalist forms of political mobilization are not only the effect of a weakly developed working class in peripheral capitalism, as the earlier analysis of Di Tella and Germani had suggested. For Laclau, the "people" is the revolutionary subject in the concrete; in popular-democratic forms of mobilization, the "class," whatever it might be (feudal, bourgeois, petite bourgeois, peasant, proletarian) acts as/through the people. This means in turn that ideological signifiers like the "nation," which in their moment of genesis might have had in their production and use a certain kind of "class-belonging," are not reducible or limited in their semantic potential to that relationship. Taken up and articulated with other signifiers, they can express quite different class and/or group interests.[10]

Let us consider Sandinismo in these terms for the sake of example, with the understanding that this argument would have to be modified considerably to fit Guatemala and El Salvador. Contemporary Sandinismo is undeniably a form of revolutionary populism, but one with, in some meaningful sense, a Marxist core. This slippage between a class-based ideology—socialism and more particularly Marxism-Leninism—and the notion of a broad, national anti-imperialist constituency is already implicit in the central signifier of Sandinismo, the figure of Sandino himself. Sandino was, on the one hand, a typical example of the frustrated Jacobin nationalism of the provincial petite bourgeoisie in Latin America, and on the other, a former oil-field worker aware that his campaign against the U.S. Marines and the Liberal/Conservative compromise depended ultimately on the peasants, artisans, and workers of Nicaragua, that it would have to be not only an anti-imperialist war but a "revolutionary anti-imperialist war" (to use a central slogan of current Sandinista discourse).

As Hodges (1986: 1–106) has detailed, Sandino drew on a variety of ideological sources in articulating his campaign: freemasonry, theosophy, Jacobin liberalism and the agrarian radicalism of the Mexican Revolution, Joaquín Trincado's "magnetic-spiritualism," ideas of an "indohispanic" racial destiny articulated by ideologues of the Mexican Revolution like José Vasconcelos (but also present in Rubén Darío's poetry), both Christian and indigenous millenarian myths involved in earlier Central American uprisings, socialist and anarchist ideas derived in part from the influence of the IWW and the Flores Magón brothers in Mexico and the southwestern part of the United States. What he explicitly rejected in his famous debate with the father figure of the Salvadoran left, Farabundo Martí, was the "class against class" thesis of the so-called Third Period of the Comintern (the period of Stalin's rise to power and of forced collectivization in the Soviet Union). This has led to attempts (for example by *contra* ideologues today) to make Sandino an anticommunist nationalist somewhat on the order of Haya de la Torre in Peru.   More pertinently, perhaps, Sandino should be seen as a precursor of the Popular Front strategy that emerged at the Seventh Congress of the Comintern in 1935 under the sponsorship of Dimitrov, and that would be represented particularly effectively in the development of the Chinese and Vietnamese revolutions.

In the years following the withdrawal of the Marines in 1933, the specific form of imperialist penetration and modernization of Nicaragua was the Somoza dictatorship, which was not only a personalist dynastic regime, but also a party dictatorship to the extent that the Nicaraguan Liberal party was transformed by the Somozas into their personal political machine. Somocismo invoked ideologically the great themes of nineteenth-century liberalism (republican institutionality, order and progress, civilization vs. barbarism) to justify its own monopoly of power and its alliance with U.S. interests in the region. This meant that something like Catholicism, even in the patrician and reactionary forms left over from the colonial and oligarchic stages of Nicaragua's development, came to constitute at both popular and elite levels an ideological space where an anti-Somocista, anti-imperialist, and by implication antibourgeois sensibility could be preserved and nurtured. This peculiarity of Nicaragua's uneven cultural modernization dovetailed in the 1960s with the emergence of Liberation Theology and the *comunidades de base* movement in Central America in general, providing the basis among other things for Ernesto Cardenal's crucial synthesis in his poetry of Marxism and Christianity, which we will look at in greater detail in chapters 3 and 4.

Literature as an Ideological Practice in Latin America

From the point of view of both classical Marxist theory and the political project of socialism, there is an evident problem, however, with this sense of how political will is constructed. If the people rather than the class is seen as the subject of a revolutionary process (and/or if the working class transforms its nature in the process of becoming hegemonic), there is a tendency in situations of national liberation struggle to see socialism as such—that is, as an ideology linked directly to the abolition of capitalist relations of production (including private property in the means of production)—as either mainly an international question, or the ideology of a component of the revolutionary bloc (the working class), or something the revolution will institute at some future stage. As is well known, this has been a central issue in discussions of the present character and direction of the Nicaraguan Revolution.[11]

But there is another kind of problem for our purposes with the concept of national-popular interpellation. Gramsci insists that in the case of

Italy he can specify the preconditions of a future national-popular culture but not its nature or content, because: (1) the terrain of popular culture is a contradictory totality, embodying both the weight of back-wardness and obscurantism as well as egalitarian, democratic elements; and (2) the separation of elite and popular culture is continually perpetu-ated and transformed by capitalist control of significant organs of each—a problem doubly intensified under first colonial then neocolonial conditions of cultural development. The logic of our argument suggests that poetry became in Central America an ideological signifier that could be transposed from its original class location to a new, popular-democratic and revolutionary context. This possibility was dependent on the fact that the figure of the great Nicaraguan poet Rubén Darío and the practice of poetry as such have become signifiers of the national-popular in the region. How can this be, especially when Darío represents a sort of poetry—*modernismo*—precisely distinguished by its distance from popular experience and culture? To answer this question, we need to trace the outline of a story that we will fill out in more detail in the subsequent chapters.

The centrality of literature in Gramsci's argument does not mean for him that it is always and everywhere a component of the national-popular (just as the concept does not dictate one form of political strategy over another). Clearly, not all cultural forms are equally important in different circumstances. What counts as a key cultural signifier, and for whom, depends on national and regional institutions and traditions and their complex interaction with international culture and with contingencies of race, language, class, gender, and generation.

It is a truism that literature is a universal form of expression that functions everywhere and at all times in much the same ways. But this is clearly not the case, either in different historical periods or at any given moment in relations between one civilization and another, one nation and another, one region and another, one class and another, one group and another (e.g., males and females), and so on. We need to understand therefore how literature in general, and also certain particular types of literature (poetry as opposed to the novel, for example), are marked as ideological forms in Central American societies.

The ideological centrality of literature in Latin America has to do with the effects of colonialism and capitalist combined and uneven develop-ment in the region, which have left intact and/or specially marked elements of earlier cultural formations that have become extinct or marginal in the metropolis. These include the rural tradition of story-telling (*leyendas*) and narrative ballads like the *corrido* with roots at once in survival of indigenous cultural forms and Spanish *mestizo* folk poetry; and the status and function of the *letrado* or "man of letters" in the colonial period, where Spanish language literacy was itself often a mark of distinction between colonizer and colonized.

Where illiteracy is widespread, as in most of Central America, poetry, song, storytelling, and speech making have the virtue of being susceptible to oral delivery and reception. They are forms of a culture of "secondary orality"—the term is Walter Ong's—which differs from both traditional oral poetry and narrative, dependent on recitation from memory in collective social settings, and the rhetorically highly elaborated written text produced for the private consumption of an elite reader or readers introduced by the Spanish colonization. The spoken word conjures together the presence of the communal and the sacred (the sacred as produced by the people rather than for them). At the same time, even among those who may be functionally illiterate or who have only limited access to written literature, the writer and writing are endowed with an aura of authority and charisma. The *letrado* as a political or revolutionary leader has a long and important tradition in Latin America, which goes from Tupac Amaru, through (for example) Padre Hidalgo, Sarmiento, Martí, Rómulo Gallegos, Juan Bosch, Neruda, Fidel Castro, and Mario Vargas Llosa. His or her person and *obra* are the place where the "unlettered" (*iletrado*) voice of the people can become or find itself mirrored in a discourse of power equivalent to and thus capable of displacing the official culture of the exploiting classes.

Literature develops in very close relation to the state in Latin America. The literature that was permitted and encouraged by the colonial authorities, particularly the kind of elaborate baroque lyric poetry and ecclesiastical prose that dominated the high culture of the viceroyalties in the seventeenth century, was a European implant, not a cultural form that represented in any important sense a continuity with the precolonial past.[12] The cultivation of literature was part of the Spanish crown's policy of religious conversion and linguistic Hispanization of the indigenous peoples, and at the same time a means of achieving the ideological coherence of the white European minority—both peninsular and Creole. Referring to the innovative, ultrabaroque poetry of Luis de Góngora, which in Spain itself was attacked as heretical but which came to be something like an official literary manner or style in the viceroyalties, Jaime Concha notes that it

... puts itself at the service of what are clearly apologetics for the colonial order, particularly its administrative and ecclesiastical superstructure. ... It is especially through education that the Jesuits appropriate rapidly the literary revolution represented by Gongorism and convert it into a powerful pedagogic instrument. ... The memorization of long passages from Góngora meant that, from childhood on, the colonial students would distance themselves from their immediate circumstances to submerge themselves, through the seductive mirage of words, in the distant metropolitan homeland. (Concha 1974: 46)

The fashion for the sort of intricate and artificial poetry represented by Gongorism involved in the colonies in part the aristocratic class-fetish of a highly wrought art form seen as noble or sublime because it eluded the comprehension of the unlettered—what in seventeenth-century Spanish would have been called the *vulgo* (i.e., in the case of colonial Latin America the overwhelming majority of the indigenous population and the mixed-bloods or *castas*)—and situated itself outside the realm of money, manual labor, or business as means of social advancement and prestige. What such a poetry transmitted to its readers was not only, as Concha suggests, a sign of connection to a distant universal metropolitan culture, but also a technique of power, an exercise or formal simulacrum of the ability to discern, organize, and control. It created between colonizer and colonized what Hernán Vidal (1985) has aptly termed a "comunidad lingüística diferenciadora"—a differentiating linguistic community.

What is also true, on the other hand, was that the language and literary models imposed by the Spanish were those that the colonial Creole or mestizo *letrados* appropriated to generate over time, and with their own more or less acute sense of differentiation from metropolitan culture, their own literature (Góngora's popularity in the colonies may have had something to do with his relatively embattled status in Spain itself in the early seventeenth century). It was out of this process that the ideological preconditions for the emergence of literary discourses of national identity and consciousness began to gestate. Literature therefore had a contradictory status in colonial Latin America: its cultivation, on which quite a lot of time and energy was spent, was a sign of the colony's connection to and legitimation by a European metropolitan center; on the other hand, it was a practical medium for the elaboration of an ultimately anticolonial and anti-European sensibility.

This Creolized literary discourse intersected in the later eighteenth century with the often clandestine influence of Enlightenment ideas and literary models in the numerous *sociedades patrióticas* that began to spring up in the wake of the Bourbon reforms. In a gesture of institutional continuity with the colony, literature was also specially marked as a form of republican institutionality during the period of independence in the early nineteenth century. Latin American Liberals—themselves formed pedagogically as *letrados*—saw the development of national literatures as a way to create a mentality appropriate for the consolidation of the newly independent republics under the hegemony of an enlightened Creole bourgeoisie aiming to bring their populations and resources under its control. In this process, as Vidal (1976) has suggested, the writer conceives of himself or herself as a sort of Moses, informing through his or her rhetoric the mass of the population, which is seen as still submerged in semibarbarism, lacking rational self-consciousness and an emancipatory will-to-power.

Literary romanticism, imported from Europe and North America, both stems from and acts as a sustaining expression, an ideological practice, of the Liberal project. Romanticism involves an implicit conception of history, society, and the role of the individual both as leader and follower, a conception expressing the need to create through a psycho-social catharsis and a prolonged pedagogical uplifting a new American character structure free from the negative inheritances of the colonial period and the remains of pre-Hispanic social and cultural forms. Romantic literature is nationalistic in the sense that it attempts to construct a vision of a new American cosmos. But within this cosmos, the human and natural elements of the new republics find their proper place and use in terms of their integration with the evolving social project of the Creole elites, which in the fashion of French Jacobinism invests itself with the character of being a movement for universal human emancipation.

Romantic literature was not only an expression of the values and interests of an emerging Creole bourgeoisie but also a cultural practice that marked it off from other social protagonists. It emerged in connection with the first generation of a Creole intelligentsia that had grown up, educated itself, and incorporated itself into the social elite under the republic, which was able to realize through its cultivation new social functions. It evolved accompanying the process of consolidation, social differentiation, and struggle for a place in society of the members of this intelligentsia. It served to define their group and individual identity, their relationship to power and to other social classes and groups, their sense of the possibilities of development of their societies, and, in a sort of feedback effect, their vision of the central role of literature and literary culture in assuring that development (Losada 1981: 60).[13]

It follows from this that the contradictions of the Liberal project, and its general crisis in Latin America at the end of the nineteenth century under the impact of increased U.S. involvement in the continent, also entail a crisis in the literary forms of representation of the national, and at the same time in the function of literature as a social institution. Among the symptoms of this crisis are the movement for literary renovation called *modernismo* that appears (mainly in poetry) in the last two decades of the nineteenth century and the subsequent development—especially after the Mexican Revolution—of a populist-realist narrative under different rubrics (*mundonovismo, novela de la tierra, novela indigenista*).

The general ideological parameters of this crisis are well known:[14] To overcome the state of economic stagnation and dependency in which it found itself and resist or mediate U.S. domination, the Latin American bourgeoisie—or more exactly those components of it interested in encouraging industrial and commercial expansion as aspects of nation-building—conceived the creation and expansion of an internal market as a precondition for the development of a national capitalist economy and a democratic state proper. As long as the rural masses remained in a situation of economic apathy and misery, at the margin of a generalized commodities market, the possibilities for nonexport production were relatively limited, not only because of the lack of an extensive buying public but also because the national enterprises could not compete in their own existing markets with imports or enterprises set up by foreign capital. Consequently, abandoning the principle of free trade that had been a key component of the ideology of oligarchic liberalism, the new bourgeois project proposed policies like import substitution and nationalization of key industries. The success of these policies was seen as depending in turn on the expansion of the possibilities of consumption within or between the Latin American countries, something that implied the transformation of the conditions of life of the rural populations, including the remaining pre-Hispanic communities. Such a transformation required at both the economic and the cultural levels agrarian reform in one form or other.

To displace the deeply entrenched structure of oligarchic power and foreign intervention, however, a new political agency was also required that transcended the limits of what amounted to an intraoligarchic Liberal/Conservative party rivalry. Hence the idea of an anti-imperialist and antioligarchic coalition or mass populist party, based on an alliance between the national bourgeoisie, the peasantry, the nascent proletariat, and sectors of the petite bourgeoisie and the professional middle strata. Though the actual or would-be national bourgeoisie aspired to be hegemonic in this alliance, political mobilization was also articulated from below by the spread of anarchist, syndicalist, socialist, and communist ideas and organizations and by the wave of peasant resistance that swept the continent after 1917, represented above all by the agrarian radicalism of the Mexican Revolution.

As in the Liberal-romantic stage, literature continued to play a crucial role in relation to this project, both at elite and popular levels. One particularly influential example was Rómulo Gallegos's novel of Venezuelan rural life, *Doña Bárbara* (1929), which was to become in effect the founding text of the hegemonic political force in modern Venezuelan society, Acción Democrática. Writers like Gallegos in the 1920s and 1930s were attempting to create a genuinely popular national literature, which would appeal in its language, style, plot situations, and characters to what they hoped was a growing reading public, which in turn would both be produced by and support the sort of democratic moral, intellectual, and educational reforms suggested by their novels. Ultimately, their ideal readers would be like their heroes, newly capacitated men of the people liberated from the situation of cultural impoverishment imposed by the colonial heritage of underdevelopment and foreign domination. The vision that these novels project of a progressive and democratic national destiny built on the integration into national life of sectors of the population previously marginalized (e.g., the mestizo) was integral with the providential logic of their plots, which, as in the case of *Doña Bárbara*, tended to pit enlightened upper or middle-class heroes against representatives of oligarchic backwardness and anarchy. In this sense, they were literary allegories of the political premise of an antioligarchic alliance between the popular classes and a reform-oriented bourgeoisie (or sectors that aspire to this status), partly defined by its literary tastes.

It follows that the context of so-called boom in Latin American literature in the 1960s was precisely one of the crisis of the bourgeois-democratic project suggested by this tradition of populist realism, which in turn the boom writers rejected as a literary model. As we have seen in the case of *Cien años de soledad*, the idea of the boom as a discourse of rupture with the past depended in part on its coincidence with two other factors: the political and cultural effervescence generated throughout the continent by the Cuban Revolution; and the very rapid levels of capitalist or state-capitalist industrialization that began to appear in the decade of the 1960s, with consequent demographic and cultural effects (rapid urbanization; formation of U.S.-style consumer society enclaves; proliferation of the mass media). From the former factor derives the identification on the part of many boom writers of their literary experiments with the vanguard function of the guerrilla *foco*, as theorized by Regis Debray or Carlos Marighella. But it is probably the latter that was decisive in determining the character of the boom in the long run.

As an English loan word, the boom designates ironically a correspondence between a cultural movement—a new sort of Latin American novel that catches on both in the regional and international literary markets—and the sometimes violent and chaotic process of capitalist modernization Latin America went through after the Second World War. The writers of the boom, like their readers, belong to the new middle strata of professional-technical intellectuals generated and sustained by the modernization process. Their books, articles, and interviews circulate by means of new mass media and publishing technologies, which tend to be dominated more and more by multinational capital. On the model of the best-seller, their works become consumption items— cultural commodities—which help define the taste and values of an expanding middle-class consumer culture in Latin America.

As a result, the political-ideological heritage of the boom has been extremely unstable and ambiguous, even in the case of individual writers (Mario Vargas Llosa, for example, who is now a spokesperson of Latin American neoliberalism and the presidential candidate of the Peruvian Right, began his career as a literary young Turk closely identified with the Cuban Revolution). As Antonio Cornejo Polar has observed, the boom responded with variable and sometimes opposed political inflections to a shared sense of the crisis of the concept of the nation itself and the ideological connotations connected with it. Liberalism understood that the category basic to nationhood was unity— linguistic, ethnic, economic, cultural, religious—a position echoed with antagonistic inflections (e.g., *mestizaje* as versus Liberal policies of *blanqueamiento*) by populist and some forms of socialist discourse. By contrast, the sort of plural, diglossic, carnivalesque text favored by the boom writers, with its characteristic mixture of fantasy and social realism, archaic and contemporary, European and indigenous cultural and linguistic forms, suggested a new metahistorical model of the Latin American national-popular founded on heterogeneity instead of unity. This model allowed in particular the incorporation of a series of voices that had been marginalized by or subordinated in the discourses of a unitary (and usually implicitly male) national subject: indigenous peoples, women, lower middle-class and popular sectors, homosexuals, the growing marginal population of the urban barrios (Cornejo Polar 1989: 47).

In the case of Central America, the impact of the boom in the 1960s and early 1970s coincided with a structural crisis of the regional political and economic system with very pronounced radicalizing effects. To close this chapter, then, we need finally to connect the general observations we have made here about ideology, literature, and Latin American development with the elements of this conjuncture.

Structural Positioning: Literature and Dependency in Central America

Dependency theorists (see, e.g., Paige 1975) have elaborated the proposition that political-economic systems—like those of Central America generally—in which (1) the principal source of wealth is agricultural production for export, and (2) the ownership of agricultural land is concentrated in a class of nonproducers, are inherently unstable. Lacking an elaborated internal national commodities market that can discipline the demands and expectations of labor and other nonoligarchic social actors, they require direct political/military control through the operation of the repressive apparatuses of the state, most particularly the army and police. Such systems rest politically on a very limited mandate, are economically, ideologically, and technologically weak, and tend to enter into crisis when there is a major change in the situation of the export sector (e.g., a drop in prices for the major export commodity or commodities; shifts in production technology; foreign debt crises with related downward pressures on already low wage levels).

In Central America, the repressive state apparatuses act upon not only rural workers and peasants, but also business sectors, teachers, service workers, labor aristocracy, and students, who have reached a certain level of development and relative privilege under the dictatorships. In this situation, shifting alliances can develop between the mainly rural poorer classes and sections of the new urban elites who have not been allowed what they consider a sufficient share of political and economic power.[15]

Concretely, the crisis of the 1970s in Central America was the result of the convergence of the rising expectations stimulated, but also unsatisfied, by the economic growth and diversification created by the Central American Common Market and the Alliance for Progress policies in the 1960s (we rely here on Torres-Rivas 1984). The growth fostered by Central American economic integration produced a situation of both economic and ideological displacements in which the equilibrium maintaining oligarchic domination became harder and harder to maintain without increased repression. But increased repression led dissenting middle sector and bourgeois groups to merge their concerns with those of the popular sectors. By the late 1970s, a radical polarization began to set in, fueled by the eruption of the popular masses into the political scene. The emerging crisis was met with vastly increased state and paramilitary repression against both the popular and bourgeois opposition. State terrorism provoked, however, a situation of what Torres-Rivas calls "collective impatience," which entailed an increased willingness to use violence against the state. What transformed a potentially revolutionary situation into actual revolutionary movements, however, was the ability of the oppositions to forge the broadest possible organizational and ideological consensus against the regimes they faced. This is where the role of cultural practices was to prove decisive.

The complex interaction between economic, political, cultural, and subjective factors implicit in such a situation was elaborated theoretically by Althusser and his school in the proposition that in certain social formations economic structures may themselves position politics as a "structure in dominance." Althusser distinguishes a series of practices (or levels/instances) that together constitute a social formation: the economic, political, ideological (cultural), juridical, and theoretical (scientific). Each of these has its own relatively autonomous history as a practice, determined by its own contradictions and possibilities, which in turn may determine or be determined by what happens in the others. A conjuncture is a particular relation of these practices in which one or another may play a dominant role (e.g., a crisis of political legitimacy may provoke a change in the economic mode of production).

From such a perspective, the economic is "determinant in the last instance" only in the sense that the mode of production of a given social formation determines which of the levels will be dominant, or what its degree of effectivity will be. The usual example adduced here is feudalism, where the effective control, as opposed to titular ownership, of the means of production by the peasantry requires that surplus be extracted by the aristocracy through extraeconomic compulsions of a legal-military nature emanating from the political-ideological level of feudal social formations.

By the mid-1970s, something like this perspective had been incorporated into advanced dependency and world systems theory analyses in the proposition that in certain peripheral social formations, whose economies are disproportionately subject to the external market, the relations of production themselves are secured and reproduced largely by political and ideological practices (see, e.g., Cardoso and Faletto 1979: 101–126; and Torres-Rivas 1984). A metropolitan capitalist economy runs by itself, so to speak, in the sense that its conditions of expanded reproduction (prices, wages, rates of profit, etc.) are determined by the normal operation of the market, which with variations here and there all social actors, including labor, accept. In the situation of a Third World agro-export plantation economy, however, the dominant class (or class fraction) governs through the mechanisms of its *political* relations with other classes—which in the final analysis depend on its control of the state, which in turn depends on its control of the police and military apparatus—rather than through the purely economic mechanisms of national, regional, and international market operations, which it does not control. Social control and its reproduction are thus at least partly an extraeconomic matter.

In Central America, the 1929 depression represented the first systemic crisis of the oligarchic model of development and the first great upsurges (Sandino, the rebellion in El Salvador, the dictatorships of the 1930s). Where, as in the case of Costa Rica, a degree of development of national financial and commercial sectors had resulted in the creation of broad rural and urban middle classes, a relatively autonomous and democratic state could emerge. Where there was not a state based on popular consensus or even on an adequate, lasting consensus among the components of the dominant class itself, as in the cases of Nicaragua, El Salvador, and (after 1954) Guatemala, however, power came to rest on an externally funded and to an extent externally legitimated police state. When this arrangement did not serve to contain domestic opposition forces, foreign intervention (concretely: U.S. intervention) became necessary to avert or, as in Guatemala in 1954 or Nicaragua after 1979, reverse revolutionary developments.

As the political level—in the characteristic form of a military dictatorship or exceptional regime—weighs on all other levels of practice, including the economic, all significant and effective forms of opposition tend to transcend their origin in particular sectors, institutions, and demands and to condense in an all-out struggle for an end to the regime as such and for control of the nation. Bread and butter economic demands (struggles over wages, franchises, shares of national or export markets, and land tenure) cannot be adequately mediated or resolved in the existing legal frameworks, which often have only a de jure existence, and become directly political, leading to increasing repression on the part of the state and/or its paramilitary extensions; repressed political energies are displaced onto both popular and elite cultural spheres; cultural forms are likely to suddenly assume explosive political force. In extreme cases, such as that of Nicaragua after the 1971 earthquake or the assassination of Chamorro, such a situation pits civil society as such against the state (Torres-Rivas 1985). This is particularly so, given that the combination of dictatorship and enclave economy implies a general underdevelopment or uneven development of the national culture itself and the displacement of components of indigenous and Creole traditions by imported metropolitan doctrines and cultural commodities. We noted before that literature in general has had a very close relation to the state in Latin American development. But there is a difference between the character of this relationship in the nineteenth century, where a national literature is generally seen as a component of the state ideological apparatus of the Creole bourgeoisie, and—excepting Costa Rica—in Central American culture after the depression, where literature is at the same time a hegemonic middle- and upper-class cultural form, but also in a certain relation of antagonism not only with the state but also with a dependent, "lumpen" bourgeoisie (to recall André Gunder Frank's apt term), which is incapable of either supporting or appreciating the national literature.

This situation has two major consequences: (1) it makes literature a means of cultural-ideological production particularly susceptible to being employed by middle sectors, or displaced or marginalized sectors of the upper classes, inserted contradictorily between the dominant groups—whose cultural model is metropolitan consumer culture (concretely in recent years, Miami)—and the repressed working population, largely illiterate or semiliterate (and in the case of Guatemala, at least in part non–Spanish speaking); (2) it passes to the left and the popular sectors the task of building the institutions of a strong national culture, including literature, that in Western Europe, the United States, or Japan was carried out by the national bourgeoisie in the nineteenth century.

This is not to say that all cultural and literary modes are or become explicitly political in such a situation. But since cultural production of any kind has to take place always in relation to powerful dictatorial apparatuses closely linked to foreign interests (with consequent problems of censorship, cultural mimicry and inauthenticity, repression or exile of dissenting voices, and underdevelopment of education and cultural services), it has a tendency to become politicized, to represent itself whether it is explicitly political or not as an alternative to the logic represented by the existing system. In turn, the very lack of a developed educational and cultural infrastructure that could sustain the broad reading public and professional writers demanded by the popular realist novel of the sort Gramsci championed (and which had in fact appeared in other Latin American countries in the 1920s and 1930s), positioned poetry, in a way we will try to explain in more detail in chapter 2, as the dominant literary mode.

Notes

1. "... an ideology is a system (with its own logic and rigor) of representations (images, myths, ideas or concepts, depending on the case) endowed with a historical existence and role within a given society." In ideology human beings express "not the relation between them and their conditions of existence, but *the way* they live the relation between them and their conditions of existence: this presupposes both a real relation and an *'imaginary,' 'lived,'* relation. . . . In ideology the real relation is inevitably invested in an imaginary relation, a relation that *expresses a will* (conservative, conformist, reformist or revolutionary), a hope or a nostalgia, rather than describing a reality" (Althusser 1970: 231, 233–234).

2. "Men 'live' their ideologies as the Cartesian 'saw' . . . the moon at two hundred paces away: *not at all as a form of consciousness, but as an object of their 'world'*—as their 'world' itself" (Althusser 1970: 233).

3. Kant's distinction between aesthetic and teleological judgment is in his *Critique of Judgment.* For a discussion of formalism, see Jameson (1972) and Bennett (1979).

4. The model often suggested for this is French psychoanalyst Jacques

Lacan's account of the "mirror-stage" in the formation of the human psyche, which influenced the work on ideology of the Althusserians. See his *Ecrits. A Selection* (1977).

5. Compare Tony Bennett (1979: 166–167): "The position of a given form of cultural practice within the disposition of a given cultural field and, accordingly, the part it plays within the wider social processes are constantly shifting and changing as the relationships which define that field are themselves constantly redefined and rearticulated. There are no forms of cultural practice which are intrinsically and forever either dominant or oppositional. Their function and effect, in political terms, depend on the place they occupy within that incessantly changing nexus of relationships which defines their position in relation to one another."

6. This is a somewhat different matter from the question of what ideological practices produce revolutionary consciousness in the exploited classes or social groups themselves, among other things because one of those practices—socialist or revolutionary rhetoric and propaganda—is that of an already constituted radicalized intelligentsia. The ideological practices that produced a Lenin, for example, are not necessarily those that might have led a Petrograd factory worker to support the Bolsheviks, although most discussion of cultural politics proceeds on the assumption that they are or should be the same.

7. The scene in part 2 of the Cuban film *Lucía*, where the two lovers involved in the insurrectionary movement against the Machado dictatorship recite to each other a love poem by Martí, dramatizes this very effectively.

8. On the relation of the emergence of uniform vernacular languages, literature, nation-states, and nationalism, see Anderson (1983).

9. As Laclau and Mouffe explain,

For, whereas political leadership can be grounded upon a conjunctural coincidence of interests in which the participating sectors retain their separate identity, moral and intellectual leadership requires that an ensemble of "ideas" and "values" be shared by a number of sectors—or, to use our own terminology, that certain subject positions traverse a number of class sectors. Intellectual and moral leadership constitutes, according to Gramsci, in a higher synthesis, a "collective will," which, through ideology, becomes the organic concept unifying a historical bloc. (1988: 66–67)

It follows that "a class does not *take State power*, it *becomes* the State, transforming its own identity by articulating to itself a plurality of struggles and democratic demands" (ibid.: 70).

10. We should note here, however, a point of difference with Laclau. While it is obviously the case that literature as an ideological signifier can be articulated as a component of a revolutionary bloc—indeed this is the central thesis of this book—this does not mean it has no class character whatsoever. As a historically concrete social institution, literature (any given literary text) has been shaped by very specific class interests and values, or served as a field of negotiation between the interests and values of antagonistic classes (e.g., between the aristocracy and the bourgeoisie in eighteenth-century Europe), such that it cannot be simply appropriated by a popular movement without some change in its nature and

audience. Even the force of literature as an ideological signifier depends on its previous articulation as a form of power connected to projects of class domination or liberation (see our discussion of literature and Latin American liberalism below).

11. See Vilas (1986) on this point. In Gramsci, the working class and class-based party retain a coherence and centrality as social agents in any project of hegemonic articulation. Laclau and Mouffe, on the other hand, argue that the working class as it is constituted as a theoretical object in Marxist discourse is not the fundamental political subject of social change, that hegemony does not "always correspond to a fundamental economic class," but rather involves a democratic plurality of variously constituted historical subjects (1985: 69–71). Orlando Núñez—writing as a theoretician of Sandinismo—finesses the problem as follows: On the one hand, "the working class is the only class that is destined by history to be the antithesis of capitalism while that system exists"; on the other, "the starting point for any contemporary revolutionary process is the shaping of broad class alliances." Consequently, "No revolution is possible without the working class. . . . But the remaining classes and sectors—the peasants, the urban masses, the social movements, etc.—are indispensable; and they constitute the social subject of all revolutions. It includes the diverse popular sectors, which along with the working class, have driven all the great socialist revolutions in the twentieth century" (Burbach and Núñez 1987: 8).

12. This is often obscured in Latin American literary history by the tendency to see continuities between pre- and postcolonial poetry, narrative, and myth. Certainly nothing like "literature" as the very special sociocultural institution this becomes in Europe in the course of the Renaissance existed in pre-Columbian America. On the colonial institution of literature in Mexico and Central America, see Irving Leonard's (1966) classic *Baroque Times in Old Mexico* and Martínez Peláez (1983).

13. Referring concretely to the Peruvian romantic writers, Losada notes: ". . . this generation of liberal-Romantic youth gets its identity not from its location in the social relations of production, nor from its interests or its privileged place in the overall social structure, *but rather from a specifically literary ideal.* It was as if they felt themselves different, and specially suited to take control of the government, because they represented literary and abstract ideas." On literature as a social-ideological institution in nineteenth-century Latin American development, see, besides Losada, Rama (1984), Molloy (1984), González Echevarría (1985), Cornejo Polar (1989), and Ramos (1989).

14. For a schematic conception of the crisis see Cueva (1977); for ideological-cultural implications see Moraña (1984), Perus (1976 and 1982), and Osorio (1985).

15. Jan Flora specifies four generalizations on the roots of Central American insurgency in the 1970s: (1) Insurgency is more likely to develop in countries where capitalist forces of production have developed to the point where there is a significant agrarian working class, at least an incipient industrial working class, and a threatened artisanry. (2) The development of an export-oriented agrarian bourgeoisie requires and results in the strengthening of the role of the state, increasing its capacity for repressive action and for exclusion of the popular classes from political dialogue. (3) As the economy diversifies, interests of the

different class fractions of the bourgeoisie diverge. (4) A situation of extensive foreign control of export agricultural production (as in the case of Honduras), or the domination of agriculture by small producers (as in the case of Costa Rica), tends to permit a relatively more representative state, which allows some participation of middle sectors and the popular classes in political dialogue, thus deflecting the tendency to insurgency (Flora 1987: 36–38).

2. Culture, Intellectuals, and Politics in Central America

The limit of the structurally oriented Althusserian-dependency theory model we invoke at the end of chapter 1 is that it cannot specify the empirical means and forms of cultural-ideological resistance, only their general conditions of emergence and effectivity. Even under military-authoritarian regimes (which are such precisely because they do not rest on effective institutionalization and consensus), cultural practices retain a degree of autonomy and indeterminacy. They tend to operate by a fluid logic of displacement and condensation in which forms elaborated on the basis of tradition and in relation to a given set of concerns are constantly modified by the ebb and flow of innovation, censorship and repression, new cultural trends and technologies (including foreign influences), and new political conjunctures to which their own effects as ideological practices at least in part contribute. To put this another way: Somocismo is an effect of Nicaragua's situation of structural dependency. But its specific character and evolution cannot be accounted for by that dependency, or for that matter can Sandinismo be explained simply as an effect of Somocismo. As Laclau and Mouffe put it, "it is impossible to specify *a priori* surfaces of emergence of antagonisms, as there is no surface which is not constantly subverted by the overdetermining effects of others. . . . [W]hat has been exploded is the idea and the reality itself of a unique space of constitution of the political" (1985: 180–181).

The general theoretical problem involved is this: how to show the relations of various kinds of cultural production to concrete social formations in evolution, taking into account local, national, regional, and international forces at work in shaping or complicating these relations. Phenomena that are said in Althusserian terms to belong to or constitute clearly distinct practices, levels, or instances in metropolitan social formations cannot always be so categorized in situations of dependent, neocolonial development, which are characterized precisely by the tendency for the relative autonomy of the political, economic, cultural, and so on, levels to collapse (perhaps we should speak of a "relative collapse"). The fragile and fragmented nature of these phenomena make them readily subject to residual influences ("survivals") from prior historical-cultural stages, as well as overlays from more advanced social formations—traditionally, Europe or the United States but now also Third World and socialist countries. Barring extremes, it is difficult to establish a given phenomenon as ideologically reactionary or progressive (veterans of Sandino's army often became Conservatives, because that was the party opposed to Somoza). The resultant ambiguity and duality are a sign of cultural weakness, but sometimes also a source of unexpected possibilities of national-popular articulation. Elements of reactionary culture and ideology can be assimilated and refunctioned by popular and progressive tendencies. The inability of both popular and elite cultures to maintain themselves as distinct levels makes them liable to politicization, and they become a space where powerful social antagonisms and impulses can condense.[1] Finally, dependency does not imply homogeneity: there are varying degrees of dependency and autonomy for each level of a given social formation, and aspects of a given level may also be marked differentially (e.g., in Latin American literature, poetry and the novel have somewhat different aesthetic-ideological connotations as forms, given the connection of the novel to Creole liberalism).

In this chapter, we would like to try to concretize at something like a microlevel the problematic about the interaction of social formation, ideology, politics, intellectuals, and literature we have been tracing. We propose to look in some detail at the literary formation of a typical middle sector Central American intellectual: Carlos Fonseca Amador, a cofounder of the FSLN in Nicaragua and its leader and most important theoretician during its formative stages, and then move to fill in some of the general parameters of Central American literary and cultural history that pertain to his example.

The Formation of an Ideology: Fonseca, Darío, and Sandino

We begin our consideration of Fonseca with what seems like an odd detail of his career:[2] according to the chronicle of his life prepared by the Instituto para el Estudio del Sandinismo, after being expelled from Nicaragua in 1965 for his political activities and just married, Fonseca dedicated himself to a study of the poetry of Rubén Darío under the direction of Edelberto Torres, an important study that he prolonged until summer of the following year when he returned to Nicaragua to prepare a guerrilla base in the mountains. A portion of his research—on the reception of the Russian novelist Maxim Gorky by Darío—was recovered after Fonseca's death and published in 1979 as "Noticia sobre Darío y Gorki" by the Cuban cultural journal *Casa de las Américas*. It suggests a good part of the ideological originality of his fusion of Marxism and nationalism. Fonseca draws attention to Darío's surprising interest in and sympathy for the 1905 revolution in Russia and to his positive evaluation of Gorky's experiments in social realism, noting "¿No será necesario pensar menos en el demasiado célebre poeta de cisnes y princesas?" (Isn't it necessary to think less about [Darío as] the too-famous poet of swans and princesses?). Because of the conditions of cultural backwardness maintained by the Somoza dictatorship, Darío is in any case barely known in his own country, Fonseca adds, concluding that "la mano de la agresión cultural norteamericana no podía estar ausente en el ocultamiento de escritos darianos de espíritu latinoamericanista" (the hand of U.S. cultural aggression could not have been absent in this repression of Darío's Latin Americanist writings) (Fonseca 1984: 407–408).

Contemporary Sandinismo gestated in part out of the process of struggle and exile during the hard years of the Somoza dictatorship in the 1950s and 1960s, which brought young Nicaraguan intellectuals in contact with left intellectual centers in San José, Mexico City, Paris, Moscow, and (after 1959) Havana. Its manifesto was Fonseca's *Ideario político de Augusto César Sandino*, a selection of quotes from Sandino's correspondence and writings, which was to have been part of a larger historical work on Sandino titled *Viva Sandino* that Fonseca was still working on at the time of his death in combat in 1976. The *Ideario* was originally published in mimeographed form in 1961 by the predecessor organization of the Frente Sandinista, the Movimiento Nueva Nicaragua. In a somewhat expanded version printed in 1966 by the Sandinista youth front, the Frente Estudiantil Revolucionaria (FER), it became the indoctrination manual of the FSLN.[3]

Fonseca was brought up in the provincial capital of Matagalpa, the center of the northern coffee-growing region of Nicaragua. Like Sandino himself and many of the later Central American poet-revolutionaries (Roque Dalton, for example), Fonseca was the product of a well-to-do father and working-class mother (his mother was a cook and his father an accountant at a U.S.-owned mine). In the company of his friend and fellow Matagalpan, Tomás Borge, he developed politically in and around the orbit of the very small Nicaraguan Communist party—the Partido Socialista Nicaragüense (PSN)—in the mid-1950s.[4]

As Hodges has detailed, Fonseca's break with the PSN came not, as in the cases, for example, of Haya de la Torre in Peru or Rómulo Betancourt in Venezuela, from the opposition of a petit bourgeois nationalism to Leninism. Fonseca believed that socialist and, more particularly, Marxist ideas had barely begun to penetrate Nicaragua, and the PSN, like many other Latin American CPs, had been strongly influenced in its origins by the reformist and collaborationist strategy associated with the North American Communist leader Earl Browder (Fonseca 1984: 352; Borge 1989b: 85–91). (The PSN was founded in 1944 during the Second World War, and initially sought an alliance with the U.S.-supported Somoza regime.) It stemmed rather from his conviction that the PSN had become too closely tied to the ameliorist strategy of the bourgeois opposition to the Somozas in the 1950s. What was needed Fonseca felt was not only a new kind of vanguard party but also a new ideology of armed national liberation struggle specific to Nicaragua's cultural and political experience. He followed sympathetically the development in the later 1950s of Castro's 26th of July Movement in Cuba; but closer at hand was the model of Sandino's campaign against the occupation of Nicaragua by the U.S. Marines from 1927 to 1933. The problem was that Sandino had all but disappeared from historical memory in Nicaragua. The point of the *Ideario* was to reactivate the image of Sandino and to show that his thought had an immediate relevance to the task of building a movement to overthrow the dictatorship. This involved subsuming under the figure of Sandino the specifically Marxist-Leninist problematic of imperialism represented by the PSN.[5]

Those familiar with Nicaragua know that it has been common for FSLN cadre members to insist, following the logic of Fonseca's revision of Sandino, that they are not *socialistas* but *sandinistas*, that *socialismo* is a "European" ideology or, in a common variant, the particular ideology of the organized working class of Nicaragua. There was and is, no doubt, a certain tactical caution in this: during the cold war it was useful in the American backyard not to be branded too quickly as Communist. But there was also a recognition that in a society with a small formal working class like Nicaragua, orthodox Marxism-Leninism of the sort represented by the PSN was going to be, at best, one strand of the national-popular, not *the* necessary and sufficient ideological signifier for all the social forces in the country capable of being mobilized against the dictatorship and U.S. domination (see our discussion of Sandinismo in chapter 1). That, and the insistence—again authorized by the appeal to Sandino—that the struggle against the dictatorship and imperialism would have to take a military form, were the essential positions Fonseca imparted to the work of the Frente.

We are fortunate to have a number of more or less direct sources that show the relation between Fonseca's involvement with literature and his development of Sandinista ideology and organization.[6] They portray him as a somewhat precocious and bookish adolescent. According to a classmate, "Carlos era sumamente estudioso, para él no existían los juguetes ni los juegos de los niños de su edad; solamente existían los libros" (Carlos was very studious, for him the toys and games of the children of his age hardly existed; only books) (Fonseca 1984: 431). He was famous in his school for being the only one to have read an apparently multivolume history of the United States. Borge credits him with a precocious senior thesis on capital and labor.

Borge recalls that as a teenager he shared with Fonseca readings of Thomas More's *Utopia*, Flaubert's *Madame Bovary*, the Spanish late-romantic poet Bécquer, Darío's *Azul*, Karl May—a German author of Westerns—Steinbeck, and Howard Fast. "Later," he adds (we are in 1953), "Marx and Engels hidden in the poet Samuel Meza's dusty old bookstore" in Matagalpa, at a time when "Lenin was no more than an inaccessible bibliographic reference" (Borge 1984: 16). He also speaks of a weekly *Spartaco*, "in which we wrote vaguely but fervently of Sandino" (ibid.: 13).

In 1954, Fonseca and FSLN cofounder Francisco Buitrago, along with a group of Matagalpan students and intellectuals, started a cultural journal called *Segovia*, which Borge describes as marked by "el estilo declamatorio y la retórica modernista," adding that its literary heroes included Darío, Azarías Pallais, María Teresa Sánchez, José Coronel Urtecho, Manolo Cuadra, Fernando Silva, Ernesto Mejía Sánchez, and the Peruvian Communist poet César Vallejo—excepting Darío, all figures associated in one way or another with the dominant literary group in Nicaragua, the *vanguardistas* (Borge 1989b: 111–112). Fonseca himself published in *Segovia* among other things a satirical poem in the style of vanguardism, "16 versos del Molendero" (Borge 1989b reproduces the text). With Borge, he also participated in Marxist study groups sponsored by the PSN, reading among other things Gorky's novel *Mother*. After graduating from high school in 1955, he got a job in Managua as a librarian and began to study for a law degree, working off and on as a stringer for the opposition newspaper *La Prensa*. In 1956, now a member of the PSN, he was arrested after the assassination of Anastasio Somoza by Rigoberto López Pérez. He wrote in a letter that the National Guard took from his residence on that occasion "innocent things like books of poetry by César Vallejo and Emilio Quintana. Novels by William Faulkner. Books on politics written by Catholics like Cardinal José María Caro" (Fonseca 1984: 433; Quintana was the author of the most important Nicaraguan social realist novel, *Bananos*).

Sponsored by the vanguardist writer Manolo Cuadra, Fonseca traveled via Costa Rica to the Soviet Union in 1957 as a delegate to a youth congress, a key formative experience repeated around the same time by other figures of the Central American left like Roque Dalton, Otto René Castillo, and Roberto Obregón. He was very much influenced by a book he read during his trip, *Report at the Foot of the Gallows* by the Czech journalist Julius Fucik. *Un nicaragüense en Moscú* (1957-1958) is the result of this trip; it has a number of observations about literature, but the most interesting is perhaps this one:

> One afternoon walking around Moscow I met a young Russian man who spoke Spanish. When I told him I was a Nicaraguan, he said:
> —Oh! Nicaragua. Rubén Darío. A great poet.
> Once again, it made me proud of our immortal Darío. His genius is so universal that it reached as far as Moscow. (Fonseca 1984: 324)

Fonseca read widely in Nicaraguan and Central American literature.[7] Besides Darío, Quintana, Cuadra, and the other vanguardists, who were writers of previous generations, he followed closely in the 1960s the work of Ernesto Cardenal, Sergio Ramírez, and the writers associated with the *Ventana* group, and, via translations by the vanguardists, he was familiar with U.S. poetry. (In *Un nicaragüense* he notes that "the Russians have had the sense not to confuse Walt Whitman with Foster Dulles," p. 311.) But the poet—unknown outside Nicaragua and only a few years older than Fonseca himself—who seems to have made the greatest impression on him was Rigoberto López Pérez, the author of the assassination—or *ajusticiamiento*, as Fonseca preferred to call it—of Anastasio Somoza in 1956. Fonseca wrote a long literary-political analysis of López Pérez's "Carta-testamento" and rearranged the text in verse form. In this format, it was to become one of the key literary documents of Nicaraguan radicalism.[8]

Fonseca was particularly attracted to books about Sandino. Borge has given us a detailed account of his reception of these in his prison journal:

> Around then (1955–56) we were semi-recruited by the Socialist Party, and Carlos led the first Marxist cell of Nicaraguan university students: Silvio Mayorga was one of its three members. A guy from León who had lived in Mexico (we never knew whether he was a Marxist or a cowboy) was sent to have discussions with us.
> "Sandino," Carlos said on one occasion, "is a path. It would be superficial to reduce him to a category or to one more date on the yearly calendar of activities. I think it is important to study his thought."
> The guy from León got scared and answered more or less as follows:
> "A path? That's poetry! Don't forget what a suspect hero certain bourgeois ideologies have made of that guerrilla. Sandino fought against foreign occupation, not against imperialism. He wasn't Zapata . . . I mean, he didn't deal with the question of the land."

Carlos expressed his doubts when faced with these arguments. He began to investigate Sandino's thought more thoroughly. I remember the joy and severity of his violent outburst when he came across the book *El calvario de las Segovias* in which the author attempts to belittle our immortal hero. That was the first biographic reference before we found *Sandino: o la tragedia de un pueblo* by the honest historian Sofias Salvatierra; a book by a Spaniard with a long name impossible to remember; Calderon Ramírez' work; and, finally, Selser's books. With precision and diligence, Carlos took notes, jotting down phrases from Sandino's rich correspondence. In these notes *Ideario Sandinista*, handbook of basic concepts that circulates among FSLN militants, was conceived. (Borge 1984: 20–22)[9]

The legend of Sandino was alive among the Nicaraguan people in various ways, particularly in and around Matagalpa, which was close to the northern mountain region where Sandino's army had operated. Borge's own father had been linked by family ties to Sandino and often recounted anecdotes of his exploits. Borge recalls in his memoirs how these stories began to merge with the adolescent literary interests he shared with Fonseca and their incipient anti-Somocismo around the anniversary of Sandino's murder in 1954:

These tales [of Sandino] began to reach our consciousness. Influenced, in addition, by readings of Victor Hugo, José Martí, Juan Montalvo, Manuel González Prada, or by the sense of discomfort with Somoza—which appeared all of a sudden—they seemed like a flowering, the discovery of something splendid which satisfied our thirst and made our hearts beat faster. (Borge 1989b: 82)

Later, Borge, Fonseca, and their contemporaries were to be strongly affected by the defeat in October 1958 of a small guerrilla band led by a veteran of Sandino's army, Ramón Raudales.[10] As Hodges notes (1986: 167–172), other veterans of Sandino's army had been in contact with a republican exile from the Spanish civil war, Colonel Alberto Bayo, who used their oral histories of the campaign to construct his own manual of guerrilla warfare, *150 Questions for a Guerrilla*, which he would use to train the members of Fidel Castro's *Granma* expedition in 1956, including a young Argentine doctor named Che Guevara. But the Sandino of Fonseca's *Ideario* is not exactly the Sandino of the veterans of his campaign like Raudales, or the popular legend represented by the anecdotes of Borge's father, and even less the real flesh-and-blood historical Sandino. He is rather, as this itinerary makes clear, a discursive production, a text constructed out of a pastiche of other texts on Sandino: in other words, a "work" of literature.

A Brief Sketch of Central American Literary and Intellectual History

It has been a commonplace that cultural and intellectual life in Central America (with the possible exception of Costa Rica) was impoverished, unstable, "underdeveloped"—that, after all, is part of what the Banana Republic caricature is about.[11] Fonseca complained about the "oscurantismo ideológico" of his country (Borge 1989b: 86). In his *Historia de las ideas contemporáneas en Centro América* (1960), Rafael Heliodoro Valle outlines the elements of disorganization of the cultural sphere in Central America, themselves related to the dependent character of the local economies and state-formations: provincialism; mediocrity; absence of institutional continuity; the shortage of teachers; the corruption, nepotism, and personalism (*amiguismo*) that determine who gets grants, scholarships, and minimal jobs; the poor quality of schools and school equipment; the lack of book publishers and of an extended market for books; the pervasive suspicion, censorship, and repression of intellectuals dating back to the times of the Inquisition; the brain drain toward more developed metropolitan centers. "Teachers who form generations have been lacking. Each regime establishes laws and regulations which make it difficult to carry out a well-planned cultural program," Valle observes. "The little that has gathered in archives and libraries tends all too quickly to be lost, sold off, allowed to fall into disorder, or left to the elements" (ibid.: 8).

Rubén Darío, representing the frustrated liberalism of the Zelaya regime, wrote of "poor Republics."[12] Roque Dalton, with his customary satirical precision, anatomized the "national" literary culture of El Salvador some fifty years later as follows:

In San Salvador
in the year 1965
the best sellers
of the three most important
book stores
were:
The Protocols of the Elders of Zion;
a few books by
diarrhetic Somerset Maugham;
a book of disagreeably
obvious poems
by a lady with a European name

who nonetheless writes in Spanish about our country;
and a collection of
Reader's Digest condensed novels.
                    (Translated by Edward Baker in Zimmerman 1988)

In such a situation, promising intellectuals—Darío and Dalton are themselves cases in point—are forced to emigrate to foreign centers, to Europe and the United States in the heyday of the dictatorships, in recent years also to Cuba, Mexico, and the Soviet bloc countries. In response, modernization projects, often tied to the ideology and practical aims of foreign—mainly U.S.—interests in the region, have penetrated and/or created educational and cultural institutions in Central America with the goal of producing a humanist and technical intelligentsia that could act as a buffer between foreign interests, the local agro-export oligarchies, reform-minded white-collar middle strata, and the illiterate or semiliterate popular classes that are the object of exploitation.

There are, however, striking exceptions to this picture of an anachronistic, impoverished, and/or dependent regional culture: Darío's achievement as the virtual founder of modern Latin American poetry; the complex intellectual synthesis represented by Sandino's thought, which Hodges (1986) has described; Fonseca's reelaboration of this we have just outlined; the striking theoretical originality and capacity for mobilization and maneuver in extremely difficult circumstances of the region's revolutionary movements. Such phenomena indicate that the achievement of Central American culture has been far deeper than formerly imagined. Since colonial times and most particularly since the inroads of the modern world economy, it has elaborated a series of powerful and complex ideological patterns of national identification, fed by diverse social classes and sectors with diverse and often antagonistic interests and orientations.

As we suggested in the introduction to this chapter, one has to be careful not to judge Central American intellectual life by standards that derive from developmental, historicist schemas often tied to colonial or imperialist projects. In Central America, as in other regions of the postcolonial world, intellectuals and bodies of ideas are not necessarily of the same sorts or located in the same places as in the metropolitan centers. We refer not only to the well-known problem of indigenous and peasant culture, but also to the Latin American form of elite humanistic-scientific culture on the European academic model. If there is a general synthesis of middle- and upper-class intellectual life in Central America, it finds its actualization not in formal philosophical systems, libraries and museums, universities, a technical-scientific establishment, but in an informal literary public sphere constituted, often quite haphazardly and precariously, by journals, newspapers, editorials, manifestos, tracts, letters, testimonios and memoirs, novels and stories, *costumbrismo*, and above all, as we will argue here, poetry. Not only has the evolution of Central American intellectual life followed a path different from the one normally associated with European development from the Renaissance onward (the rise of secular humanism and scientific research; technical-professional thought and training proper to advanced industrial and service economies; modernization of the bureaucracy), it has been in some senses *opposed* to such a path.

If talented people are unable to develop in technical and scientific areas, or if those areas are occupied only by those willing to serve an oppressive political apparatus, then intellectual energies will be displaced to other levels. However cosmopolitan given cultural movements in Central America may appear, intellectual life of any lasting significance from the nineteenth century on has been tied not to developing "universal" scientific or philosophical knowledge, but to lyrical and narrative embodiments of an oppressed national culture (or cultures), to the language, rhythm, memories, visions, and dreams of provincial and often illiterate groups seeking to react to or escape from forces of domination as they experience them in their daily lives. This has made literature the main cultural form of the "national."

The conquest and colonization of Central America by the Spanish entailed the destruction or repression of indigenous cultural forms and their substitution by their European counterparts in language, religion, education, philosophy, urban art and architecture, clothing, furniture and decorations, music, dance, and so on. Literature, however, was something new—a specifically colonial implant with no real equivalent in pre-Columbian culture. Generally speaking, the control of literature by the Spanish crown—for example, the well-known prohibition on the importation or publication of novels—seems to have been more pronounced in Central America than in the rest of Latin America. Both university life and publishing houses appeared relatively late (the first printing press in Central America was established in 1660, the first university, San Carlos in Guatemala, in 1678). In Guatemala (more than in the other regions), there was an extensive production—mainly by the clergy—of religious poetry and sermons, *autos* and *loas* (short didactic plays), *historias* and *crónicas*, written in the baroque style, but little development of the secular literary forms that were becoming central in the emerging bourgeois culture of seventeenth- and eighteenth-century Europe, particularly the novel (for a time Cervantes's *Don Quijote* circulated only as an article of contraband). The most important Mexican/Central American writer of the colonial period was perhaps the Jesuit Rafael Landívar, famed as the "American Virgil" for his poem

Rusticatio Mexicana (1781–1782) depicting the daily life of the American countryside, including aspects of the Indian communities, but written, characteristically, in Latin.

In contrast to this sort of literature produced and consumed mainly by the colonial upper classes, songs and stories from the oral tradition like the *cuentos de camino* (something like the Uncle Remus stories of the North American South), and indigenous or mestizo theater pieces like Nicaragua's famous *El Güegüense* retained elements of precolonial cultures and in certain conjunctures could generate a critical or contestatory force. But even these popular forms could also function as successful modes of co-optation and containment by serving as safety valves for lower class anxiety and discontent.

As the presence of foreign, particularly British, capital and trade increased in the late eighteenth century under the impact of the Bourbon reforms, the more commercially oriented sectors of the Creole gentry, urban merchant and financial groups, *letrados* and professionals, began to coalesce into something like a proto-bourgeoisie. They looked for intellectual guidance generally to the *philosophes* and reformers of the Enlightenment and to British political economy. Their main innovation in culture was the development of periodicals and newspapers, and it was in connection with this medium and the new reading public it created that the first modern novel as such appears in the region, the picaresque, anticlerical *El periquillo sarniento* (1816) by the Mexican journalist José Joaquín Fernández de Lizardi.

Expanded coffee production and export in Central America challenged the semifeudal *hacienda* system and the surviving Indian communal lands—both sustained by ideological and administrative superstructures left over from the colony. Following independence, struggles between Conservatives and Liberals, *colonos* and coffee entrepreneurs (many of them recent immigrants), Indians and army, gave rise to a series of coups, uprisings, invasions, and intrigues that broke up the Central American Confederation by 1838. By the second half of the nineteenth century, the Liberals had more or less consolidated their hold on the states throughout the region, using them to disentail or expropriate church and communal lands, which were then sold to investors for the production of coffee or other export crops. The economic basis of the regional oligarchy was thus constituted; an aggressive agricultural capitalism began to displace the somnolent patriarchy of the colonial *hacienda*, without, however, transforming the property form of the *latifundia* itself.

Central American liberalism has come to seem both a cause and a symptom of dependency (among other things, it was a Liberal initiative that led to Walker's occupation of Nicaragua in the 1850s). But it also had a progressive side, expressed in, for example, the democratic, anticolonial satire of *El periquillo sarniento*; the visionary idealism of Francisco Morazán, the first president of the Central American Confederation; the abolition of slavery in 1823; the ultimately failed attempt at Central American unity; or José Santos Zelaya's effort to promote a Nicaraguan canal and his reform program at the beginning of the twentieth century. Despite its connection with the formation of the agro-export oligarchy, this has made liberalism—in its more "Jacobin" variants—still a strong ideological current in Central American nationalism (Sandino was a nominal Liberal).[13]

The contradiction between Liberal rhetoric and the actual forms of social and economic organization it produced, which is a feature of bourgeois culture generally in the nineteenth century, became particularly acute in the situation Central America entered with independence. Ramírez notes in this regard that the point of departure for modern Central American culture is "the rupture of the unity of cultural norms imposed by the Spanish colony, a rupture which fully materializes not with the 1821 independence proclamations, but in the second half of the nineteenth century, through the expansion of the world capitalist system and the place assigned Central America in the international division of labor by the entry of coffee and other other products in the world market" (1983a: 42–43).

Liberal ideology consolidated itself juridically in new constitutions that, with a high-sounding and sometimes radical rhetoric, ended up legitimizing the dispossession of church and Indian lands and their concentration in the hands of a coffee-producing bourgeoisie. The connection with the world market generated by free trade policy meant that products manufactured in Europe and the United States were imported into the region and began to affect the tastes and attitudes of the new agro-export oligarchies.

The ambition of these groups—some of them formed by recent immigrants—was above all to be considered part of the metropolitan bourgeoisie. It was a desire, Ramírez observes, that also came to determine their permanent frustration, since they were unable as a class to carry foward the development of their nation-states on the model of their European and North American peers. Hence their feelings of inadequacy, provincialism, and anachronism. They designed and decorated European-style homes, churches, offices, clubs. They sought to legitimize their project by rejecting regional values and fostering cosmopolitan cultural standards. But they were unable to create, even at the level of language, a unified national culture, because such a culture would have contradicted their class economic basis in cheap agricultural labor. Their laws left the native population on the margins of the national body politic and history. As a social group, they were ethnically and culturally alien to the project of national unification they sought to champion. Even in terms of their own needs, their adaptations of European models were not creative or extensive enough to produce a satisfactory life-style. They depended on imports, as much of ideas as of consumer goods.

In Europe, literature—centered after romanticism around the novel, lyric poetry, and the theater—was the major cultural form of the bourgeoisie in the nineteenth century. It follows that the contradictions of dependent Liberalism reproduced themselves with special force in the development of a Central American literature. In Central America, the role of literature was to legitimize the new oligarchic order, to act as an intermediary between the emerging inadequate "national" culture represented by the agro-export bourgeoisie and the culture of the metropolitan centers. By imposing writing and literacy as standards of cultural performance, the cult of literature put the predominantly oral cultural practices of the indigenous communities and the mestizo peasantry and farm workers in a relation of subordination and domination.[14]

However, there were also contradictions in the situation of literature and the writer, just as there were problems with the *colonos* and Indian communities who balked at submitting to a form of "progress" that dispossessed, uprooted, and impoverished them. The hegemonic intellectual currents of the period of consolidation of the Liberal oligarchies toward the end of the nineteenth century tended to be versions of positivism, Social Darwinism, and classical political economy tailored to the peculiarities of Central American development. But the very ideologues who fostered these doctrines were often themselves clerically educated, humanist literati—sometimes of mestizo origin—who found these doctrines limiting and abhorrent to their own personal values, which incorporated elements of feudal and precapitalist cultures. They were prone to distance themselves in their writing from what they regarded as the more "vulgar" (democratic and/or explicitly commercial) aspects of the new order in the name of "higher" values based on an idealization of the immediate or distant Latin American or European past as a time of harmony and beauty.[15]

The intrigues and struggles around independence and confederation consumed potential writers like Morazán in proclamations, speeches, editorials and pamphlets. Central American literature thus comes into being, Ramírez points out, as a modern literature, not so much with independence itself as with the region's insertion into the world market sytem in the mid and later nineteenth century. The first important writers of the postindependence period were both Guatemalans: Antonio José de Irrisari, author of two semiautobiographical novels in a picaresque mode, *El cristiano errante* (1847) and *Historia del perínclito Epaminondas de Cauca* (1863), which are the Central American equivalent of *El periquillo sarniento;* and the narrative poet and satirist, José Batres Montúfar.

Two major literary systems developed in the context of agro-export dependency: *costumbrismo* and *modernismo.* Fostered by the rise of periodical journalism, *costumbrismo* designates narrative sketches (sometimes strung togther to form a longer story), usually in prose, of manners and social customs (the first Central American *costumbrista* writing is attributed to the Guatemalan José Milla). The *costumbristas* shared the same general vision of a romanticized rural world, a sort of timeless tropical Arcadia with no essential contradictions or complications. In Liberal *costumbrismo* there was sometimes a mildly satirical or critical note directed against the backwardness and *caudillismo* of the older sector of the oligarchy, but rarely a critique of the system as such. As Ramírez puts it, the *costumbristas* "saw the countryside from the balcony." The Central American reality closest to the image was perhaps Costa Rica's, where *costumbrismo* reached its apogee in the work of the so-called Generation of 1900.

In 1894 there was a major debate in San José over the kind of literature the Central American writer should produce. The protagonists of the new literary movement represented by Darío, the *modernistas*, attacked the *costumbristas'* concentration on rural themes, arguing the need for a literature with a more urbane, up-to-date (hence their sobriquet), cosmopolitan character. Their reference point was Darío's enormously popular first book of poems and prose sketches, *Azul* (1888). Though they explicitly rejected the notion that art and literature should serve politics, their literary program paralleled the desire on the part of some sectors of the oligarchy for reform and modernization of the state along the lines suggested by Zelaya's presidency in Nicaragua. On both sides of the debate, however, the terms were essentially Eurocentric and elitist. Even those who supported *costumbrismo* did so from the perspective of romantic conceptions of the folkloric and popular. Despite their apparent confrontation, both tendencies represented strategies related to the nature of the oligarchy's own contradictory insertion in the world economy.

Marcos Kaplan has pointed to a "dialectic of cosmopolitanism and nationalism" (albeit with a predominance of the first over the second) in Latin American culture and politics of this period generally. He notes that

> on the one hand, the dynamic of incorporation into the international market system and the relation of dependency lead to a

tendency towards europeanization. On the other, the oligarchy needed to keep intact its own room for maneuver in relation to keeping the relations of exploitation intact, assuring internal cohesion and its own hegemony, and establishing a negotiating position with foreign interests and the Great Powers. (Kaplan 1969: 194–195)

The point may help to explain the continual oscillation in Central American literature and individual Central American writers like Darío between localism and cosmopolitanism, "pure" poetry and the older Liberal-romantic idea of literature as a civic function. Ramírez argues that in Central America the "detour" of *modernista* cosmopolitanism was necessary to the evolution of a fully developed regional literature. *Costumbrismo* in both its Liberal and Conservative variants was a more or less direct expression of traditional oligarchic interests; *modernismo* was more contradictory. At a minimum it appropriated for Latin America literature the formal and technical resources of the most advanced European and North American literature (writers like Neruda or García Márquez would not have been possible without *modernismo*).[16] In the case of Nicaragua, Darío's poetry represented a pioneering synthesis of aesthetic and ideological elements derived from the crisis of the regional oligarchies provoked by the building of the Panama Canal and by U.S. intervention generally at the end of the nineteenth century, a synthesis related ideologically to the nationalist liberalism of the Zelaya regime.

The question of the ideological effects of *modernismo* is still subject to debate, as we will detail in our discussion of Darío in chapter 3. What is clear is that to the degree that Central American writers were able to throw off the Eurocentrism implicit in both *costumbrismo* and *modernismo*, they began to develop a genuine regionalism, as in the stories of the Salvadoran writer Salarrué (b. 1899). What intervened in Central American culture to break apart the Liberal/Conservative, *modernista/costumbrista* antinomies was the impact of the Mexican and Russian revolutions, and the particular form the general crisis of the Latin American oligarchies in the years from the First World War through the depression took in the region. In Central American literature, this was the moment of a tentative movement toward social realism, very much influenced by the novels (and to some extent the political perspective) of Rómulo Gallegos in Venezuela; of Nicaraguan and Salvadoran Vanguardism; and of Miguel Angel Asturias's *Leyendas de Guatemala* and *El señor presidente*, which marked the beginnings of a literary engagement with Indian culture.[17] This is also the moment of the initial formation of a revolutionary anti-imperialist left in the region.

Intellectuals and Modernization in the 1960s and 1970s

We return here in a context specific to Central American development to the issue we raised in chapter 1 of the distinction between Marxism as a "science" (in Althusserian terms, as a form of *theoretical* practice) and the articulation of actual ideologies and corresponding political movements of revolutionary popular struggle. In Central America the role of the populist mass parties that develop elsewhere in Latin America (APRA, Acción Democrática, the Argentine Radicals) is played in a very different way by Farabundo Martí, Sandino, and intellectuals like Asturias and the Guatemalan Generation of 1930. These figures should be seen as elaborating responses to imperialism that challenged its cognate ideological justifications in positivist and historicist schemas of rationalization, "universal progress," racial *blanqueamiento*, and the like.

The connection of scientific ideology and science itself with imperialism repositioned religion, the humanities, and the fine arts, which were beginning to become secondary spheres of ideological production in the metropolitan centers, as hegemonic cultural forms in Latin America and the periphery in general.[18] Intellectual activity tended (and tends) to find expression, variously, in modes of philosophical idealism or irrationalism, spiritualism and religious thought, both right- and left-wing political radicalism (including several varieties of socialism and Marxism), in the fine arts, and in literature. As Françoise Perus (1973) has suggested, even the cult of positivism itself was an ideological symptom of the oligarchy's differential relation to European culture, in the sense that it expressed more a utopian wish than an actual state of events or possible policy.

The relative sophistication of Latin American literature after *modernismo*, contrasted to the relative absence or underdevelopment of scientific-technical culture, can be seen then as both a consequence of and a response to dependency. The uneven development of bourgeois institutionality in the early decades of the twentieth century produced in Latin America a situation where the division of intellectual labor characteristic of the metropolitan countries had not yet fully appeared. As a result, Perus argues, "the novel and poetry take on functions which in the 1950s or 1960s will fall to the social sciences proper." In the periphery, literature is valorized "primarily for its (aesthetic-ideological) use value," rather than as in the formalist aesthetics dominant in the metropolis for its autonomy from politics and economics. In particular, the development of cultural apparatuses (newspapers, magazines, presses, reading circles, and the like) connected with the new political parties and organizations opened up for literature the possibility of a new, *actual or potential*, reading public, which would be qualitatively different from the traditional elite one, among other things in its aesthetic expectations. With the appearance on the cultural scene of this new public, which is more directly linked to the world of work and of everyday life . . . arise demands for new forms of literature more closely related to the conditions of life of these sectors and, with these new forms, the championing of a "realist" (when not explicitly "socialist" or "proletarian") aesthetics. (Perus 1982: 108)

We are close here to the empirical situation represented by the adolescent literary enthusiasms of Fonseca and his Matagalpan chums, deep in the provinces of Nicaragua in the early 1950s. What the lists of Fonseca's readings show (see in particular note 7), among other things, is that his consciousness and knowledge of Marxism were as much shaped by literature—social realist novels like Steinbeck's *Grapes of Wrath* or Gorky's *Mother*, the poetry of Vallejo and Neruda, Joseph Davis's memoir of Stalin's Russia, *Mission to Moscow*—as by such Marxist tracts as the *Communist Manifesto, What Is to Be Done?, The Origins of the Family, Private Property and the State*, or Mao's essays.

The period of the dictatorships (in Nicaragua and El Salvador after 1932; in Guatemala between 1932 and 1944 and after 1954) meant a general repression or restriction of not only Marxist, but also technical-scientific and secular humanist culture, including literature. The appropriate symbol of this was General Martínez's encouragement of theosophy in El Salvador—which extended to, among other things, his prohibition of inoculations for children and his belief that a revival of traditional handicraft production would be the key to El Salvador's economic future. The new cultural factor that began to intervene more and more in the post–World War II era was U.S. involvement in the creation of a modernized educational and intellectual infrastructure in the region.

The penetration of Central American education by U.S. private and government programs occurred at a number of different levels (we rely here on Monteforte Toledo 1972). The cultural sections of the embassies gave grants, extended invitations of travel to intellectuals, promoted professional interchanges, edited and distributed books, provided non-commercial films, organized exhibitions, and worked closely with local newspapers and media. American schools were set up for the children of the urban bourgeoisie and the North American colony. In the context of the Alliance for Progress and the Central American Common Market, AID and other funding sources poured in millions of dollars for school construction, equipment, and books and sent experts to plan educational campaigns with the collaboration of Central American teachers. Responding to the economic difficulties of higher education and the weaknesses in technical and scientific areas, the Ford Foundation and similar organizations gave grants for teaching, research, and the purchase of equipment and buildings—either directly to the universities or through the Consejo Superior Universitario Centroamericano. The center of Central American cultural and intellectual life, which had traditionally been Guatemala City, shifted to Costa Rica in response to the relatively open and democratic situation that developed there in the 1950s.

The purpose of this policy was the formation and the control of a prodemocratic, reformist middle- and lower-middle-class technical-professional intelligentsia that could serve as an alternative to the reactionary sectors of the local bourgeoisies tied to the regional dictatorships, and at the same time act as an intermediary between the interests of the bourgeoisie as a whole, U.S. and other foreign interests, and the peasantry and working class. Implicit in this goal, of course, was the creation of an alternative and a counter to the influence of Marxist ideas and the organized political left in the region (contemporary Salvadoran Christian Democracy would be a good example of what the policy aimed at).

But educational modernization had contradictory results, partly because it was a kind of cultural imperialism that could be resisted as such, partly because in some ways it was more progressive than the regimes it was channeled through. The majority of active intellectuals in Central America come from middle- or upper-class backgrounds. Some—the children of older oligarchic dynasties, embittered by a foreign presence in their country that marginalized their own cultural heritage and values—became part of a nationalist opposition while at the same time sometimes retaining very close ties to certain aspects of U.S. culture (e.g., the cases of Ernesto Cardenal in Nicaragua or Claribel Alegría in El Salvador). Others identified with and participated in the modernization programs, but began to sense precisely on that basis that the existing power structures were incapable of implementing real reforms in this direction. Others were connected more or less directly with the groups in power, but came to feel that these betrayed or didn't fully represent their interests.

In the 1960s, the main base for political opposition came from precisely the group targeted by the modernization programs: students and young professionals from middle-class backgrounds who had their main institutional ties with the universities in their home country or in Mexico or Costa Rica. Of this group, those intellectuals who eventually radicalized tended to be those, like Fonseca, whose professional interest was concerned more with questions of "culture" than "civilization": lawyers (as a sort of general form of university-educated intellectual), writers, artists, religious intellectuals, sectors of the social sciences relatively independent from policy, teachers. The majority of intellectuals not directly involved in business, technical, or policy areas found themselves caught up in a cultural-political activism whose consequences often went beyond their own immediate ambitions and projects and came increasingly to imply participation in, collaboration with, or sympathy for the revolutionary organizations or their fronts.

A key intermediary between university life and revolutionary activism was the increasingly radical student groups that begin to appear in the late 1950s and early 1960s in both the secondary school system and the universities. Whatever the initial class, political, and religious formation of the individuals concerned, these involved, as we noted in the case of Fonseca, sharing in the production and consumption of a nationalist, left-inflected counterculture constituted very centrally around novels, poetry, songs, ephemeral literary magazines and student journals, and the like. In these terms, perhaps the single most important institution in the development of this counterculture among the intelligentsia was the Editorial Universitaria Centroamericana (EDUCA) created in San José by the Confederation of Central American Universities under the auspices of the regional common market and the educational modernization programs. EDUCA became the main publisher of the new generation of left-oriented writers and literary critics represented by figures like Claribel Alegría, Roque Dalton, and Manlio Argueta in El Salvador; Otto René Castillo in Guatemala; and Sergio Ramírez in Nicaragua.[19]

Paradoxically, then, the limited but real space opened for Central American education, universities, and publishing ventures in the 1960s by U.S.-inspired and funded programs served to promote the development of a radicalized sector of the humanist-technical intelligentsia strategically positioned to react to the new contingencies generated by the rapid socioeconomic change and crisis in this period. Pressures for structural change from modernizing sectors of the bourgeoisie and the middle strata combined with the displacement of large sectors of the rural population and the rapid growth of an urban working class to create the context in which this new church and university-bred intelligentsia began to function. Fonseca's revision of Sandinismo in Nicaragua, the various Cuban-style guerrilla movements in Guatemala in the 1960s, the popular organizations of what would eventually become the FDR-FMLN in El Salvador, and throughout the region the spread of Liberation Theology base communities, provided the broad political and organizational bases for this intelligentsia in its complex, and often internally contradictory, orientations. The kind of poetry and testimonial narrative we will be looking at in the remaining chapters, which constitute the historical and descriptive portion of this book, were its catalyst.

Poetry and Politics

Restating a point we have made several times already, Central American literature in general fails to achieve a significant degree of relative autonomy from other levels of social practice; it operates under the constant and more or less direct pressure of political and ideological circumstances and in turn is itself a factor in determining those circumstances. Even *modernismo*, the most extreme effort at aesthetic autonomy, was both an expression of and reaction against the inroads of capitalist modernity into the bucolic and patriarchal cultural world of the Latin American oligarchies. As we will see in chapter 3, in Darío's own work aesthetic autonomy broke down under the pressure of the social forces it sought to elude. But in the process, aestheticism itself came to acquire an implicit ideological cast as a signifier of a possible "Indo-Hispanic" counterlogic to the discourses of modernization and foreign domination. What the achievement of Darío's poetry—and more generally of *modernismo* as a literary movement—did secure was the position of poetry as the dominant mode of cultural production in Central America. The breakdown of the *modernista* system and the development of literary regionalism and then vanguardism in Central America resulted in a contradictory situation where the basis of the literary system as such became dependent on its integration with the national problematic. An aesthetic ideology privileging poetry as a cultural form became in turn a component of nationalist ideology.[20]

In the chapters that follow, we posit the following general stages of development out of the *modernista* frame established at the turn of the century by Darío: (1) Central American *vanguardismo* and related tendencies in the 1920s and 1930s; (2) the literary groups and figures that develop during and after the Guatemalan October Revolution (1944–1954); (3) the emergence of Roque Dalton and El Salvador's *Generación comprometida*, and Ernesto Cardenal and exteriorist poetry in Nicaragua in the 1950s; (4) the radicalization of the political situation in the 1960s and 1970s, with consequent development of a poetry closely connected to the emergence of armed struggle in the region; (5) the impact of Liberation Theology and women's liberation discourses in Salvadoran and Guatemalan combat poetry and in the postrevolutionary Nicaraguan poetry in the later 1970s and early 1980s; and (6) the contingent shift toward testimonial forms in both poetry and narrative prose, itself a consequence of shifts in the situation, theory, and strategy of the revolutionary movements in recent years.

We should reiterate that we do not see this literature simply as an *expression* of left revolutionary currents, but as an active force invoking these. This involves us in the question of the conjuncturally determined cultural consumption or reception of literature. Even texts or elements of the previous literary system whose intention and formal configuration are not political may be appropriated by a process of radicalization that transforms their meaning in terms of its own functionality. In turn, this process (which entails the elaboration of a revolutionary "horizon of expectations" with regard to poetry) feeds back on literary production itself, so that writers may very easily find themselves creating works whose political implications are far more radical than their own overt ideological positions.

One final note in this respect: In holding that poetry is the dominant literary mode in Central America, we are far from wanting to romanticize it as a uniquely progressive or revolutionary cultural form, as is often the case in discussions of its role in Central America (e.g., by poets themselves, as in the passage from Coronel Urtecho we cite in note 20). As we have tried to show in these two chapters, poetry has the kind of centrality it does in Central America precisely as the effect of a situation of cultural "combined and uneven development" characteristic of many—but by no means all—postcolonial countries. Among other things, it is a uniquely portable form of literature capable of being produced and circulated in conditions of poverty and clandestinity, unlike the novel or scientific-technical writing, which require large-scale publishing and distribution apparatuses.[21] As these countries modernize and/or undergo revolutionary change, however, narrative forms like the testimonio or the novel tend to become more important than poetry, and literature itself will begin to be displaced as a hegemonic cultural medium by the mass media, particularly television and radio, and new forms of popular culture whose nature it is difficult to predict.

Notes

1. Michael Taussig's (1987) account of the culture of shamanism in Latin America is a brilliant elaboration of this phenomenon in the sphere of popular culture and religious ideologies.

2. In what follows we are obviously indebted to Donald Hodges's *Intellectual Foundations of the Nicaraguan Revolution* (1986), particularly his chapter "From Sandino to Sandinismo," although our focus on discursive production is somewhat different from his political science approach, which does not take into account Fonseca's literary interests and ambitions.

3. The *Ideario* was supplanted in 1974 by Sergio Ramírez's much more extensive anthology, *El pensamiento vivo de Sandino*.

4. Borge's memoirs, *La paciente impaciencia* (1989b), offer a richly detailed reconstruction of their Matagalpan childhood and adolescence.

5. The *Ideario* was paralleled and complemented by Ernesto Cardenal's important long poem *Hora 0* (1957, 1959), which reconstructed for the generation that was coming of age in Nicaragua in the early 1960s the narrative of Sandino's campaign in terms of the post–Cuban Revolution emphasis on the role of the guerrilla *foco* as the vanguard form of national liberation struggle. We will discuss *Hora 0* in greater detail in chapter 3; for the moment, we should note that this is the title Fonseca chose for his important 1969 manifesto of the FSLN.

6. These are: the chronology of Fonseca prepared by the Instituto para el Estudio del Sandinismo mentioned above (in Fonseca 1984: 431–440); his own travel journal, *Un nicaragüense en Moscú* (ibid.: 275–344); Tomás Borge's account of their friendship in his prison journal and memoirs (Borge 1984 and 1989b); the recollections of Humberto Ortega included as a preface to the *Obras* (Fonseca 1984: 14–16); and a testimony by writer and fellow Matagalpan Guillermo Rothschuh cited by Hodges (1986: 164).

7. The most complete account of Fonseca's early readings is in a 1981 lecture by fellow FSLN cadre member Humberto Ortega reproduced as a preface to Fonseca's *Obras* (1984: 15). It borrows partly from the sources noted above, but adds a number of other materials. We reproduce it here in full for its documentary value.

Para esa época, se devoraba con honda pasión y sensibilidad humana el *Canto general* de Pablo Neruda; *Viñas de ira*, del novelista norteamericano John Steinbeck; *La enfermedad infantil del 'izquierdismo' en el comunismo* de Lenin—adquirido en la librería del consecuente opositor antisomocista Adán Selva—; *La madre* de Gorki; *Historia de los Estados Unidos* y otras lecturas como las de Tomás Moro, William Faulkner, César Vallejo, el libro *Misión en Moscú*, de Joseph Davis, exembajador de Estados Unidos en la Unión Soviética; el *Manifiesto del Partido Comunista* y un resumen de *El Capital*, lo mismo que *El origen de la familia, la propiedad privada y el estado* de los sabios revolucionarios Carlos Marx y Federico Engels. En 1955, al bachillerarse Carlos en el Instituto Nacional de Matagalpa, presenta la tesis "El capital y el trabajo." Libros, folletos, revistas, periódicos eran cazados con gran agilidad por el joven Fonseca y a la altura de 1956, Carlos, además de los textos ya citados, contaba en su poder decenas de textos relativos a distintos tópicos como la ley de reforma agraria, "El socialismo argentino y las reformas penales," *Utopía, El príncipe,* "Ensayos sindicales de inspiración católica en la República Argentina," "El cristianismo y los nuevos tiempos," "Sobre el derecho de autodeterminación de la naciones," "De la neutralidad vigilante a la mediación en Guatemala," *La hora de la clase obrera, La epopeya de Stalingrado, La nueva democracia* de Mao Tse Tung, ¿*Que hacer!* de Lenin, *La revolución histórica de México, La cuestión indígena en América,* Balzac, *Declaración Universal de los Derechos del Hombre, Boletín de estadísticas,* textos de Rubén Darío, y revistas de la época como *Visión, Life, Venezuela, Seguridad social campesina.*

8. The text is reproduced in Fonseca (1984: 393–406). The "Carta-testamento" was a personal letter Lopéz wrote to his mother, explaining the reasons for his action against Somoza and asking her to settle his affairs should he be killed in the course of carrying it out. Fonseca's study and version of it appeared initially as a special supplement of *Casa de las Américas* in 1972.

9. There is another version of this anecdote in Borge's memoirs (1989b: 186–189). The phrase "Sandino is a path" comes from a poem by Rigoberto López Pérez's coconspirator in the Somoza *ajusticiamiento*, Edwin Castro, also an associate of Borge. The "guy from León" refers to Nöel Guerrero, Fonseca and Borge's tutor in Marxism who subsequently broke with them. *El calvario* is the official history of Sandino commissioned by the Somozas; the "Spaniard" was Ramón de Belausteguigoitia, author of *Con Sandino en las montañas* (1934); Calderón wrote *Ultimos días de Sandino* (1934); "Selser's books" refers to Gregorio Selser's two-volume *Sandino: general de hombres libres* (originally published in 1957), with an extensive selection from Sandino's correspondence and writings—one of the texts that has most influenced contemporary Central American radicalism. Rothschuh (cited in Hodges 1986, p. 164) adds that while he was living in Managua, Fonseca worked through Emigdio Maraboto's *Sandino ante el coloso* (1929), Carleton Beals's *Banana Gold* (1932), and Gustavo Alemán Bolaños's *Sandino el libertador* (1951).

10. Fonseca saw Raudales's group as "the beginning of the reactivation of armed struggle, with its principal base in the rural areas . . . with the object of achieving a definitive popular and national liberation" (Fonseca 1984: 356).

11. In much of what follows in this section, we depend on Sergio Ramírez's seminal essay on Central American cultural history, "Balcanes y volcanes" (1983a: 11–115).

12. "Pobres repúblicas. . . . Es duro decir que en aquella tierra, apenas conocida por el canal y por el café, no hay, en absoluto, aire para las almas, vida para el espíritu. En un ambiente de tiempo viejo, el amor de un cielo tibio y perezoso reina la murmuración aúlica; el progreso material va a paso de tortuga, y los mejores talentos, las mejores fuerzas, o escapan de la atmósfera de plomo o mueren en guerras de hermanos, comiéndose el corazón uno a otro porque sea presidente Juan o Pedro" (*Prosa dispersa*, cited in Valle 1960: 13).

13. We should note that in general analyses of Latin American cultural history that derive from dependency theory—including Ramírez's, which we follow here—have a tendency to underestimate the progressive dimensions of at least certain aspects of national bourgeois culture and the degree of ideological contradictions within the Latin American bourgeoisies themselves.

14. See Rama (1982) on this point. Ramírez cautions that in dealing with the relation of oligarchic Liberalism to indigenous and mestizo popular cultures in the nineteenth century, one cannot even speak of a "clash of cultures," since the two barely converged.

15. Françoise Perus's portrait of Darío (1976: 100–139) gives a good sense of this.

16. In the 1920s, Mariátegui had argued similarly in his *Siete ensayos* that the shift in Latin American literature from a narrowly nationalist perspective to even an artificial cosmopolitanism, as in the case of *modernismo*, could be a

progressive stage in the development of a literary language and culture that transcended Creole Liberalism and suggested the necessity or possibility of a socialist solution to the problem of Latin American development.

17. On the transition from *costumbrismo* and *modernismo* to Latin American literary realism and vanguardism, and the connection of this with more general ideological shifts, see Perus (1982: chap. 3), and Losada (1979).

18. For a good discussion of this point (though oriented toward Indian nationalism), see Chatterjee (1986).

19. For a history of Central American student movements and an analysis of their role as incubators of revolutionary ideology see P. González (1985). The rector of the National University of Nicaragua in Managua (UNAN) in the late 1950s, Mariano Fiallos Gil, was an important figure in promoting the emergence of a left intelligentsia in both Nicaragua and Central America generally. From 1957 to 1961, Fonseca was heavily involved in student activism at the UNAN, among other things editing the student newspaper *El Universitario* and organizing a demonstration against a visit to the university by then U.S. President Eisenhower's brother Milton to receive an honorary doctorate. Fonseca participated in the founding of the Juventud Democrática (later Patriótica) Nicaragüense (JPN) in 1959 and in 1961 of the Frente Estudiantil Revolucionario (FER), the student front of the Movimiento Nueva Nicaragua, the predecessor organization of the FSLN.

20. The following remarks by the Nicaraguan vanguardist poet José Coronel Urtecho suggest one way this linkage could be articulated:

> In reality, all people are born more or less poets and Nicaraguans are almost all natural poets, who stop being poets to the degree that life deforms them or separates them from poetry. This means that . . . the system, or if you wish the regime, is in itself a war against poets and the poetry of Nicaraguan life or of human life itself. It is, in any event, a struggle against the poets, and all those who fight the system which in Nicaragua has taken the worst form imaginable, are poets. At least this is one way one could describe . . . the Nicaraguan struggle against imperialism. (1979: 9–10).

21. When we complained to a group of social scientists during a 1989 visit to Nicaragua about the effects of the new austerity program (*compactación*) on literary activity, we were reminded by them that publication of poetry still commanded a higher priority and greater resources than work in the social sciences or professional disciplines, not to speak of the natural sciences.

3. Nicaraguan Poetry from Darío to Cardenal

While the novel became the crucial form of literary nationalism in most of Latin America, in Central America, as we have noted, poetry assumed that role. In no Central American country has poetry been as important an element of the national culture as in Nicaragua, however. This situation is both constituted and represented by the central place of Rubén Darío in modern Nicaraguan literature.

Whatever the political and artistic inconsistencies of Darío as the poet laureate of a fin de siècle oligarchy, fascinated and repelled by the United States at the same time, Sandinismo invents a cult of personality around him similar to that of Martí in Cuban revolutionary culture. Darío, and the practice of poetry as such, become for the Nicaraguan Revolution forms of expression of the national-popular. Sergio Ramírez observes:

> The revolution rescues Darío, not from oblivion but from false idolization, because Darío has always been authentically present in the popular imagination as the source of a pride more intuited than understood, as the figure of the "great poet," the genius of unknown acts who could triumph over any rival, over death itself: the poet of poets, the fabulous creator of impossible rhymes and images.
> Because poetry as such, and poetic inspiration, are values which the Nicaraguan people esteem without limit. (1983a: 198)

Ramírez argues that the Sandinista Revolution should itself be seen as a cultural revolution, stemming at least in part from a specifically literary project centered on poetry. He links this to Nicaragua's ". . . limited tradition of individual cultural creation. Within the real conditions of social development, this tradition was only given in poetry, and very slightly in painting or narrative, not to mention music, where the absence is almost absolute." Ramírez adds that since the Nicaraguan bourgeoisie "failed to consolidate its own line of cultural creators, the most important artists in our contemporary history emerged in contradiction with this bourgeoisie, . . . with imperialism or the dictatorship" (1982b: 50).

As we have seen, Darío's prestige established poetry as the hegemonic form of literature and as the major vehicle of intellectual expression in the Central American area. From this point on, a modern poetic system took form, which of necessity registered major changes in politics and ideology. At the same time, this system served in turn as a medium for the generation of ideological and intellectual transformations that inspired political mobilization and struggle. Following the logic of the argument we have developed in the last two chapters, to the degree that the force of a foreign intervention and then Somocismo made the political character of the state an essential fact of social life, and to the degree that poetry was a central mode of intellectual expression and resistance, politics came to dominate poetry, and political poetry came to dominate Nicaraguan literature as a whole. In this chapter, we will sketch the evolution of Nicaraguan poetry out of Darío's *modernismo*, passing through the work of the vanguardists in the 1930s and 1940s into Cardenal and the writers, like Ramírez, who were the literary fellow travelers of Fonseca and the Sandinistas. In chapter 4, we will look more closely at developments in Nicaraguan poetry during and after the revolution itself.

Darío and *Modernismo*

Modernismo, as its name suggests, represented a complex reaction to the experience of modernity in Latin America at the turn of the century.[1] Though somewhat incoherent in both its artistic and political programs, it succeeded in producing a general renovation of Latin American literature, above all, of poetry. The *modernistas'* literary model was the esoteric poetry of the French symbolists and the hyperaestheticism of the art nouveau movement championed in Europe by figures like Baudelaire and Oscar Wilde; their cultural sign was the figure of Ariel in Shakespeare's *The Tempest*, celebrated by the Uruguayan writer Rodó as the incarnation of the refinement of the Latin American Creole elite as against the menacing Prospero represented by North American cultural and economic imperialism. The movement was cosmopolitan, francophile, bohemian, pan-American (in the sense that the *modernistas* sought to write for a general rather than a national or regional Latin American reading public); it stressed the separation of art from the worlds of politics and commerce, the power of fantasy and the imagination, sensuality, the idealization of the past, above all the careful cultivation and enrichment of poetic language and form itself. In consequence, *modernismo* has the reputation of being a Latin American form of "art for art's sake," fundamentally elitist, formalist, and apolitical in character, particularly when compared with the contemporary Generation of '98 in Spain.

Modernismo was not without any connection to ideology and power, however. For one thing, its appearance as a cultural phenomenon coincided with the advent of imperialism in Latin America and signaled Latin America's growing role both in world literature and in a developing world-market system. As Octavio Paz put it concisely, the movement's "passion for modernity is not simply a catering to fashion: it represents the will to participate in a historical plenitude previously denied to Spanish Americans" (cited in Fernández Retamar 1984). In the recent critical literature on the movement, two general characterizations have predominated, both of which assign it a negative or at least ambivalent political character with respect to Latin American nationalism: (1) as a form of cultural modernization, closely tied to the emergence of a new oligarchic order, which in turn is a function of the new markets and the restructuring of the domestic economies by foreign capital; (2) as an artistic or more generally a cultural reaction to and possibly against imperialist penetration by an idealization of precapitalist oligarchic cultural models opposed to British and then U.S. hegemony.[2]

These perspectives are synthesized by Françoise Perus (1976) in her study of Darío, the most important of the *modernistas* and the prime source of the negative view of the movement's political significance. For Perus, *modernismo* should be understood as a superstructural effect of the retrograde, dependent development of Latin American economies, which brings in its wake an oligarchic order without any genuine transformation of social relations or of ideological perspectives, or for that matter, of the character and function of intellectuals.[3] For all its cosmopolitanism, dynamism, and innovation, Darío's *modernista* revolution simply meant the articulation at the level of poetry of an ideological practice ultimately confirming this oligarchic power structure in the context of the new opportunities and dangers it had to deal with at the end of the century. Darío, Perus points out, was like most of the major *modernistas*, a functionary (diplomat, minister, bureaucrat, senator, etc.) of the oligarchic state apparatus itself.

But, as we have noted, these oligarchies were themselves positioned in contradictory ways in relation to the inroads of foreign, particularly U.S., capital and personnel, and the changes these provoked in Latin America. On the one hand, they saw themselves as the agent or collaborators of the doctrine of progress, a would-be comprador bourgeoisie; on the other, they, or fractions of them, were in some ways its actual or potential victims. Darío's poetry reflects this ambivalence. Darío was wary of the new currents of materialism, positivism, and naturalism entering Latin

American culture. He feared a growing loss of spirituality and imagination, qualities he, like Rodó, associated with Latin American civilization. But, Perus argues, while Darío sought to restore and secure these values, he equated the exaltation of the spirit with luxury, the most extreme forms of sensuousness and exoticism, a glorification of the lifestyle of the oligarchic families, and a quest for aesthetic forms and experiences deliberately distanced from the masses. Darío's sometime opposition to particular aspects of U.S. influence and oligarchic rule stemmed not from a revolutionary grasp and exploration of the contradictions implicit in capitalism and imperialism, but from a nostalgic sense that the new order was eroding elements of a partly real, partly mythical quasi-feudal value world of which the practice of poetry and the figure of the great poet themselves were ultimate symbols.

Perus places Darío against the Latin American bourgeoisie as a whole at the turn of the century, a role and status he indeed sought by expanding his activities beyond Central America to Chile, Buenos Aires, and eventually Europe. (In most Latin American literary histories, it is almost incidental that Darío was a Nicaraguan.) She suggests a general ideological dichotomy within this bourgeoisie in the contrast between Darío and the Cuban poet and revolutionary Martí, with Darío representing an ambivalent but ultimately reactionary response to the experience of modernity, Martí a renunciation of *modernista* elitism in favor of a more popular-democratic conception of Latin American culture and development.

But a rather different picture emerges if we look at Darío in relation to Nicaragua itself, among other things because of his very close relation with Nicaraguan liberalism and the Zelaya regime in particular. As Ramírez has suggested (1983a: 44–67), for all his cosmopolitanism Darío was first and foremost a Nicaraguan of a certain time and place, formed essentially by the social and ideological circumstances of his childhood environment. Even his exile should be seen in this light. Compared to Guatemala and El Salvador, Nicaragua was a relatively late entry in the coffee production-export system, the economic base of Central American liberalism. As a result, the great Conservative dynasties of the city of Granada were able to maintain a patriarchal and Catholic hegemony over the national culture, one of the reasons for the Liberals' initial pact with Walker. Darío, raised in the Liberal university city of León, was sensitive to this situation, which he described as a "lamentable state of embryonic civilization." His self-imposed exile to the great urban centers of the Southern Cone meant a rejection of the provincialism and *costumbrista* localism of Nicaraguan culture, a choice in both his poetry and his journalism for a cosmopolitan, universalizing perspective. But even in this function he remained, in the image of the vanguardist poet

José Coronel Urtecho, the "inevitable paisano" of Nicaraguans in their relations with the outside world.

Darío's connection with Zelaya's project to stimulate the development of a national bourgeoisie is particularly significant in this respect. Darío was in the terms of the time an *extranjerizante* or "Europeanizer"; but the upshot of this posture was his creation of a flexible, sophisticated literary manner capable of defending itself against, indeed of competing with, the threat represented by U.S. cultural penetration, on the one hand, and the domination of European cultural models, on the other. His writing represented a struggle to free Latin American Spanish from the domination of the "mother tongue" and Spanish literature, but also from the encroaching influence of English. Darío aimed to be for Nicaragua and Latin America as a whole what Whitman had been for U.S. culture: the creator of a national voice in literature. But to do this he had to adopt a perspective outside the immediate limitations of Nicaraguan nine-teenth-century national culture itself.[4]

It is in the nexus between Darío's aesthetic system and the question of the defense against or adaptation to imperialism that the Central American and Nicaraguan significance of his multivalent cosmopolitanism must be located. Darío's search for an authentic Latin American spirituality is at the root of his view that "if there is poetry in America, it is in old things." In the famous introduction to his *Prosas profanas*, he writes that he was not born of his age, that he draws the inspiration of his poetry from a past Golden Age, sometimes identified with a feudal chivalric age, sometimes with pre-Columbian America, sometimes with the life of the great absolutist courts, sometimes with rural idylls of the days of the *hacienda*. But the elements of these different idealizations of a precapitalist value world are also connected to a form of democratic Liberalism that went far beyond even the most open and progressive Latin American governments of his day. In Darío, exotic fantasies of the past function paradoxically as a quasi-utopian social vision, projecting images of human possibility into the future beyond the immediate pressure to accommodate to U.S. power and interests. This may account for the particularly intense escapist opulence of his poetry as well as the ironic ambivalence with which it negotiates between the celebration of an older, oligarchic agrarian order and the sociocultural effects of industrialization and what the Cuban *modernista* Julián del Casal called "el impuro amor de ciudades"—the impure love of cities.

Darío saw *modernismo* as "el movimiento de la libertad." If, in a very broad sense, European romanticism was the form political Liberalism took in literature and the fine arts, *modernismo* was both an artistic strategy and consequence of Latin American Liberalism. It based itself on the principle of absolute artistic freedom, on the separation of religious and secular culture. This explains Darío's affinity with the democratic vision of Victor Hugo and such New World figures as Washington, Bolívar, and Whitman (cf. his "Su soberbio rostro de emperador"). In "A Colón," he blames the Spanish conquest for producing in America a corrupt world of disorder and strife, but also projects in racial-cultural *mestizaje* a synthesis of the Indian with the positive values of Spanish civilization, and the incorporation into the New World of the libertarian promise implicit in the French Revolution—a theme he shares with Martí and later Latin American progressive and populist ideologies (see Ellis 1986).

Modernismo responded to the cultural penetration of imperialism by assimilating the romanticism of the revolutionary bourgeoisie with the movements engendered by the writers marginalized at the apex of nineteenth-century economic development (Baudelaire, Verlaine, Mallarmé, Oscar Wilde, Bécquer), recasting these elements in a highly original cultural mode that in its very cultivation of aesthetic refinement closed itself off from the commercialism and utilitarianism of the more specifically capitalist side of Liberal ideology. Darío made the swan (*cisne*) the symbol of *modernista* aestheticism. If Latin America was the *cisne*, then the United States was the bird of Jupiter, the eagle (*águila*), whose enormous power and productive energy Darío both feared and, as a creator and innovator himself, admired. Sometimes—for example, in his infamous "Salutación al águila"—he tried to see virtue in an influence that seemed in any case inevitable. Darío hoped for a creative syncretism between what he saw as the democratic materialism of North America and the aesthetic and spiritual values of Latin America. "Hoy el rayo de Júpiter Olímpico es esclavo de Franklin y de Edison" (today Jupiter's bolt of lightning is the slave of Franklin and Edison), he writes. In his poem "Calef" he notes that America could challenge "senile Europe" if only its Latin part would add an "arm with a heart" to the "strong arm" of the North ("si el norte es fuerte brazo, agregaría el latino / un brazo con corazón").

The openness and energy of the Whitman's "democratic vistas" can also turn into a weapon of U.S. manifest destiny, however. The Latin American "heart" weakens and allows penetration. The hope of the Latin American Liberal for fraternal synthesis is overwhelmed by the North American desire for domination. In the most famous of his explicitly anti-*yanqui* poems, "A Roosevelt," the eagle appears as a hunter threatening the swans. Darío always feared that the relation between North and South America, the nexus between Jupiter and Leda, between power and poetry, would not be a harmonious "pan-American" union but the violent rape of a vulnerable people by a voracious eagle that might engender a monstrous, English-speaking Caliban. His poetry cautions against the danger posed by the uncritical celebration of material progress, but also shows an understanding of how that delusion becomes a part of the colonized mentality of a dependent bourgeoisie. The military occupation of Nicaragua by the marines in 1909, the consequent downfall of the Zelaya government, and the failed Liberal rebellion of 1910–1912 must have obliged him more and more to see the negative dimension of U.S. civilization, without at the same time a compensating hope for a viable Latin American alternative. Hence the tone of desperation and disillusion of his later poetry.

Darío was not a writer who projected to the popular sectors of Latin American society: in this sense Perus is correct to contrast him with Martí.[5] But his cosmopolitan aestheticism certainly contained elements of a radical form of Latin American bourgeois nationalism, suggesting a path of development different from simple assimilation to U.S. hegemony on the one hand or oligarchic immobilism on the other. It is from this perspective that we may glimpse in Darío and *modernismo* anticipations of the more popularly inflected anti-imperialist discourses that will find their first political and military expression in Nicaragua with Sandino.

The Vanguardists and Sandino

After Darío, *modernismo* became the fashion in Nicaraguan poetry (and still is, in a lot of bad Nicaraguan poetry). But the most important successors of Darío—Alfonso Cortés, Azarías Pallais, and Salomón de la Selva—represented, in general terms, a move away from the verbal sensuality and love of surfaces of *modernismo* toward a more meditative, philosophical poetry. Cortés was famous for his metaphysical poems with titles like "The Dance of the Stars," "Dirty Souls," "The Song of Space," written between or in bouts of the insanity that kept him institutionalized his entire life. Totally apolitical himself, he nevertheless projected a very powerful sense of cosmic utopian subjectivism that is still an important strain in Nicaraguan political poetry.

Pallais was a forerunner of Liberation Theology. A classicist by training, he became a priest and was fond of denouncing in his sermons capitalism and the evils of wealth and power. According to Ernesto Cardenal (1973: 3), he was one of the first Central American intellectuals to speak of socialism. His poetry echoes Darío's in its extreme disgust with the modern world and its tendency to idealize the Catholic Middle Ages, but with a religious and libertarian note that is almost totally absent in his predecessor.

Of the three, de la Selva was to have the most direct influence on the development of Nicaraguan political poetry. He was raised as an adopted child in the United States (his first book of poems was published in

English: *Tropical Town*, 1918). Writing in a wide variety of genres, including historical, erotic, and autobiographical poems, de la Selva was the closest of this group to the nineteenth-century tradition of "civic" poetry that Darío adopted in some of his poetry. His service as a soldier in World War I produced a volume of antiwar poems, *El soldado desconocido*, with illustrations by Diego Rivera (1922). A long poem on Alexander Hamilton, *Sonata de Alejandro Hamilton*, anticipated the historical "documentary poems" developed by Pablo Antonio Cuadra and Cardenal. An early progressive, de la Selva worked as a secretary for Samuel Gompers and later as adviser to Henry Wallace, Cárdenas, and several other Mexican presidents. In 1930, he led a press campaign in the United States in support of Sandino.

Like Darío, Cortés, Pallais, and de la Selva were from León, reflecting the cultural impetus given to this Liberal center by Zelaya's presidency. By contrast, the movement that would come to be the dominant force in modern Nicaraguan literature until the 1960s, the *vanguardistas*, was associated with Granada, the seat of the great Conservative family dynasties. This circumstance of origin marked the group and its evolution deeply.

The vanguardists included at different times Luis Alberto Cabrales, José Coronel Urtecho, Pablo Antonio Cuadra, Manolo Cuadra, Joaquín Pasos, Alberto Ordóñez Argüello, Octavio Rocha, María Teresa Sánchez, and José Román. Politically they defined themselves variously as nationalist, antiliberal, Catholic, ultrareactionary, futurist, pro-Sandinista, and fascist; aesthetically they attacked Darío and the heritage of *modernismo*, identifying with the European and American poetic avant garde represented in the 1920s by figures like the Chilean poet Huidobro, Apollinaire, the Spanish Generation of '27, Ezra Pound, T. S. Eliot, and William Carlos Williams.[6]

Paradoxically, given its extreme anti-Americanism, the group owed its origins to José Coronel Urtecho's contacts with the new currents in North American poetry during the 1920s, when he lived in San Francisco. On his return to Nicaragua in 1927, Coronel Urtecho joined with Luis Cabrales, recently returned from France, to publish a series of manifestolike poems and commentaries. The most important of these was "Oda a Rubén Darío," which developed what was to be the central idea of the group: that the renovation of Nicaraguan poetry and literary language along the lines suggested by the new European and American avant garde would be the key to renovating Nicaraguan national culture and ultimately the nation itself.

The goal Coronel Urtecho announced in his "Oda" was to transcend the poetic system established by *modernismo*, to break down existing metrics and forms, to forge a new kind of poetic symbolism. But the vanguardist aesthetic project had from the start an ideological dimension too. In 1927, Nicaragua was in a state of virtual civil war complicated by the intervention of the U.S. Marine Corps. The vanguardists coalesced as a group in the midst of Moncada's compromise with the United States and the beginnings of Sandino's campaign in the Segovia mountains. Almost immediately, they sensed in Sandino a kindred spirit, becoming in effect the literary fellow-travelers of his movement.[7]

The logic of this identification was a curious one. Both Sandino and the vanguardists were products of a failed Liberal project of national autonomy and development. Both were nationalist, anti-*yanqui*, and antibourgeois. Both accepted the need for armed struggle against U.S. intervention. Both placed great value on Nicaragua's indigenous past and the peasant base of the nation. Both had a sense of the transformative role of culture in the process of national liberation. Politically, however, if Sandino represented an internal evolution of and break with liberalism toward a left nationalist populism, the vanguardists were by contrast a sort of sui generis New Right seeking to revamp what they considered the outmoded Conservative tradition corresponding to their Granadan base and their class and family backgrounds. In the process, several of them came to identify with Catholic corporativism and in some cases directly with fascism. In 1934, Coronel Urtecho and Pablo Antonio Cuadra briefly edited a proto-fascist cultural journal, *La Reacción*, which was shut down by the Liberal government of Sacasa. As a group, they gave unconditional support to Franco in the Spanish Civil War.

Like the Generation of '98 in Spain, the vanguardists were ideologically incoherent and unstable. With some individual variations—Manolo Cuadra was one of the intellectuals associated with the founding of the PSN—they would turn first to Sandino, then to fascism, then to Somoza-García, then to the opposition to Somoza-Debay in the 1960s for political correlatives of their project. What unified them in the final analysis was their common rejection of U.S. intervention and the Liberal-Conservative "compromise" that tolerated it, and their aesthetic iconoclasm.

The zeitgeist of the movement in its formative period may be suggested by this passage from one of Coronel Urtecho's articles for the journal *Criterio* in 1932:

There are many things to destroy and we don't have to finish in a minute. But we also have to replace and build on our own account. We begin with ourselves. We think that in the battle our hatred for the enemy unites us for a moment, but in peace it is only discipline. And the discipline of youth is culture. . . . We must seem like revolutionaries in the face of the exhausted criteria of the

Liberals who believe in the "progress" of mankind, of the pious
Conservatives who imagine that the Church is on their side, of the
faint-hearted and rancid lambs that democracy brings to market.
(in Arellano 1969: 13)

Referring to "Sandinista atmosphere" in which the vanguardists coalesced in the 1930s, Ernesto Mejía Sánchez notes that they

. . . didn't find what some other parallel generations in Latin America discovered: socialism, Marxism, the APRA party in Peru, etc.
They were seeking what was traditionally Hispanic in order to
oppose imperialism. They were looking for folklore, romances,
riddles, and popular theater. Through that Hispanism and nationalism, Pablo Antonio Cuadra and José Coronel Urtecho contaminated
themselves with Franco's political beliefs. (In White 1986: 39–40)

Elaborating on the point, Pablo Antonio Cuadra has commented recently:

. . . in our cult of the new, we wanted to get involved in a new kind
of politics that was against what had gone before. Fascism had a
strong influence over some of us. In others, such as Coronel, the
doctrine of Ramiro de Maeztu and of Charles Maurras and the
Action Française was more influential. We were obsessed with a
nationalism that we wanted to be ultra-original. And, of course,
Communism repelled us, because our movement was nationalistic.
We were a movement parallel to Sandino, and the Communists at
the time were deeply internationalistic. In Nicaragua, during their
first public demonstrations, the Communists burned the Nicaraguan flag and sang the "Internationale." And that repelled us. We
were disgusted with Stalin's Russia from the start. This feeling
pushed us into symphathizing with anti-Communist movements
even though socialism and Christian communalism attracted us. (In
White 1986: 19–21)

In one sense, the vanguardists' turn to fascism paralleled the impulse
inherent in Sandino to transcend the very structure of the Liberal/
Conservative dynamics in Nicaraguan political life. They opposed the
Liberal-*modernista* world of León, but not on the basis of the older
Conservative ideology and interests of their fathers, which they also
considered bankrupt. They saw the "bourgeois spirit" in general as
destructive to the formation of a viable national culture. The problem
of *modernismo* for the vanguardists was not simply that it was an

outmoded style associated with León and Zelaya's liberalism, but that by its cult of aesthetic hermeticism and cosmopolitanism it inhibited an adequate exploration of linguistic and poetic possibilities of the national tradition, particularly the incorporation of historical, folk, and vernacular elements into literature. The vanguardist project was to build a new culture and new nation on an ideological basis that transcended the framework of oligarchic politics. They conceived of their work in poetry as a means of advancing this goal by creating a new national mythology and imagery that would express a positive Hispanic and Catholic appropriation of indigenous and popular Nicaraguan culture. But their upper class, *granadino* backgrounds made them skeptical of the collectivist and democratic project Sandino ultimately represented. They saw him more as a Mussolini who would bring a renovating elite represented ideologically by themselves to power in Nicaragua than as a Lenin. In Arellano's judgment, even the their hypernationalism did not extend beyond a folkloric appropriation of the popular and indigenous.[8]

Perhaps the most curious, although short-lived, ideological metamorphosis of the vanguardists was their transformation into supporters of Somoza García after Sandino's assassination in 1934. "At the time," says Mejía Sánchez, "there was a kind of universal ambience of fascism, Nazism, and the Vanguardists thought they were going to manipulate old Somoza into being a leader [like Franco]" (in White 1986: 39–40). Pablo Antonio Cuadra remembers the pro-Somoza turn as follows:

Coronel . . . convinced us to sign a manifesto supporting the person who was at that time the young head of the army—Anastasio Somoza—in order to take power with him and realize our political ideas. Coronel's Machiavellian thesis was that it would be easier to conquer one man than to conquer a people, Somoza said that he would make our ideas his. What he really did was deform them and take advantage of our idealism. He showed his claws soon enough. A few months later, I was imprisoned after being accused of putting up posters in honor of Sandino. And from that time on, I was against Somoza. (In White 1986: 19–21)

As Cuadra suggests, soon after Somoza became president in 1937, the vanguardists began to go their separate ways. Several followed Coronel and Cabrales along the road to fascism; Manolo Cuadra, on the other hand, took a leftward path that led him eventually to membership in the fledgling Nicaraguan Communist party, the PSN. Pablo Antonio Cuadra cultivated a blend of pre-Columbian mythology, Greco-Roman classicism, Catholicism, and right-wing nationalism. Strongly anti-Communist, he was one of the intellectual pillars of the bourgeois opposition to Somoza in the 1950s and 1960s; after the revolution he became perhaps the most prominent intellectual figure of the anti-Sandinista forces represented by *La Prensa*. Coronel Urtecho, by contrast, would spend many years at least nominally supporting the Somoza regime, only to eventually transform himself into one of the major literary fellow travelers of the FSLN.

The various vanguard-related literary journals established in the late 1930s and early 1940s like *Centro*, edited by José Román; *Ya*, edited by Alberto Ordóñez Argüello; and *Nuevos Horizontes*, edited by Paolo Steiner and María Teresa Sánchez, frequently sidestepped politics altogether to keep publishing. During these years Cuadra organized in Granada a poetry workshop, the Cofradía del Taller San Lucas, with a corresponding journal, *Cuadernos del Taller San Lucas*, both of which were to serve as incubators for a new group of poets that would come to be known as the Generation of 1940.

The Generation of 1940 and the Crisis of 1954–1959

Like the other Central American dictatorships, the Somoza regime began to lose flexibility in the mid-1940s, attracting in particular the animosity of new middle sectors—including artists and intellectuals—whose emergence was due to the relative prosperity that accompanied import substitution economics during the Second World War. As Somoza began the third term of a presidency that was starting to appear eternal, Cuadra's *cofrades* organized the First Congress of Nicaraguan Intellectuals in July 1950, with the aim of "taking cultural power so as to officially establish national cultural work under their control." The effort, articulated in the pages of *Semana*, a literary supplement to the increasingly popular Managua daily, *La Prensa*, failed, but it signaled the growing inability of many of Nicaragua's writers of varying political tendencies to work with the regime.

In the 1950s Nicaraguan cotton production began to expand. In tandem, the Somoza regime grew in size and power, extending its scope to banking and credit, as well as to the growing number of civil and military employees who depended on it. The regime was able to achieve a degree of support and legitimacy by making concessions to the more dynamic sectors of the business community like the cotton growers, who could develop their industry only with state subsidies and protection. But this also had the effect of pushing the Conservatives and less-favored sectors of the agro-export bourgeoisie into open opposition.

The regime's ability to mollify, co-opt, or repress dissident groups contributed to an appearance of stability. In response, the opposition became more desperate, attempting a series of abortive coups like the so-called April Conspiracy of 1954 or the assassination of Somoza García by Rigoberto López Pérez in 1956. Pedro Joaquín Chamorro, the Conservative editor of *La Prensa*, had been involved in a number of these. In 1954, Chamorro asked Pablo Antonio Cuadra to edit a weekly literary supplement, *La Prensa Literaria*, which would develop a cultural perspective consonant with the paper's anti-Somocista stance. Using *La Prensa* as a platform, Chamorro began to take steps to form a coalition of the legal opposition composed of the Partido Liberal Independiente, the Partido Social Cristiano, the PSN, and the important trade unions.

This was the general context for the emergence of the Generation of 1940, which began, as we noted, under the influence and patronage of the vanguardists, to whom some of the younger writers were related by ties of family and class. Informally, María Teresa Sánchez (1918), Enrique Fernández Morales (1918), Guillermo Rothschuh (1928), Fernando Silva (1927), Ernesto Gutiérrez (1929), and Mario Cajina-Vega (1929) were associated with this group. But its three major figures, all poets, are Carlos Martínez Rivas (1924), Ernesto Mejía Sánchez (1923), and Ernesto Cardenal (1926).

The Generation of 1940 writers turned quickly into opponents of the regime, and several of them became important in different phases of the development of the Somoza opposition. Martínez, who is considered by Cardenal and most Nicaraguans the master poet of the group, was the most bohemian and overtly apolitical (a good portion of his work remains unpublished). But he was also the writer who most firmly established the image of the poet as iconoclast and rebel, particularly in his aptly titled collection of 1953, *La insurrección solitaria*. It has often been hinted that Mejía Sánchez, who eventually became a university professor, was party to several of the conspiracies against the regime in the 1950s. Certain of his political poems, carefully crafted, often complexly symbolic and ironic, are among the strongest statements of opposition during the period. Fernando Silva was perhaps the closest to approximating something like a social realist poetry, centered in the depiction of peasant and working-class life and incorporating spoken Nicaraguan as a literary language. In Ernesto Cardenal's judgment, "es el más nicaragüense o al menos el más *popular* de nuestros escritores" (he is the most Nicaraguan or at least the most "popular" of our writers) (Cardenal 1973: 291). Not formally connected to the group, but an important poetic voice in the 1950s was Edwin Castro, Rigoberto López Pérez's co-conspirator in the *ajusticiamiento* of Somoza García, who was killed in prison afterward.

But the figure of the Generation of 1940 most centrally involved in the transformation of the vanguardist aesthetic into the generalized Sandinista cultural ethos that would emerge in the 1960s, and by all accounts the major figure in contemporary Nicaraguan cultural life, was Cardenal himself. In what follows, we sketch the formative stages of his work, leaving a consideration of its later, explicitly Sandinista, stages to chapter 4.

Ernesto Cardenal

Cardenal was born in 1925 in Granada. He earned his high school diploma at the Colegio Centroamérica in his hometown and then went on to study literature, first in Managua, then, from 1942 to 1946, at the National Autonomous University of Mexico, where he earned his degree with a series of essays on Nicaraguan poetry. As a *granadino* interested in literature, it was natural for Cardenal to become a protégé of the vanguardists, particularly of José Coronel Urtecho, from whom he derived his close familiarity and contact with U.S. poetry. From 1947 to 1949 he studied at Columbia University in New York and traveled in France, Italy, Spain, and Switzerland. He returned to Managua in 1950 where he came in contact with anti-Somocista opposition.

Cardenal joined a clandestine group made up of young people from good Conservative families, much like his own. Their meetings led to the April Conspiracy of 1954, headed by Adolfo Báez Bone and Pablo Leal. The conspiracy was betrayed early on, and the two leaders, as well as several other close friends of Cardenal, were killed. Cardenal was forced into hiding and then into exile. In 1957 he entered a Trappist monastery located in Gethsemani, Kentucky.

His decision to study theology and eventually to become a priest surprised those who knew Cardenal as a promising young poet with very strong political convictions. He had begun publishing in the 1940s, establishing his reputation with a series of epigrams modeled on Catullus that openly attacked Somoza. Cardenal's subsequent concern with religion is hardly evident in this early work. It seems probable that the influence of Pablo Antonio Cuadra's "national" Catholicism, combined with his experience in the April Conspiracy, led to his turn toward religion. In any event, the death of Báez Bone, linked in Cardenal's mind to the drama of Sandino's campaign and eventual murder by Somoza, would become the constituent theme of what is perhaps the founding text of literary Sandinismo, Cardenal's great poem *Hora O*.[9]

At Gethsemani, Cardenal served as a novice under the famous poet-priest Thomas Merton. The two men came to know and translate each other's poetry, and the influence of Merton on Cardenal was considerable. However, Cardenal's health was too fragile to endure the demands of Trappist discipline. He left the monastery in 1959 to study theology in Cuernavaca and, after 1961, in Colombia. He continued writing poetry throughout these years, publishing *Gethsemani, Kentucky* in 1960 and *Salmos* (Psalms) in 1964.

The period of Cardenal's stay in Colombia corresponded with the growing influence of Liberation Theology among younger priests in Latin America. Here he came into contact with Camilo Torres, one of the most influential figures in the new developments. Cardenal admired Torres's decision to give up his ministry and join the guerrilla movement, but rejected the choice of arms himself in accord with his adherence to Merton's principle of nonviolent resistance to evil.

In 1965, at the age of forty, he was ordained as a priest in Managua. The same year he and two friends founded a Christian commune based on concepts that had their roots in the teachings of Merton on the archipelago of Solentiname in the south of Lake Nicaragua. Solentiname had at the time a population of fewer than one thousand peasants and fishermen. Cardenal and his friends built a church that they named Our Lady of Solentiname. There, Cardenal taught a new interpretation of the Gospels, calling for an active struggle against worldly evil and the establishment of the Kingdom of Heaven on the earth. Each Sunday families from the neighboring islands and shoreline villages came to the church to attend mass. Gradually, a small permanent community began to develop, mainly drawn from the local rural population and centered around the production of a number of collectively run workshops devoted to handicrafts, primitive painting and sculpture, and, later, poetry. In the evenings, the members of the community and visitors would read, interpret, and comment collectively on Gospel texts, often in relation to current events and their own lives. Cardenal's collection and transcription of some of these dialogues—*El evangelio de Solentiname* (1975)—became a key text for grass-roots Liberation Theology work, particularly the *comunidades de base* movement.

It was during the Solentiname years (1965–1977) that Cardenal began to merge the artistic, political, and religious dimensions of his life work. At first, Cardenal argued on a Mertonian basis that a community constructed according to Christian principles—including nonviolence and community of goods—would infect by example the world surrounding it without needing to resort to armed struggle. But these were also the years of rapidly escalating resistance to the Somoza regime, as the political and military fortunes of the FSLN waxed and waned, and for all his pacifism, Cardenal was still very much an opponent of Somoza. As the Solentiname project evolved, his sympathy for revolutionary options began to intensify, especially as younger members of the commune brought Sandinista politics with them.

A transition between the Mertonian idealism of Solentiname and the Marxist-Christian synthesis of Cardenal's later, explicitly Sandinista, work may be found in his poetry of the late 1960s, especially *El estrecho dudoso* (1966) and *Homenaje a los indios americanos* (1969). These are both products of Cardenal's intensive studies (perhaps influenced by Pablo Antonio Cuadra's earlier work in the same vein) of pre-Columbian Amerindian cultures and his increasing involvement with Marxism. Like Mariátegui in his articulation of the Inca *ayllu* as a prototype of communist society indigenous to America, Cardenal came to posit the classic Mayan cities as peaceful, classless societies whose values more or less coincided with the Christian utopia he was seeking to propagate in Solentiname. What was missing, however, was a perspective on how the values he had come to admire (and perhaps overidealize) in pre-Columbian society and primitive Christianity might be realized in a contemporary context. Such a perspective would emerge only later, as Cardenal moved toward a more direct identification with Sandinismo in his poetry after his trip to Cuba in 1970. In the meantime, Solentiname began to confront the problem of all utopias: it was successful only to the extent it remained relatively isolated from the outside world. The Sandinistas sometimes criticized it as a dangerously illusory alternative to the brutal realities of power in Nicaragua.

In ideological terms the basic achievement of Cardenal's poetry has been its interpolation of a Marxist vision of class and national struggle through the belief structures and corresponding discursive practices (prayers, sermons, psalms, homilies, etc.) of Catholicism. The possibility of this was already latent in certain aspects of the vanguardists' antiliberalism. In social formations like those of Central America where liberalism rooted late and/or unevenly, the possibilities of a crossover between Catholic traditionalism—historically a breeding ground of reactionary ideologies and movements—and popular insurrections have been rich and varied. Cardenal inherits from vanguardists the idea of a poetry that could project an image of Nicaraguan national destiny, but precisely in a context where the founding assumptions of Liberal historicism have collapsed, where the expected apotheosis of democracy and modernization reveals instead the torture cells of Somoza's prisons. In Cardenal's poetry, the experience of the present is of time-without-hope: the seeming eternity of the dictatorship, the sense of a past that has been canceled, of the failed epic of a dominated and dependent Banana Republic. But there is at the same time a countermotion, which derives from Cardenal's representation of Nicaraguan and Central American history through the narrative frame of Christian eschatology. Despair is lit up from within by the promise of an imminent redemption from evil, a time when "the last shall be first," when human beings will attain a new community and a new body.

Hora 0, written immediately after the April Conspiracy but not published until 1959, was an attempt to portray Sandino's war against the United States and his assassination by Somoza as the central passion—in the evangelical sense—of modern Nicaraguan history. The poem is in four parts: (1) a short introduction describing the mood of Central America during the "night" of the dictatorships in the 1930s; (2) a textual collage on the economics of the Banana Republics, including a history of the United Fruit Company; (3) a long central section reconstructing Sandino's campaign, culminating in a description of his assassination; (4) a final episode describing the April Conspiracy and the capture and assassination of Báez Bone by the Somocista police. The "zero hour" is the moment of the hero's death, but also the time before dawn, the moment that separates disaster and redemption, the point where history turns on its axis, as in the poem's famous opening evocation of Central America in the 1930s:

Tropical nights of Central America
with lagoons and volcanoes under the moonlight
and lights of presidential palaces,
military barracks and sad bugle calls at curfew.
"Often as I smoked a cigarette
I've decided that a man should die,"
says Ubico smoking a cigarette. . . .
In his palace like a pink cake
Ubico has a cold. Outside, the
people were routed with phosphorous bombs.
San Salvador, under the night and spies,
with anxious whispers in homes and boarding houses,
and screams of torture from the police stations.
The palace of Carías stoned by the people.
One of the windows of his office has been broken,
and the police have fired on the people.
And Managua the target of machine guns
pointing from the windows of the chocolate pastry palace
and steel helmets patrolling the streets.

Watchman, what of the night?
Watchman, what of the night?
(Translation adapted from Zimmerman 1980)

Like the Christian passion, the stories of Sandino and Báez Bone are annunciations, the prophetic figuration of the possibility of a future epic of national liberation. The description of Sandino's "barefoot army" in *Hora O* anticipates the Sandinista guerrilla *focos* that Carlos Fonseca and his comrades would begin to construct some years later:

and though they had a military hierarchy they were all equal
with no distinction of rank when they shared their food
and their clothes; they all had the same rations
And the leaders had no lieutenants:
it was more like a commune than an army
and it was not military discipline that unified them but love
though there was never such unity in an army.

The concern with recovering and giving narrative form to a tradition of struggle reflects the experience of a national history that has been falsified, driven underground, marginalized. Cardenal's poems are a sort of palimpsest in which fragments of a past that has been written over by previous stages of historical domination resurface. Imperialism in the realm of culture depends on the destruction of collective memory, the imposition of forms of amnesia, the corruption of language and values under the pressure of commercialization and modernization. ("There are also crimes of the CIA in the realm of semantics," Cardenal writes in his "Epistle to Coronel Urtecho.") In the official histories of Somoza's Nicaragua like *El Calvario de las Segovias*, Sandino figured as a renegade and an outlaw. The loss of the past is the loss of revolutionary possibility; the revolution is the return of the repressed. For Cardenal, the classless society is already *inside* history, prefigured in the communitarian societies of pre-Columbian America or early Christianity.

Partly in recognition of William Carlos Williams and the objectivist movement in U.S. poetry, Cardenal called the new way of doing poetry represented by *Hora 0 exteriorismo* (exteriorism), explaining:

Exteriorism is objective poetry, narrative and anecdotal, made with elements of real life and with concrete things, with proper names, details, data, statistics, facts and quotations. An *impure* poetry, in short. A poetry that for some is closer to prose than poetry. . . . In contrast, interiorist poetry is a subjectivist poetry made only with abstract or symbolic words: rose, skin, ash, lips, absence, bitter, dream, touch, foam, desire, shadow, time, blood, stone, tears, night. . . . I think that the only poetry which can express Latin American reality and reach the people and be revolutionary is exteriorist. . . . Poetry can serve a function: to construct a country and create a new humanity, change society, make the future Nicaragua as part of the future great country that is Latin America. (1973: vii–xi)

We can recognize here a clear echo of the vanguardist project of a concrete poetry that would break down the separation of art and life and embody and project a new sense of national identity. What Cardenal was seeking was a political poetry rooted in the Nicaraguan national-popular—particularly in the peasant elements of precolonial corn-centered culture—that was also holistic, metaphysical, and cosmic. Gone in this poetry is the sonorous, vatic, and not incidentally patriarchal voice that Pablo Neruda affected in his epic reconstruction of Latin American history, *Canto general*. Similarly, there is a rejection of complex metaphor toward what Roberto Márquez (1974) calls the "objectivist immediacy" of a metonymic figural chain formed by a textual collage of the elements Cardenal enumerates ("proper names, details, data, statistics, facts and quotations"). The interplay of anticipations, partial affinities, and identifications this sets up (e.g., in *Hora O* Christ-Sandino, Sandino–Báez Bone, Sandino–the Cuban–inspired guerrilla of the late 1950s) is meant to generate relational patterns suggesting the linkage of all things past, present, and future in an ever-extending associative web, centered on Sandino and the possibility of the revolutionary transformation of Nicaraguan society. What Cardenal creates in effect is a new sort of revolutionary historicism that shuttles between the universal and the immediate, the cosmic and the regional, death and rebirth, the individual and the community, the facticity of history and its transfiguration in moments of great crisis and tension, the realms of nature and culture. This relates his work to the initial efforts at Christian-Marxist synthesis founded on the special characteristics of postcolonial societies rather than an abstract theological universalism that was being elaborated in scriptural exegesis by Latin American Liberation Theology around the Second Vatican Council of 1962–1965.

Cardenal's efforts to revive the vanguardist project of cultural revolution, as well as his own participation in Báez Bone's failed coup, *Hora O*'s proto-Sandinismo, the *ajusticiamiento* of Somoza, the anti-Somoza protest poetry of the older vanguardists and the Generation of 1940 poets, Fonseca's literary-political evolution that we sketched in chapter 2: all these developments anticipated a growing unity of political poetry and revolutionary action that would reach new levels in the 1960s. For Cardenal's exteriorism to become the literary correlative of the revolutionary movement itself, however, it had to undergo a transformation corresponding to the political and ideological changes involved in the development of Sandinismo itself; this implied in turn both a revision and ultimately a turn away from the vanguardist project. Important in this transformation were a series of new literary tendencies appearing elsewhere in Latin America like Nicanor Parra's "anti-poetry," the "conversational poetry" of the poets of the Cuban Revolution, the poems and testimonios produced by the numerous guerrilla experiments that sprang up between 1960 and 1968. In Nicaragua, the primary role in assimilating these new influences and relating them to the developing revolutionary movement would be played by a group of writers and intellectuals that comes to be known as Ventana (Window) or Frente Ventana.

Frente Ventana

Though its short-term consequences were disastrous, the assassination of Somoza García by Edwin Castro and Rigoberto López Pérez was a turning point in the development of the political opposition in Nicaragua. In the wake of the fraudulent elections that confirmed Luis Somoza as his father's successor, the regime suffered a crisis of legitimacy exacerbated by a fall in the world market price of cotton, now the country's chief export crop. There followed a series of abortive coups and guerrilla actions, perhaps the most significant of which was the battle of El Chaparral in 1959, where a guerrilla column formed—apparently with Cuban support—by veterans of Sandino's campaigns and young radicals was ambushed and massacred in a joint military operation by the Nicaraguan and Honduran National Guards. Hearing of the massacre, the students who had recently won autonomy for the National University (UNAN) staged a protest demonstration in Managua that was attacked by the Guard, leaving four dead and some seventy wounded.

These failed military adventures of the late 1950s served to cement the alliances between old and new Sandinista tendencies and to define an alternative to the reformist strategy of the bourgeois opposition and the Communist party. In 1961, the FSLN was founded, in part by the survivors of El Chaparral (Carlos Fonseca was wounded and, along with future FSLN leader Daniel Ortega, captured in the battle). Many of the students who had fought for university autonomy and participated in the demonstrations of 1959 became involved at the start of the new decade with organizations like the Frente Estudiantil Revolucionario (FER) or the Juventud Patriótica Nicaragüense, which acted as conduits between the student world and the urban cells and rural guerrilla *foco*s of the FSLN.

Several new literary projects appeared in this context: the FSLN magazine, *Trinchera*; Praxis, an informal coalition of politicized artists and writers that enjoyed a period of popularity before breaking up in the early 1960s; the Bandoleros from Granada; Grupo "M" from Managua; and Grupo Presencia from Diriamba. Unquestionably the most important of these was Frente Ventana, founded in 1960 on the heels of the demonstrations at the National University.

Defining itself loosely as a group of intellectuals and cultural workers committed to the "reality of the Nicaraguan people," Ventana aspired to be the vanguard of a new ideological and cultural movement among the

nation's young people in tandem with the specifically political organizations directly tied to the FSLN. The organization owed its origins to
two brilliant university students, Fernando Gordillo and Sergio Ramírez.
Several other writers joined the group in short order, and many more
were to come under the influence of its positions. Its activities included
the journal, *Ventana*, which published nineteen issues between 1960
and 1964; the first round table of young poets of Nicaragua organized at
the National University in October of the same year; and poetry contests
in 1961 and 1962.

Speaking of the situation in which the group emerged, Sergio Ramírez
noted many years later:

> The magazine and the group were born with the wounds of the [El
> Chaparral] massacre. We were repulsed by the dictatorship and had
> a militant conception of literature—not socialist realism or any-
> thing like that. But from the beginning we did reject the position
> that had reigned in Nicaragua up to that time in terms of artistic
> labor: the famous story of art for art's sake; the artist's sworn
> aversion to political contamination. . . . It's important to see how a
> new revolutionary culture that began to emerge in the country
> during the 1960s had to make its way between two closed walls: a
> degenerating and obtuse Somocism (which had produced no impor-
> tant cultural movement of its own), and the elite literary culture
> represented by the legacy of the Vanguardists. . . . At the end of this
> narrow passage, imperialism was cutting off and blocking our path.
> The Ventana group began to break with all this. (In White 1986: 80,
> 82)

As Ramírez notes, Ventana's sense of the need for a decisive break with
the tradition represented by the vanguardists was central to its project.
Pablo Antonio Cuadra's journal, *La Pez y el Serpiente* and other van-
guardist-related publications such as *Revista Conservadora* also began
to publish in the early 1960s. *La Prensa Literaria*, still directed by Cuadra,
would be the journal of record for Nicaraguan poetry throughout the
decade.[10] Almost from its origins, Ventana entered into a struggle with
a group of Managua writers who were protégés of *La Prensa Literaria*.
Headed by Edwin Yllescas and Roberto Cuadra, and including Beltrán
Morales, Iván Uriarte, and other young poets, the group was called the
Generación Traicionada or Betrayed Generation. It modeled itself on
existentialism and the U.S. Beat Generation, posing a kind of apolitical
bohemianism against what it regarded as the materialism and vulgarity
of modern life, and attacking *Ventana* in particular for contaminating
literature with partisan politics. The highly charged atmosphere of the

early 1960s, as the Frente Sandinista began to consolidate its influence among the emerging generation, weighed against the Betrayed Generation's stance of disaffection and cynicism, and the group quickly dissolved, with Roberto Cuadra becoming an apologist for the regime and Morales and Uriarte moving increasingly to the left.[11]

Though the work of the Ventana group was crucial in the elaboration of a generalized Sandinista ethos in the 1960s, it remained independent of the FSLN as such. Nevertheless the political tendency of the group was explicit enough, as Ramírez explains:

> We took a very clear ideological position, and in our rejection of [the Betrayed Generation's] dependence on foreign cultural models . . . we proposed political commitment. We spoke of the miners with silicosis in Siuna, the poor who lived in Acahualinca and other parts of Nicaragua, and we tried to resolve this political position in artistic language. One could say that in literature and art these were already the positions of the recently created Frente Sandinista, which was nourished by the radicalized youth movement headed by our generation. In 1962 when Carlos Fonseca . . . secretly spoke with us in León, he reminded us of the political importance that the Frente already had and of the need to maintain it. Looking back on those years of literary and political agitation, one could say that they were a contribution—a link—in a period of definitions necessary to break with the past. (In White 1986: 80–81)

By 1964, Ramírez had left the university to pursue his remarkable career as a writer, critic, and politician. Gordillo had written a small group of poems that showed a politicization of the formulas of exteriorism—above all, his poem on Sandino, "La circunstancia y la palabra"; but he was already suffering from the disease that would take his life in 1967. The journal stopped publishing, though the influence of the group's ideas continued to spread among students, teachers, writers, and intellectuals. The last issue was edited by Michele Najlis, who would later produce with future Sandinista comandante Jaime Wheelock a journal published by the UNAN Student Center, *Taller*, which began to publish the poetry of young FSLN militants like Carlos Guadamuz and Daniel Ortega.

The Sandinista Poets

Throughout the 1960s, the Frente Sandinista continued to gather strength and support, particularly among young people. But its armed struggle component was something less than a real threat to the regime, now bolstered by its participation in the Central American Common Market and the counterinsurgency regional military framework created by the United States, CONDECA.

In military matters, the Sandinistas drew initially on Che Guevara (who had befriended Fonseca during one of the latter's visits to Cuba) and on Regis Debray's interpretation of Che in what came to be known as *foco* theory, to develop a practice based primarily on establishing small guerrilla columns in remote parts of the country. For reasons they debated over and over, the results—in El Jícaro, Bocay, and elsewhere—were disastrous; the low point was the defeat at Pancasán in 1967, which coincided with the death of Che in Bolivia. The same year, Luis Somoza died, and his brother Tacho, the architect of the National Guard's counterinsurgency program, became president, bringing the Guard and its program to the very heart of state power.

In 1968, after intense discussions, the FSLN began to move toward a more flexible strategy called the "accumulation of forces," which placed greater emphasis on ideological and cultural work among diverse social sectors in an effort to build a broad revolutionary bloc (see Hodges 1986: 218–225). Among other things, the new line encouraged the production of literature by the Frente itself (or failing that, about its activity), as a means of representing its cause and attracting the sympathy of possible recruits. In the process, the Sandinistas analyzed and adapted many of Ventana's proposals about the need to construct an ideological front that could involve intellectuals and cultural producers directly in revolutionary activism. Lizandro Chávez Alfaro's novel *Trágame tierra* (1970) and Carlos Guadamuz's Y . . . *"Las casas quedaron llenas de humo"* (1982), which we discuss in our chapter on testimonio, are key prose texts of this conjuncture. Most strikingly, the important new voices in Nicaraguan poetry will tend to come now from within the ranks of the FSLN itself. They include important Sandinista leaders like Tomás Borge and Daniel Ortega.

Two major figures, both killed in combat, stand out in the transition period between 1968 and 1973: Ricardo Morales Avilés, a former university professor and member of the FSLN National Directorate, and Leonel Rugama, a young seminarian active in the FSLN urban underground in Managua. An intellectual, Morales spent the early 1960s studying at the National University of Mexico. He returned to Nicaragua in 1967, the year of Pancasán, joining the Frente and rising quickly to a leadership position with particular responsibilities for the development of the student front, the FER. He was arrested, tortured, and imprisoned in 1968. After his release in 1971, he joined the guerrilla component of the Frente and was killed in combat in 1973. While in prison, he wrote a group of poems addressed to his lover and fellow FSLN cadre member, Doris Tijerino, speaking mainly of his experiences in the movement and in prison, and of his faith in the future of the struggle. There has been some dispute over their value as poetry (Pablo Antonio Cuadra refused to publish them in *La Prensa Literaria*). Morales was not a poet by training or vocation, but rather someone who turned to poetry in a difficult moment in his life. Whatever their shortcomings, his poems do display two characteristics that were to become more and more evident in Nicaraguan literature in the ensuing years: (1) the emergence of a poetry produced within the revolutionary organization itself rather than by cultural "fronts" like Ventana or fellow travelers like Cardenal; (2) the related fusion of testimonial situations (imprisonment, participation in the guerrilla component) with poetry.

Morales was perhaps more important to the FSLN as a theorist than a poet. In a series of essays he wrote from 1967 to the eve of his death (1981), he set forth a Maoist-influenced analysis of contradictions within the Nicaraguan bourgeoisie that posed the possibility of conjunctural alliances with certain bourgeois sectors as valuable to the revolutionary struggle. The question of class alliances was part of the new strategic orientation toward broader popular mobilization and modified forms of what was called—on the model of the Chinese and Vietnamese revolutions—"prolonged popular war" *(guerra popular prolongada)*. Even in Morales's rejection of *foquismo*, he sought to maintain the visionary side of Che Guevara's thought represented by the concept of the "new man" and the emphasis on ideological and cultural issues. Morales argued for, on the one hand, the strictest revolutionary commitment and orientation from Sandinista writers and cultural workers, criticizing Cardenal's Solentiname utopia on this basis; on the other, like Che, for toleration of ideological pluralism (including toleration of religious beliefs) as important to the strategy of alliances (see Hodges 1986 203–210, 214–218, 257–258).

The figure who was to come to symbolize the combination of poetry and Sandinista militancy most dramatically for the generation that was coming of age in Nicaragua was Rugama, killed in a shootout in Managua with the National Guard in 1970 at the age of 20. In one sense, Rugama's continuing importance within the Sandinista movement is a mystery: he wrote only a handful of significant poems, and the circumstances of his death were associated with the errors of the discredited *foco* strategy that the Frente was trying to move away from. In the hagiographic portrait Cardenal would invent for him in *Oráculo sobre Managua* (see next chapter), Rugama emerges as a simple, almost average, young middle-class Nicaraguan, a seminarian whose love for his fellow citizens—especially the poor of Acahualinca and other slum areas of Managua—leads him to accept the need for armed struggle.

Yet Rugama was an unusually powerful and original poet. Very much in the spirit of Ventana's injunction to move from "talking about" revolution to making it, his poems are records, by turns satirical, impassioned, tragic, or sentimental, of a process of very rapid and deep politicization. Among other things they prophesy his own martyrdom, projecting it toward the reader as a symbol of the ultimate depth of his commitment to revolution. Perhaps his best-known poem, "La tierra es un satélite de la luna," is a sardonic version of the kind of religious incantation Cardenal liked to use, which counterposes the vast techno-logical power represented by the U.S. space program to the life of the slum dwellers of Acahualinca, a Managua *barrio*. His longest poem, "El libro del Ché," moves in the direction of Cardenal's efforts to construct a national narrative, but with very different means suggested by Pablo Antonio Cuadra's "Indo-Catholic" poems. In biblical fashion, it invokes the names of saints, martyrs, bandits, and heroes of the resistance to both the Spanish Conquest and the westward expansion of the United States, Bolívar, Zapata, Che, Sandino, and the heroes of past and recent FSLN defeats in an imaginary revolutionary genealogy that skips back and forth in time and place, from the 1500s to the twentieth century, from Nicaragua to Mexico to the American West to Nicaragua again, ulti-mately extending, in what seems like the poet's anticipation of his own epitaph, to Rugama as a sort of Nicaraguan everyman facing the need to commit himself to the armed struggle:

> leonel rugama
> gozó de la tierra prometida
> en el mes más crudo de la siembra
> sin mas alternativa que la lucha.

> (leonel rugama
> tasted of the promised land
> in the cruelest month of the harvest
> with no choice but to struggle).

Another poem, "Las casas quedaron llenas de humo," reconstructs vividly the death of a group of young Sandinistas at the hands of the National Guard in a Managua shootout similar to the one that would take Rugama's own life a year later. The refrain of the poem was "Los héroes nunca dijeron que morían por la patria, sino que murieron"—a poetic slogan that, like "sin otra alternativa que la lucha," would be written on the walls of buildings throughout the insurrection. The words were actualized in Rugama's own death in combat. "Be like Che! Be like Che!" Omar Cabezas remembers Rugama constantly saying (White 1986: 87). After his death, Jaime Wheelock would edit a selection of his poems for *Taller*, including tributes from several emerging political poets, and Cardenal would tell the story of his death in *Oráculo sobre Managua*, relating it to the disaster of the earthquake and the possibility of national redemption represented by the Frente.

What is striking about the new conjuncture represented by Rugama's precocious martyrdom is that cultural hegemony passes decisively to the Sandinistas and the left in general. The Sandinista counterculture that had very gradually developed in the 1960s, maintained in the schools, churches, and small journals during the lowest ebb of the movement, would come in the 1970s to redefine the whole sphere of literature, so that even non-Marxist and nonrevolutionary writers were co-opted or reread in relation to the insurrectionary project of the Frente. This situation, which extends into the role of poetry during the postrevolutionary period of national reconstruction, as it is called by the Sandinistas, is the subject of our next chapter.

Notes

1. We use the Spanish form *modernismo* to preserve the distinction with the English term "modernism," which is more appropriately, but still not quite exactly, translated as *vanguardismo* (vanguardism) (not quite because *vanguardismo* has a specifically Latin American connotation that modernism—as a term conceived in relation to European and North American culture—does not). Similarly, we retain the Spanish term post-*modernismo* to designate a transitional pre-*vanguardista* current in Latin American literature between 1910 and 1920, and to distinguish it from "postmodernism" as a concept designating certain features of international cultural production today (see our brief discussion of postmodernism in the preface).

2. The recent literature on *modernismo* has been extensive, but Rama (1970), Perus (1976), Achugar (1985b), and Ramos (1989) may give some idea of the range of positions involved.

3. Perus relies on (or anticipates) the characterization of oligarchic development in Latin America between 1870 and 1900 provided by Cueva (1977).

4. Hence, in part, *modernista* francophilia in matters of art and culture, which has become a feature of modern Latin American literary culture. France, for the Liberal oligarchy, represented in contrast to Spain an advanced civilization (positivism was, after all, a French doctrine), but one that was still "Latin" and at least nominally Catholic. French foreign policy in turn encouraged this identification (from which derived the notion of *Latin* America) as an adjunct of its own interests and designs in the region.

5. Something Darío recognized himself in the preface of *Cantos de vida y esperanza*: "Yo no soy un poeta para los muchedumbres." But he adds immediately: "Pero sé que indefectiblemente tengo que ir a ellas" (I am not a poet for the masses. But I know with certainty that I have to go to them).

6. Jorge Eduardo Arellano's *El movimiento de vanguardia de Nicaragua: Gérmenes, desarrollo, significado 1927–1932* (1969) is our primary source for our

characterization of the vanguard in what follows. The Nicaraguan group was part of a general vanguardist movement in Latin American literature in the 1920s and 1930s; for an overview of this in relation to the new sociopolitical conjuncture of these years, see Osorio (1985).

7. According to Arellano, vanguardist meetings would begin with a salute to the portrait of "the Liberator." Coronel Urtecho argued that "Sandinism, which is nothing other than revolutionary nationalism, will not disappear from Nicaragua"; Pablo Antonio Cuadra wrote poems and even began a novel describing Sandino's campaigns, corresponding with Sandino about the project. José Román interviewed Sandino in the Segovias mountains and published some of his impressions in Managua newspapers (see chap. 7); Cabrales proposed in 1932 a solution to the national crisis that involved a major role for Sandino.

8. "The people for the group was not the marginalized and economically exploited campesinos, nor the worker who now was coming to be a reality in Nicaragua, but rather . . . a more or less literary abstraction. On the contrary: the people as a socio-economic mass had no importance in their political plans" (Arellano 1969: 70–71).

9. Cardenal has connected the development of his poetry to the April Conspiracy in a passage that is worth quoting at length:

> I was always obsessed by my hatred of Somoza. From the first Somoza. And I always wanted to write political poetry, attacking Somoza. But I couldn't figure out how to do that. There didn't seem to be any models for writing political poetry. I didn't want to write propaganda, tracts . . . I wanted it to be poetic and political at the same time. The first poem I wrote that satisfied me poetically *and* politically is one of the epigrams: "En la tumba del guerrillero." Years later, Carlos Mejía Godoy put it to music. That's an important poem for me, not just because it's my first successful political poem, but because I wrote it [after] taking part in . . . the April Conspiracy. It was a plan we had to take the presidential palace, capture Somoza and take power. . . . I was very close to one of the leaders of the plan, one of its martyrs: Adolfo Báez Bone. I'd written that poem of mine for Sandino, and the idea was that no one knew where the guerrilla was buried, but the whole county was his tomb. And I was thinking of showing it to Báez Bone. . . . Later mutual friends of Báez Bone's and mine said why didn't I dedicate that poem with the guerrilla's tomb to him instead of to Sandino. Sandino was a well-known figure, they said, while Báez Bone was relatively unknown. And no one knew where he had died, either, nor where he was buried. He was an unknown hero and martyr. . . . I gave the poem a new name, "Epitaph for Adolfo Báez Bone's Tomb." And I began to feel I had found a way of writing political poetry. (In Randall 1984: 97–99)

10. Ramírez recalls that Cuadra was the "pope of letters" who

> . . . ruled the world from the pages of *La Prensa Literaria*. And we all published there as well. But *La Prensa Literaria* virtually demanded that we be apolitical. Or, more accurately, rather than apolitical—because you

could always publish a poem or two against Somoza there—it was a kind of ideological asepsis as far as literature went. . . . When we began taking shots at that position of theirs, we were immediately accused of degenerating literature. . . . [W]e were told it was impossible to make good literature . . . with . . . committed prose or verse . . . literature that involved social struggle. So it was out of that contradiction that *Ventana*'s political vision was born. (In Randall 1984: 29)

11. Morales himself noted later that the generation had been a failed experiment, "while the spark lit by the Frente Ventana can ignite the entire field" (Morales 1975: 140).

4. Nicaraguan Poetry of the Insurrection and Reconstruction

The earthquake of December 1971 and the subsequent scandal over the misdirection of the international relief aid by the Somozas and their close allies were major factors in destabilizing the regime. Even to the conservative church hierarchy and business community it was becoming clear that the nation had become a captive of a corrupt, self-perpetuating clique. In 1974, Pedro Joaquín Chamorro founded a coalition, the Unión Democrática de Liberación (UDEL), which brought various (though not all) sectors of the opposition into a common front. During the Christmas season of the same year the FSLN abandoned its strategy of "accumulation of forces" and carried out under the leadership of Eduardo Contreras a sensational kidnapping of several prominent Somocistas at a private home in Managua. The action won them a number of direct concessions from the regime and, more important, reasserted their presence as a force in national life; however, it also led to three years of fierce repression against Frente-related student groups, trade unions, and cultural organizations, and to the death in combat of several key FSLN leaders, including Fonseca.

As a consequence of the wave of repression, in 1976–1977 the FSLN split into its three famous tendencies. Guerra Popular Prolongada headed by Tomás Borge, descended from the post-*foquista* strategy of building support among the peasantry in the rural areas suggested by the Chinese and Vietnamese experiences; Tendencia Proletaria, headed by sociologist Jaime Wheelock, emphasized the increasing concentration of capital and proletarianization of the work force as the key to revolutionary development; the third (*tercerista*) or insurrectional tendency headed by the Ortegas, was the most heterogeneous ideologically, emphasizing broad alliances in combination with an escalating military-political campaign aimed at attracting further internal and international attention and support until Somoza's continuing presence would be untenable.

The *terceristas* began seeking a pact with the dissident bourgeois sectors represented by UDEL. The economy began to go into recession, alienating sections of the business community that had stuck with Somoza during the relative prosperity of the late 1960s and early 1970s. In 1977 the FSLN made a try at launching a nationwide popular uprising, which failed in part because of hesitation on the part of the bourgeois opposition. Chamorro's assassination by agents of Somoza in January 1978 and the subsequent general strike, however, left this opposition with no place to turn but the militant organization they had feared in the first place. Meanwhile, Carter's human rights policy placed restrictions on U.S. support to the regime. The stage was set for the insurrection of 1978–1979.

The young people who would play key roles in the insurrection were reading Fonseca, Morales Avilés, Rugama, older writers like Cardenal, Fernando Silva, Sergio Ramírez, and Lizandro Chávez Alfaro, and the first testimonios of the armed struggle like Doris Tijerino's *"Somos millones"* (1975); even nonrevolutionary writers like Carlos Martínez Rivas and Pablo Antonio Cuadra were appropriated by the rising tide of radicalization and nationalist enthusiasm. A generation of Sandinista poet-combatants began to take shape, including for the first time a growing number of women. Ernesto Cardenal remained, however, the decisive figure in the transition.

Cardenal in the Early 1970s

In 1970, Cardenal went to Cuba to serve as a judge in a poetry contest sponsored by Casa de las Américas. The visit changed his life dramatically. Invited for a few weeks, he stayed three months, visiting all parts of the island, talking to everyone he could. *En Cuba* (1970; 1972), the journal of the experience—including an anthology of the new Cuban "conversational poetry"—was situated politically somewhere between left Christian Democracy and revolutionary Marxism. It became a popular text among Catholic students and social activists throughout Latin America but especially in Nicaragua. In it Cardenal looks critically at certain aspects of Cuban society, but he is struck by what he considers to be the fundamentally Christian orientation of this overtly anti-Christian revolution. As he puts it (in a letter to Marc Zimmerman, dated November 19, 1984), "I never considered the Cuban Revolution to have lacked a Christian basis, but rather that this revolution was the Gospels put into practice, and what had to happen was for the Christians in Cuba to understand this revolution." After his Cuban trip, Cardenal believed, according to Robert Pring-Mill, that "the New People 'that is going to be born' would be a people made up of the New Men whom Che Guevara predicted, but the values of their 'communism' would coincide with those of the earliest Christians" (Pring-Mill 1980: xii–xiii).

This was the vision that gradually came to answer the questions Cardenal left pending in *El estrecho dudoso* and *Homenaje a los indios de América* and which increasingly informed his work in Solentiname in the 1970s. Cardenal began to hold clandestine meetings with Tomás Borge and Carlos Fonseca in which they discussed the future of Nicaragua and the ways to achieve it. "From the beginning, I agreed with everything they said," he recalls. "But I thought the method should be nonviolence . . . In any case, I told them, as a priest, I cannot take part in armed struggle" (in Randall 1984: 106). If Cardenal was led to abandon the Mertonian ideal of strict nonviolence it was because he came to the conclusion that in Nicaragua, as in other parts of Latin America, nonviolent struggle was not possible.

However, this transformation was anything but immediate. It was not until the mid-1970s that Cardenal began actively supporting the Sandinistas and not until the destruction of Solentiname in 1977 by the Guard that he accepted personally the principle of armed struggle. *Canto Nacional* (1972) and *Oráculo sobre Managua* (1973) are his major works of this conjuncture. They appear alongside his anthology of Nicaraguan poetry, *Poesía nicaragüense* (1973), which itself was a quasi-political intervention in its reconstruction of the canon of Nicaraguan poetry under the rubric of exteriorism and anti-imperialism.

The political and aesthetic pressures that had been building in Cardenal's work produced a final break with the vanguardist tradition. This was not accomplished without the mediation of the new political poetry and narrative emanating from Ventana and figures like Rugama, who provided the bridge to a direct identification with the FSLN. *Canto nacional* reiterates the image of Sandino found in *Hora O*, now "resurrected" in the FSLN guerrilla, in combination with an elaborate reconstruction of Nicaragua's history, landscape, and flora and fauna (there is a long section dedicated to the Nicaraguan bird songs, for example). Although Cardenal was not yet abandoning his principle of nonviolence, the poem was dedicated to the FSLN.

Oráculo sobre Managua was Cardenal's most crucial work of transition. It portrays the devastation of the earthquake and the oppression of the Somoza dictatorship, using as a narrative center a heightened retelling of the life and death of Leonel Rugama, who becomes a kind of symbolic equivalent to the idealized Sandino/Báez Bone figure of *Hora 0*. The poem has a highly complex metahistorical structure that extends back to the evocation of a prehistoric volcanic eruption that created the land on which one of Managua's worst slums, Acahualinca, was located (Rugama had worked as a seminarian in Acahualinca and written about it in his poetry). For Cardenal, Rugama—and thus by extension the

Frente—becomes a Christlike figure: both the earthquake and the emerging armed struggle are the culmination of a long process of geological-historical metamorphosis. The poem announces: "We enter into the Easter of the Revolution," where "we shall be reborn together as men and as women."

Cardenal's vision of history and revolution in these texts, which Pring-Mill has grouped together with *Hora 0* under the rubric of "documentary poems," stems in part from Teilhard de Chardin's concept of an intertwining of biological, historical, and cosmic process having at its center a Christian teleological perspective. For Chardin, matter is light whose source is a divine love that wends its way through time and space, through the vicissitudes of natural and human history. Rather than being external or opposed to this process—this is Cardenal's personal version of Liberation Theology eschatology—social revolution is part of its agency. Some sense of what Cardenal is up to may be gotten from the following section of *Canto nacional* (the last line refers to a famous photograph of the face of Che Guevara taken after he was killed in Bolivia):

> I say that iguanas lay their eggs . . . It's the process. They
> (or the frogs) in the silence of the carboniferous age
>   made the first sound
>   sang the first love song over the earth
>   sang the first love song under the moon.
>   It's the process.
> The process started in the stars.
>   New relations of production: that too
> is part of the process. Oppression. After oppression,
>   liberation.
> The Revolution started in the stars, millions
>   of light-years away. The egg of life
>   is one. From
> the first bubble of gas, to the iguana's egg, to the New Man.
> Sandino was proud he had been born "from the womb of the
>   oppressed"
> (from the womb of a Niquinohomo Indian woman)
> From the womb of the oppressed the Revolution will be born.
>   It's the process.
> To attract the female, the male pelican puffs out his chest
>   before mating.
> But the process continues still further:
> In death Che smiled as if he had just left Hell.
>   (Translation adapted from Zimmerman 1980)

The Solentiname Poets and the San Carlos Uprising

Reflecting on his transformation, Cardenal was to write in 1976: "I became politicized by the contemplative life. Meditation is what brought me to political radicalization. I came to the revolution by way of the Gospels. It was not by reading Marx but Christ. It can be said that the Gospels made me a Marxist" (p. 20). But, as we have seen, it was not just "the contemplative life" but the organized presence and activity of the Sandinistas in the midst of Nicaragua's developing crisis that turned Cardenal to direct involvement with the revolution. The transformation was complete just a few months prior to Fonseca's death in action in November 1976 and the subsequent Sandinista split. "I considered myself a member of the FSLN," Cardenal notes, "from the time I accepted my first mission: going to the Russell Tribunal in Rome, in 1976. The organization sent me to denounce the beastly crimes being committed against the peasantry there" (in Randall 1984: 107).

The same transformation was to occur in the Solentiname commune at large. If in its first phase it was also marked by an adherence to the principle of nonviolence, it could not remain immune to the convulsions of Nicaraguan society and the growth of the Sandinista movement after the earthquake. After a long process of discussion and debate, in 1977 the commune became Sandinista, identifying in particular with the insurrectional tendency. As part of the FSLN's general uprising of 1977, on October 12 members of the commune joined with units of the FSLN in an attack on the National Guard garrison in the nearby town of San Carlos, close to the border with Costa Rica. The fighting went well at first, but the Guard, using airplanes, launched a counterattack that placed the civilian population in danger. The Sandinistas decided to retreat to avoid a massacre. The Solentiname group was forced to abandon the island and disperse. Some of the group were killed in the attack, others captured, others escaped into exile in Costa Rica or to join combat units of the Frente. Cardenal's commune was destroyed by the Guard; all the buildings were razed except for the church, which was converted into a barracks.

Apart from Cardenal and his immediate collaborators, the members of the Solentiname commune were fishermen, peasants, primitive painters, artisans, and craftsmen drawn from the region of Lake Nicaragua. The majority were young people in their late teens or early twenties, but there were also children and older persons. Even after the success of his handicraft and painting workshops, Cardenal found it hard to believe that it was possible to teach the young people of Solentiname how to write poetry. It was his friend, the Costa Rican poet Mayra Jiménez, who apparently convinced him to give her a chance to develop a poetry workshop. The project began in late 1976 and lasted until the destruction of Solentiname a year later.

In the preface to her anthology of this experience, *Poesía campesina de Solentiname* (1980), Jiménez describes the activities of the workshop as follows:

> [P]oetry in Solentiname emerges as a collective artistic product. In the first sessions we dedicated ourselves to reading the great poets of Nicaraguan and world literature. . . . We read and commented texts from the early afternoon until dusk. . . . I never asked any one to write. The poetry began to emerge very quickly and in a natural way among the people. . . . The first poems they wrote were discussed between the author and me but always in the presence of other individual members of the group. Immediately we began to discuss them with the whole group, with everyone participating in deciding what seemed good and what didn't. Sometimes the authors defended their positions, sometimes, they modified their work, and there were times when they tore up their original version and began again from scratch. . . . The important thing to underline is how this poetry was among them and how it appeared—as Ernesto Cardenal says—like a miracle. That is, it's a peasant poetry, from the people and for the people and therefore it has resulted in being an eminently social, political and human production. Above all, revolutionary and testimonial. (Pp. 7–10)

As Jiménez suggests, the poetry workshop focused largely on technical and pedagogic issues and included visits by José Coronel Urtecho, Pablo Antonio Cuadra, Luis Rocha, and other writers. But its development also paralleled the radicalization of the Solentiname community as a whole. It both represented and was a means of the gradual evolution of political consciousness on the part of the young people of this special community (Jiménez believed that "this peasant poetry will be an example for the proletarian classes of the world"). In the workshop poems collected by Jiménez, we can see these young people reacting to conditions in their immediate lives; learning to love and care for each other; beginning to develop a sense of place; combining this with a growing sense of a possible role in national and universal history; springing into action as idealistic militants in an insurrectionary action; mourning their dead and the loss of the community that nourished them; and pledging themselves to continue the struggle for a new Nicaragua.

Some of the commune participants who survived the San Carlos assault worked with Jiménez in exile in Costa Rica afterward on developing workshop poetry techniques. Others passed into the FSLN and continued writing as guerrilla combatants or in prison. Some days before the attack, Cardenal had left Solentiname to go on tour for the Sandinistas. Word reached him of the events and of the fact that his special immunity under Somoza was at an end. Declared an outlaw, he published an open letter—*Lo que fue Solentiname* (The meaning of Solentiname)—accompanied by a press release proudly acknowledging that he had been a full-fledged member of the FSLN since 1976. Written in the wake of Solentiname's destruction, Cardenal's letter indicated that collective meditation on the social relevance of the Scriptures had played a leading role in the radicalization of his commune, ultimately inspiring its members to join in the armed struggle "for one reason alone: out of their love for the kingdom of God. Out of their ardent desire for a just society, a true concrete kingdom of God here on this earth."[1]

Paradoxically, it was only after its destruction that the significance of Solentiname and the poetry workshop project began to connect with the general dynamics of Sandinista cultural radicalism in the dramatic period between 1977 and 1979. Cardenal wrote a series of poems describing the unfolding of the revolution, moving from Solentiname and the San Carlos assault to portraits of the *muchachos* who built the barricades and battled the Guard in the streets of Managua, Estelí, and Masaya during the first insurrectionary offensive of 1978. He went on one speaking tour after another in Latin America, Europe, and the United States, raising money for the Sandinistas and winning new recruits for solidarity work. He also took part in the deliberations over the new junta of reconstruction that was being readied in Costa Rica to take power after the fall of Somoza. In his open letter he summarized the transformation of his position as follows: "I have given no thought to the reconstruction of our little community of Solentiname. I think of the far more important task, the task for all of us: the reconstruction of the whole country."

Gradas and the New Women's Poetry

La Prensa, the cornerstone of the bourgeois opposition to Somoza in the 1970s, continued to publish political poetry in its literary supplement as part of its campaign against the regime. But Pablo Antonio Cuadra was careful about what he included, attempting to keep out of his pages anything that seemed to veer too much in the direction of the FSLN. As we noted, he rejected Morales's poems, and the work of many, though not all FSLN-identified writers, met the same fate. Partly because of this, partly because of a more general sense of the exhaustion or irrelevancy of the vanguardist mode, a series of new cultural groups emerged to take the place of the suspended *Ventana* project.

The poetry and prose testimonios of Sandinista martyrs, prisoners, combatants, and fellow travelers began to appear in the pages of the new UNAN-based magazine, *Taller*, directed by Michele Najlis and Alejandro Bravo, or circulated more informally in mimeographed sheets among revolutionary cells, student organizations, and clubs. Ethnologist Carlos Alemán Ocampos, poet Francisco de Asís Fernández, and painters Alejandro Aróstegui and Leonel Vanegas revived the Praxis group in 1970. Connected with the FSLN through Camilo Ortega, their journal published two issues before being shut down in 1973. In 1972, a group of young writers including Rosario Murillo, David McField, Guillermo Menocal, Eric Blandón, and Bayardo Gámez, along with Nicaraguan *nueva canción* writer and performer Carlos Mejía Godoy, established a cultural "brigade" of politically committed artists called Gradas (Steps). Guided by the slogan that "the struggle for culture is the struggle for social change," Gradas reached out to all cultural workers, recruiting critic Winston Curtis and painters like Genaro Lugo, Alfonso Ximenes, and Efrén Medina. In a series of manifestos issued in 1974, the group rejected the commercialization of intellectual or artistic work, attacking in particular the elitism of previous Nicaraguan literature. They proposed instead the concept that culture exists to serve the people, and on this basis they invited the participation of popular sectors in their programs and activities, demanding "a change toward a more just and egalitarian system, a change toward the new man" (see Arellano 1982: 84).

Rosario Murillo, already linked personally to Sandinista leader Daniel Ortega, was one of the main forces behind the group. She recalls the difficulties of balancing her writing and political work during her "Gradas years" as follows:

My poetry was imbued with the necessity I lived everyday in communicating with the masses. In Gradas we tried to change the concept of cultural work so that people were not merely receivers but *creators* of culture. At that time, my poetry responded to the need of immediate communication. When the situation changed and we were persecuted and jailed by the dictatorship, we adopted a different strategy. My work went from being open to playing a part in the clandestine network. Publicly I had to be careful so that the place where I lived could be used as a safe house. On the one hand, my poetry reflected the need to continue communicating; but, on the other, I had to communicate in such a way as not to catch the attention of the censors who read the newspapers. (In Anglesey 1987: 395)

Murillo's testimony points to the growing role of middle-class women in clandestine activism for the FSLN and the breakdown of autonomous cultural work as the revolutionary situation intensified, both aspects of the Gradas project. Murillo herself was a major protagonist of a new Sandinista women's poetry that began to appear in the early 1970s. Its forerunner was the 1969 collection, *El viento armado*, by Michele Najlis, who had been part of the Ventana and Praxis groups. It quickly became one of the most important literary expressions the insurrectionary period produced.

The more prominent figures of this new women's poetry—Murillo, Najlis, Yolanda Blanco, Vidaluz Meneses, Gioconda Belli, and Daisy Zamora—are known in Nicaragua collectively as "The Six" (Ana Ilce is sometimes also associated with the group, although her work has been less explicitly political). Generally, they came from well-to-do families, passed through exclusive private Catholic schools and the university, were influenced by the vanguardists and Cardenal, whose poetry helped to radicalize them, published in both *La Prensa Literaria* and *Taller*, and eventually came into the orbit of the Frente. In part, their formation as a group was related to the expansion and modernization of Nicaraguan education in the 1960s, which allowed women greater access to universities and career training, in part to the influences from the emerging international women's movement.

Gioconda Belli echoes Murillo's account of the strange double life many of these women began to lead, as they shifted between their literary careers and clandestine work for the Frente:

> After the 1972 earthquake, Somoza's security police got wise to me and I began to be followed. At that time I was working as a messenger between René Núñez and Eduardo Contreras. The people where I worked at that time told me that the head of Somoza's security force had told them to fire me because I belonged to the FSLN. I didn't let on there was anything wrong, and I remember that my poetry was a useful cover with them, because that was how I justified my hanging around with a few "strange" people, as they called them. (In Randall 1984: 146–147)

Belli's first book of poetry, *Sobre la grama* (On the grass) appeared in 1974 with a preface by José Coronel Urtecho. "The only conflict I had," she says, "was making sure I didn't publish anything that would give my real sentiments away. That's why *Sobre la grama* is not a book of political poetry as such, although it is certainly a book that dealt with society's hypocrisy toward women" (in Randall 1984: 148). Belli served in a support group for the December 1974 hostage taking by the FSLN in

Managua—her recent novel, *La mujer habitada* (1988), is a fictionalized account of the action—so that when the Frente finally recognized her publicly as a militant, she had already become so "burnt" that she had to leave the country.

In 1978, Belli shared the Casa de las Américas poetry prize for her collection, *Línea de fuego*, which now overtly drew the connection between a passionate eroticism and Sandinista politics. Marked by evocations of protracted lovemaking and warfare, the collection surges in rhythms of intense anger, pain, and sexuality. Disalienated and sexually liberated, woman becomes for Belli the allegorical representation of the revolutionary process.

Speaking about the dramatic politicization of her work, Belli explained:

> I saw that it was possible to write love poems which were also
> revolutionary, which could integrate personal and collective experi-
> ences. . . . At first I had problems with the so-called political
> poems. They always came out of my own individual experiences,
> and I considered that to be a limitation. But when one lives collec-
> tive experiences as an individual . . . the truth is that one expresses
> feelings or ideas which have the force of many experiences born
> from collective practice and struggle. . . . I wrote *Línea de fuego*
> during the first four months of my exile in Mexico. . . . [E]verything
> I'd been accumulating throughout those years, my deepest feelings,
> the pain of the repression we had suffered, exile, the separation
> from my children—all this came out in my poetry, poured out in
> that book. (In Randall 1984: 148)

The effect of *Línea de fuego* was remarkable, not only because of its outspoken eroticism and feminism but also because of Belli's rumored love affairs with various Sandinista leaders.

But it was only the most sensational of a cluster of *poemarios* by Sandinista women that appeared during and just after the insurrectional period. These include Najlis's attempt at a "Marxist" didactic poetry, *Augurios* (1981); Murillo's *Gualtayán (Amar)* (1974), *Sube a nacer conmigo* (1976), and *Un deber es cantar* (1981), centered on the death of her child in the 1972 earthquake and her subsequent radicalization; Vidaluz Meneses's *Llama guardada* (1974), with the widely admired feminist satire "Cuando me casé"; Ana Ilce's *Las ceremonias del silencio* (1975); Yolanda Blanco's, *Así cuando la lluvia* (1974), *Cerámica sol* (1977), and *Penqueo en Nicaragua* (1981)—which the author described as "como un testimonio" of the insurrection; and Daisy Zamora's *La espuma violenta* (1983).

Among the male poets who belonged to the writer groups of the late 1960s and early 1970s, one of the most active was Francisco de Asís Fernández, who after his experiment in reviving *Praxis*, left for Mexico City, where he edited an important anthology of Sandinista and proto-Sandinista poetry, *Poesía política nicaragüense* (1st ed., 1979), and worked with poet Thelma Nava, head of the Mexican Nicaraguan Solidarity Committee. A black writer from Bluefields, McField, along with Carlos Rigby, the novelist Lizandro Chávez Alfaro, and the historian Ray Hooker, represented those Atlantic coast intellectuals who supported the FSLN from the early 1970s. More spectacular was the role of Carlos Mejía Godoy and his brother Luis, who staged solidarity concerts and even recorded a commercial hit in a multicountry fund-raising and support-building campaign for the Sandinistas, using poems by Cardenal, others as texts for songs done in the *corrido*-influenced style of Nicaraguan folk music.[2] A protégé of Ernesto Mejía Sánchez, Julio Valle-Castillo continued Cardenal's vein of exteriorist, historically inflected poetry, but in general the production of these years marks a shift away from the formulas of narrative exteriorism to the more emotionally and personally inflected testimonial voice represented by Rugama and the women poets.

In some cases there was a correspondence between the work of these writers and the different tendencies of the FSLN. Mejía Godoy and Belli, for example, were said to be associated with the position of *guerra popular prolongada.* Murillo, Daisy Zamora, Sergio Ramírez, the Solentiname poets, and Cardenal himself identified with the *terceristas.* The *proletario* tendency lacked poets of its own, but its leader, Jaime Wheelock, attempted to claim Rugama at least in spirit. These sectarian nuances meant little in the long run, since the poetry worked more in generating an overall revolutionary ethos than it did in fighting for specific political-strategic lines. Where there were later differences about cultural politics—for example, as we detail below, between Cardenal and Murillo over the poetry workshops—they don't necessarily correspond to the pre-1979 splits. We should note, however, that the majority of the poet combatants of the insurrection period were *terceristas* in tendency and often were directly influenced not only by the poetry and theology of Cardenal but by his voluntaristic post-Solentiname political line as well. Both the Ministry of Culture under Cardenal and Zamora, as well as the cultural section of *Barricada, Ventana,* and the cultural worker's union, the Asociación Sandinista de Trabajadores la Cultura (ASTC) directed by Murillo, would be dominated by *terceristas.*

The Combat Poets of the Insurrection

While Cardenal could continue to speak ex cathedra from Solentiname until the end of 1977, many of the cultural organizations and publications associated with the Sandinistas like Gradas or Praxis disappeared or went underground between 1975 and 1979. Many of the writers who developed around Ventana in the 1960s were in exile, working with international solidarity groups; those who remained in Nicaragua were wrapped up in immediate political and military tasks, and their writing would begin to appear only after the final insurrection. Literary texts that affected the political process often appeared clandestinely, as mimeos circulated by hand, graffiti (what Nicaraguans call *pintas*), or song lyrics passed on by memory from one person and group to another.

While the poets in exile like Belli or (after 1977) Cardenal had both the freedom and professional formation that enabled them to fashion elaborate verbal structures, the poet-combatants inside the country wrote more simply, using short verse forms as a means of recording and commemorating the rush of events and emotions affecting them directly. A focus on poetic restraint and minimalism, testimonio, camaraderie, and militancy is found in almost all their work, which in turn began to influence the style of the more established writers.

Striking in this body of poetry from the insurrection are veteran writer/poet Mario Cajina Vega's poems written while he participated as a combatant in the defense and liberation of Masaya; the poem-diary by a housewife, Magdalena de Rodríguez, written as a day-to-day account of the fighting in and around Estelí; Luis Vega's poems on the street fighting in Managua in the last hours of Somoza's regime. A remarkable number of Sandinista leaders—Carlos Guadamuz, Dora María Téllez, Hugo Torres, Daniel Ortega, and Tomás Borge, among others—wrote poetry during the final insurrection. But most significant in terms of revolutionary mobilizations, which often centered around demonstrations commemorating Sandinista martyrs, was the poetry written by poet-combatants killed in the struggle. By the time of the insurrection, Nicaragua already had a poetic canon of martyrs of the revolution, including Rigoberto López Pérez, Edwin Castro, Rugama, Morales Avilés, José Benítez Escobar, and several of the Solentiname poets.

One of the most famous of the poet-combatants was Ernesto Castillo, a young man who died fighting at the age of twenty in León, during the September 1978 fighting. A nephew of Cardenal, Castillo was to become especially important in the insurrection as a link to the FSLN martyrs like Rugama and Morales of the previous period. The poems of his that survive explain why he wrote, what he thought of life and the struggle, and what he hoped for in the future he sensed he would not live to see.

The first book of poetry published by Cardenal's Ministry of Culture after the revolution was a collection of the work of Gaspar García Laviana, *Cantos de amor y guerra* (1979). Although Spanish by origin, García Laviana was a priest who became so identified with the Nicaraguan struggle that he joined the guerrillas, eventually becoming an important Sandinista leader before being killed in combat. His poems are expressions of his spirit of combative Christianity, his feelings of solidarity with the peasantry, his growing conviction of the necessity of armed struggle, his vision of a time after the victory that his own sacrifice would help to make possible. Like Camilo Torres in Colombia, his personal example and work symbolized the synthesis of religious commitment and national liberation struggle that was an important part of Sandinismo's ideological mobilization.

We should mention some lesser known figures among the poet-combatants: Oscar Antonio Robelo (nephew of the Alfonso who eventually ended up a spokesperson of the contras), killed in combat in August 1978; Felipe Peña, a veteran of the Solentiname poetry workshop, captured and killed in Nueva Guinea; Ricardo Su Aguilar, who left three poems before dying in the battle for Masaya; Juan Carlos Tefel, also killed during the final insurrection, on July 14, 1979, in La Calera, on the Southern Front. "I haven't read Cardenal's poems," Tefel wrote, in a poem that seems to summarize the stance and tone of the poet-combatants, "But I've felt the flame / which ignites outraged desire / singing songs of death."

On July 18, 1979, as the columns of the Sandinista army began to make their way toward a Managua suddenly abandoned by Somoza, Sergio Ramírez, Cardenal, and other figures of what was to be the provisional revolutionary government flew into the city from Costa Rica. Seeing the lights of the Managua airport, Cardenal recalls the moment he had anticipated in the image of Sandino in *Hora 0*:

> That top secret flight at night
> We might have been shot down. The night calm and clear.
> The sky teeming with stars. The Milky Way
> so bright behind the thick pane of the window,
>   a sparkling white mass in the black night
> . . . .
> Out there, in the north, I think I see Sandino's campfire
>   ("That light is Sandino")
> The stars above us, and the smallness of this land
> but also its importance, these
> tiny lights of men. I think: everything is light.
> . . . .

And the airport lights at last.
We've landed. From out of the dark come olive-green clad
   comrades
to greet us with hugs.
We feel their warm bodies, that also come from the sun,
that also are light.
   This revolution is fighting the darkness.
It was daybreak on July 18th. And the beginning
   of all that was to come.

                (Translation from Cardenal 1985a)

Poetry in the Reconstruction

A question that confronted all Sandinista activity in what came to be
known as the period of reconstruction was how long the broad-based
unity forged in the insurrection around the focus of opposition to
Somoza could last; how long could the euphoria of revolution keep
together sectors that had ultimately different historical projects and
goals? Poetry had served as a nexus between anti-Somocista sectors of
the bourgeoisie, radicalized middle sectors, and the popular masses.
What would be its place in a postrevolutionary situation, especially as it
passed from being an oppositional mode to a hegemonic one, now
inscribed in the state apparatus itself?

The Sandinistas recognized early on that they had to build on and
deepen their popular consensus through the development of work in
culture and education. Such work, they believed, would not only keep
alive the revolutionary ethos, but also serve to stimulate new forms of
consciousness and organization in the development of postrevolutionary processes of social transformation. In Carlos Vilas's description of
this conception:

> Education in the Sandinista revolution is not a mechanism of
> reproduction . . . but on the contrary a dimension of the process of
> *liberation of the great popular majorities from the material and*
> *ideological conditions in which they were reproduced as exploited*
> *and oppressed classes.* . . . The whole society becomes the active
> subject of the educational process, and to the extent that it is a
> process oriented by the popular classes themselves, education is
> progressively converted into a gigantic process of self-education.
> (Vilas 1986: 216, 218)

Carlos Tünnerman and Sergio Ramírez were to argue along these lines that the revolution was first and foremost one in education and culture.[3]

One of the first acts of the new revolutionary government was to set up a Ministry of Culture under the direction of Cardenal in a private estate on the outskirts of Managua that had belonged to Somoza's wife. Cardenal's project there was to develop the Solentiname model of cultural democratization on a national level. What this required was, he said at the time, "to bring culture to the people who were marginalized from it. We want a culture that is not the culture of an elite, of a group that is considered 'cultivated,' but rather of an entire people" (Cardenal 1981a: 15–16).

In the first days of the reconstruction, the dominant cultural and educational forms consisted of countless demonstrations, rallies, and ceremonial events to commemorate the martyrs of the revolution. Within a few months, political education seminars and orientation sessions began to proliferate in neighborhood centers and work sites throughout the country. Cardenal's ministry embarked on an ambitious program to develop cultural workshops (Casas de Cultura and Centros Populares de Cultura) in poor neighborhoods and rural areas, theater groups, folklore and artisanal production, song groups, new journals of creation and cultural criticism, training programs for cultural workers. In the area of mass communications, the Sandinista newspaper, *Barricada* and its weekly cultural supplement *Ventana* appeared, along with *Televisión Sandino, Radio Sandino*, and the new Nicaraguan film production unit, INCINE. A political split over the revolution among the staff of *La Prensa* produced the independent but pro-Sandinista newspaper *El Nuevo Diario*, with its literary supplement *Nuevo Amanecer Cultural*. A state publishing house for literature was created: Editorial Nueva Nicaragua (the more politically oriented publishing house of the FSLN itself is Editorial Vanguardia). The Mejía Godoy brothers trained new musicians, singers, and composers. Public poetry readings and contests, cultural festivals, concerts by groups of the *nueva canción* movement became everyday events.

Of the different forms of cultural mobilization, the one that overshadowed and conditioned the functioning and effect of the others, however, was the Literacy Crusade of 1980–1981, developed under the auspices of the Ministry of Education headed by Cardenal's brother Fernando. The crusade represented an even broader mobilization than the insurrection itself: of the more than eighty thousand literacy workers participating, only seven thousand were professional teachers, the rest students, housewives, professionals, and workers. Popular adult education programs had seventeen thousand teachers by 1981; in the countryside popular education collectives (CEPs) began to spring up in the wake of the crusade. School enrollments at all levels more than doubled between 1978 and 1984.

Given the presence of Cardenal in the revolutionary state apparatus, there could be no doubt that poetry would be expected to play a major role. Early in the reconstruction, the ministry began collecting and publishing much of the poetry we have been discussing here. Through its Literature Section (first directed by Daisy Zamora and then, with her promotion to Vice Minister, by Julio Valle-Castillo), the ministry among other things cooperated in the publication of the political poetry of the insurrectionary period; developed a new anthology of Darío in tune with his redefinition as an anticipatory voice of Nicaraguan national liberation; established the Rubén Darío poetry prize for Latin American writers and the Leonel Rugama prize for young Nicaraguan writers; organized the first annual dawn-to-dusk poetry marathon broadcast nationally from the public stadium of Ciudad Darío, birthplace of the poet; established on the lines of *Casa de las Américas* its own journal of literary creation and criticism, *Nicaráuac*; and helped to facilitate the formation of the organization that eventually would become its rival, the Asociación Sandinista de Trabajadores de la Cultura (ASTC), which incorporated under the banner of Sandinismo many of the nation's established writers and artists.

The ministry included poetry education in the programs it developed to train facilitators who would help establish cultural centers and contribute to the literacy campaigns. But its major effort in this field was the establishment of the poetry workshops.

The Poetry Workshops

In 1980, Cardenal commissioned his poetry specialist from Solentiname days, Mayra Jiménez, to launch a series of popular poetry workshops (*talleres de poesía*) under the auspices of the ministry throughout the country. The goal was the decentralization and democratization of cultural production. The workshops would be for ordinary working people and would be set up in their places of work, homes, and communities. Thousands of people took part in the workshops, finding, as in the earlier experience of Solentiname, in their efforts to learn how to write poetry also a laboratory for ideological development and struggle.

Julio Valle-Castillo became the editor of the workshop's artisanally produced journal, *Poesía Libre* (the issues were printed on coarse brown paper and bound with string). He provided both a characterization of and a manifesto for the movement in his presentation of one of the first collections of workshop poetry in that journal:

[Workshop poetry] is a direct and profound poetry, it is the life of the people with their language, it is physical geography, it is the history of our Sandinista Revolution written in verse. A poetry full of emotions, of testimonio (war, love), it is neo-epic. We believe that this poetry in its language, in its way of relating people with the world, has a great value: it is a poetry written by the peasants of Niquinohomo, of Condega, of San Juan de Oriente, of Jinotega, Palacagüina; by construction workers; by Monimbó artisans; by militia soldiers, by literacy *brigadistas*, by members of the Sandinista Workers Central. By the people.

The language they use is the same the people use while talking under a manocú tree, in the Cantagallo guerrilla camp, in the port of San Miguelito, or to write a letter to Nilda García, a literacy campaign worker killed near Espino.

It is the same technique as the poetry of William Carlos Williams, or the poetry of the Polynesian islands, or actual Salvadoran combat poetry. (*Poesía Libre* 2, 1981: 1)

The program thrived initially, in spite of the difficulties of the revolution's first years. Workshop poems began to appear in mimeograph, then in the major cultural organs of Nicaragua, and then in the workshops' own *Poesía Libre*. (A key feature of the program was to have the poetry produced by the workshops actually published, in order to break down the distinction between amateur and professional writers conferred by publication.) By the end of 1982, the workshops had entered into the areas developed by the literacy campaign and into every mass organization and assembly created by the revolution. At their high point, there were some seventy workshops nationally meeting on a weekly basis; local, regional, and national poetry contests; a national radio show; and besides *Poesía Libre*, countless local publications in mimeo.[4]

The critical response to the production of the *talleres* was enthusiastic. Eduardo Galeano believed that the new workshop poetry stood with the testimonio as the two most important innovations in recent Latin American literature. Venezuelan writer Joaquín Sosa argued that "for the first time, the means of poetic production have been socialized." Cardenal himself boasted, "The production of new poetry is startling. There are poetry workshops in the poorest neighborhoods, in factories, in the Army and even in the police precinct offices. I think that Nicaragua is the only country in the world where poetry produced by the police is published. . . . Our people have expropriated their culture, which is now their own, as they are owners of their land and of their history" (1981a: 15–16).

And yet, like everything else that emerged in the course of the Nicaraguan Revolution, workshop poetry became a matter for criticism and debate. Even confirmed Sandinistas complained about it, labeling it bad, artificial, too derivative of Cardenal, too prosaic, too propagandistic. Some claimed that the flexible principles of exteriorism had now taken on an academic, institutionalized air, become an official style for writing poetry. A rigid and imitative posture of "revolutionary virtue and commitment" was said to dominate and stultify the workshops' efforts. Cardenal perhaps invited the attack by his inculcation of a virtual formula for workshop poems in a text, "Some Rules for Writing Poetry" (1981c), produced in mimeograph for the use of the poetry workshop coordinators.

Trying to dismiss the force of the criticisms, Cardenal noted: "There are always different tendencies and movements among artists and these are often at odds with each other.... With a country in revolution, where art and culture come to the forefront and are in a position to play a significant social role, then naturally you are going to have arguments" (in Johnson 1985: 12). But the issue touched some of the deepest concerns about artistic pedagogy and values and the direction of Nicaragua's cultural revolution, and the arguments didn't go away.

The attack on the workshop poetry came mainly from the established poets and writers represented by the ASTC, and from the pages of *Ventana*, both headed by Rosario Murillo.[5] It was first broached in a major way in "Entre la Libertad y el Miedo," a discussion organized by Murillo among several major Latin American and Nicaraguan intellectuals—including Francisco de Asís Fernández, Eduardo Galeano, and Juan Gelman—which was published in *Ventana* on March 7, 1981. It centered on the poetry workshops and "the fear that a single poetic language promoted by an official organization was being imposed on young writers." Guillermo Rothschuh Tablada, himself a poet of Cardenal's generation, criticized the workshops for attempting to establish a school, but admitted that the exteriorist mode "lends itself most readily to express things that certain sectors are trying to say for the first time." All the participants agreed that the revolution should promote a number of different forms of cultural democratization, not just the workshops, that young writers should be exposed to the whole range of poetic styles and resources developed in Nicaragua and internationally.[6]

A year after the *Ventana* discussion, a mimeographed document signed by former instructors in the workshops appeared, criticizing the "almost mechanical" way the model of the Solentiname workshops was applied to the entire country, and taking issue in particular with the authoritarian teaching methods of Mayra Jiménez. The document reflected the larger discussion of workshop poetry going on in the Union of Nicaraguan

Writers, an affiliate of the ASTC. It claimed in part that

> . . . political, social and historical poetry is nothing new in Latin American literature. It has been considered an extremely dangerous kind of poetry because one needs a high mastery of expression in order to preserve quality. And it is dangerous since it falls so easily into realism or into the language of political pamphlets. . . . The enemies of the Nicaraguan Revolution are neither exteriorism nor surrealism. . . . We believe that it is healthy for diverse literary currents, within the framework of the revolution, to be cultivated simultaneously with an open mind. (In White 1986: 100–101)

Finding the attacks "specious and false," Cardenal countered in a 1983 interview that the primary aim of the workshops was to democratize literary culture, not to build or reinforce a particular style or "movement":

> In the beginning the participants are given some general principles. I call these principles "rules," using the term with full knowledge that it might provoke the misunderstanding that we are attempting to impose a certain method and style of writing. . . . What are these rules? In more or less general terms, they call for the preference of the concrete to the abstract; for not binding oneself to imposed patterns or rhymes that can limit poetic expression—in other words, traditional meter; for avoiding unnecessary words; for referring to the things, places and people familiar to the poet by their common names; and for paying attention to one's senses, given that poetry arrives essentially through the ear, the eye, touch, taste and smell. These guidelines have the intention of helping to overcome some of the difficulties and inhibitions which the beginning writer is naturally confronted with. In no way are they offered with the intention of imposing a single method or style on the participants. . . . Some said that the poets in the Workshops were forced to write poems with an explicitly political or revolutionary theme, and that is false, because . . . at least half the poems are about other themes—love, nature, sex, other things. Another criticism was that the Workshop poetry was too uniform in its style. . . . The Cuban writer Fina García Marruz touches on some of these questions. . . . She assumes that the poets will gradually and naturally individualize their styles as time goes on. She also points out something she considers historically unique: that the working people of Nicaragua have begun to appropriate the heritage of "cultured" poetry to better express their own past and present,

when . . . the reverse had always been the case: "cultured" poets
had appropriated the people's language and poetry to better express
their individuality. (In Johnson 1985: 10–12)

The most important person to join the debate was Mayra Jiménez
herself, the Costa Rican poet who with Cardenal's blessing maintained
ironclad control over the organization, procedures, and standards of the
talleres. Discussing the workshops with Steven White in July 1982,
Jiménez noted:

The poetry . . . is eminently revolutionary. The poets, owing to
their proletarian origins, use a concrete, simple, and direct language. The images are closely related to the immediate reality and
the experience of each of the poets. And that gives poetry a certain
tone. It's a testimonial . . . poetry. A permanent feature . . . is the
presence of nature: the names of trees, rivers, and birds. The poets
also use the names of our leaders, the heroes who died, the people
who served in the literacy and health brigades. The names of the
brothers and sisters who didn't survive are used, too. In other
words, this poetry has gathered in verse a large part of Nicaraguan
history. (In White 1986: 110)

Pointing to the connection between workshop poetry and exteriorism,
Jiménez argued that what it shares with Cardenal's narrative poems like
Hora 0 is a "concrete, descriptive, and conversational" language found
in "great poets such as William Carlos Williams and Carl Sandburg."
Addressing the repeated complaints about flatness of tone and language,
she replied:

We don't have anything against . . . metaphorical or . . . conceptual
[poetry]. It's simply [that the workshop poets are] campesinos and
workers. The language they use for poetry is the language they use
in their everyday lives. They write that way and nobody tells them
they have to. When they begin to discover that they have things to
say, the language they look for to express these things comes from
their day-to-day life. What we do in the workshops is give the
language the profundity it needs to become art. . . . It hasn't been
very long since the triumph. The poets . . . in the workshops are
young people who have participated in the war. The experience
that forms the major emotional burden at this time is still closely
related to what was going on before, during and after the war. They
haven't looked for ways to bring to their poetry that other world
related to legend, myth, superstitions, symbols and the interpreta-

tion of different phenomena. That's the way these young people
write. . . . They're searching for a testimonial form they can use to
express in poetry their most recent experiences. (Ibid.: 111–112)

The attack on the poetry workshops and on the political-testimonial
tendency in postrevolutionary literature continued in the pages of
Ventana and elsewhere in Sandinista cultural circles. It involved in part
an unspoken issue of national pride: the extent of the resources and
authority over cultural policy given by Cardenal to a Costa Rican
apparently not noted for humility or charm. But Cardenal's own status
and power as, in effect, the cultural patriarch of the revolution were also
at issue, and it was tacitly understood that the real struggle was between
Rosario Murillo—as editor of *Ventana* and head of the ASTC (Asociación
Sandinista de Trabajadores de la Cultura)—and Cardenal and the Ministry of Culture for general control over the future development of Sandinista
literary and cultural policy.

As the debate raged, the contra war and the growing internal problems
of the revolution meant a reconsideration of national priorities. Many
of the instructors and participants in the workshops volunteered for
military duty. By 1983, the number of regularly functioning workshops
had fallen to around thirty. But a much deeper disruption of Cardenal's
overall project was also under way. First, with not unconcealed rejoicing
among many Nicaraguan cultural workers, Mayra Jiménez yielded to
the growing pressure against her and returned to Costa Rica in 1983.
Then, Julio Valle-Castillo, the editor of *Poesía Libre* whom Cardenal had
appointed to head the ministry's literature section, also came under
attack by *Ventana* and other journals. The workshops were reorganized
and began to function under the auspices of the ministry's twenty-four
regional popular culture centers throughout the country. The centers
were much less beholden to Cardenal and the literature section, and
responded more directly to popular concerns and the influence and
participation of local Sandinista partisans. The reform kept the project
alive for a time, but it implied a waning of Cardenal's influence on
Sandinista cultural policy and the growing power of the woman who was
also the revolutionary government's First Lady: Rosario Murillo.

Murillo and the ASTC

Formed after the revolution in 1980, the ASTC served as an umbrella
organization for unions of writers, painters, musicians, photographers,
filmmakers, theater people, and circus workers. Though not formally
part of the Frente, its name indicated its political affiliation clearly
enough. (Its roots seem to be in some aspects of the Gradas project,

which Murillo had been involved in during the 1970s.) While some of its members worked for the Ministry of Culture or in ministry-related programs, they tended to represent the urban-based professional cultural workers who participated in the struggle against Somoza, including both those who had been Sandinista cadre and independent figures. The ASTC had no independent funds beyond dues, and at times competed with the ministry in the search for state subsidies and foreign aid. It began essentially as a combination of trade union and professional association, and its initial work focused mainly on problems of working conditions for cultural workers: health, education, and the like. Then it sought to develop a subsidized system of professionalization and patronage that would grant salaries to those artists recognized as having the sufficient skills and records to qualify. The new interest marked an ambiguity between its role as a union and as a conveyor belt of state policy in the field of culture.

Increasingly, the ASTC began to involve itself in work that impinged on the Ministry of Culture's turf. For example, it embarked on a project to upgrade Nicaragua's private circuses, an important form of popular culture, creating an organization called La Carpa Nacional to deal with circus company problems, coordinate programs, and serve as a conduit for national and touring international circus performers. For the fifth anniversary of the revolution and the fiftieth anniversary of Sandino's death, it organized theater and circus performances, song and dance festivals, contests and exhibits in different arts, mural-painting projects, and a forum, "Art and Literature Five Years after the Revolution." Responding to the escalating war with the contras, the ASTC began to organize and send cultural brigades to the war zones on the border with Honduras, an activity that, by reaching out to sectors of the population living in rural areas under very difficult circumstances, seemed to steal the thunder from the ministry and its poetry workshops.

Explaining the cultural brigades project, Murillo drew a clear distinction with Cardenal and Mayra Jiménez's emphasis on grass-roots poetry and handicraft production:

There's a tradition here of the artist and intellectual participating in the struggle of the people. While it's true that the artist can train in the militia or get involved in productive work . . . , the artist's main contribution to the defense of the Revolution lies in the field of culture itself. This is something we deeply value. We see it as a continuation of the participation of the artists in the struggle waged by Sandino and the Frente. . . . First of all we have to be ready militarily . . . to defend this Revolution with weapons. . . . But also . . . as artists. And so we go to the different fronts of the war . . . to do theater, music, poetry and painting for and with the soldiers. And if we have to go into combat, then we do it. (In White 1986: 125–126)

Whether because of the war and the economic austerity measures it imposed (*compactación*), or Cardenal's own advancing age and impatience with his bureaucratic responsibilities, or a shift brought about by the play of political forces within the revolution, the tension between the Ministry of Culture and the ASTC reached a breaking point after 1985. Though the debate had repercussions inside the Frente, the Sandinista leadership was reluctant to take a firm stand one way or another on cultural policy, for fear of making the mistake of the Cubans in the late 1960s of favoring one cultural "line" over others. But this commendable commitment to pluralism also meant that cultural policy was made ad hoc, without any real budgetary priorities or control. While *Ventana* and *Nicaráuac* both had to stop publishing from time to time because of paper shortages, it was the former, less costly publication that remained in circulation as the official expression of Sandinista cultural taste. More significantly, as part of the *compactación* the Ministry of Culture itself was disbanded in 1987–1988, with many of its resources and functions passing over to the Ministry of Education and the ASTC. Cardenal was left with a figurehead National Cultural Council.

The Veterans

Despite the debates over the workshops and what now seems like a decline of his influence and authority after 1983, Cardenal remained the central figure of Nicaraguan poetry during the period of reconstruction. If before the revolution Cardenal sought a language and expressive modes suitable to a broad audience, this seems even more the case in the poems, especially the shorter ones, he wrote during his tenure in the Ministry of Culture. In this we may perceive the influence of workshop poetry on Cardenal's own work, his sense of wanting to produce a poetry useful to the new social sectors only recently brought to a level of minimal literacy, able to capture the everydayness of the revolution.

The complex vision of human and natural transformation linked to an articulation of Nicaraguan national identity that Cardenal projected in his "documentary poems" is precisely what is missing in his recent work. All is too joyous in Waslala, in spite of the real difficulties of bringing the Miskito Indians into the revolution. The leap from insurrectional victory to the solution of the problems of a backward, struggling, multiethnic, fragmented country is too easily elided.[7] Nevertheless, Cardenal's affirmative poems pose a profound, undaunted faith in the revolution and the people's capacity for resistance and victory. They have been particularly important in the context of the struggle of the Nicaraguan Popular church to keep a religious perspective alive within the revolutionary process against the admonitions of the pope and the Catholic hierarchy. (Cardenal, along with his brother Fernando and Foreign Minister Miguel D'Escoto, was suspended as a priest by the Vatican in 1985 for refusing to give up his position with the government.) The decision to write "for the people" is to risk the parochial, the trite, the excessively obvious. But Cardenal has been clearly more preoccupied with the people's discovery of its own voice and life than with a need to give intellectual and literary respectability to the revolution. This was a key difference in the debate with Murillo.

To round out our account of Nicaraguan poetry in the reconstruction, we should note briefly what happened to some of the poets of the prerevolutionary generations. The male writers who had begun their careers more or less in the orbit of the Frente Ventana and/or the FSLN like Francisco de Asís Fernández, Julio Valle, Luis Rocha, Octavio Robleto, David McField, Carlos Rigby, Carlos Guadamuz, or Roberto Vargas became cultural or bureaucratic functionaries. José Coronel Urtecho, in yet another of his political mutations, went with the Sandinistas and wrote a series of poems and meditations celebrating the reconstruction process. (He is perhaps the most important literary intellectual of the older generation besides Cardenal to have thrown in his lot with the revolution.) Carlos Martínez Rivas became, briefly, a cultural coordinator for the agrarian reform program, before lapsing back into bohemianism. Ernesto Mejía Sánchez served as ambassador to Spain until his death. As we have noted, Coronel's colleague from the vanguard, Pablo Antonio Cuadra, turned against the revolution, continuing to write a rich poetry full of pre-Columbian and Christian myth patterns and championing from the editorial pages of *La Prensa* an ultraconservative Catholicism that resonated with the position of the church hierarchy as an ideological center of resistance to the Sandinistas.

Although all these writers continued to produce significant poetry, the more important developments were elsewhere: in workshop poetry and, partially as a response to the model represented by workshop poetry, the continuation and eventual hegemony of the new Sandinista women's poetry.

Sandinista Women's Poetry after the Revolution

AMNLAE, the Sandinista mass organization for women, grew mainly out of middle sector women's opposition to Somoza and only gradually linked itself with peasant and workers' opposition. The same evolution was true with the related movement of women's political poetry, whose origins in the early 1970s we sketched earlier in this chapter. The "Six"—Gioconda Belli, Vidaluz Meneses, Rosario Murillo, Michele Najlis, Yolanda Blanco, and Daisy Zamora—are simply the best known Sandinista women poets in a field that included many others. Their work after the 1979 victory is represented by Belli's *Truenos y arcoiris* (1982), her anthology *Amor insurrecto* (1984), and *De la costilla de Eva* (1987); Meneses's *El aire que me llama* (1985); Blanco's *Aposentos* (1984); Murillo's anthology *Amar es combatir* (1982) and *En las espléndidas ciudades* (1985); Najlis's *Ars combinatoria* (1988); and Zamora's *La violenta espuma* (1981) and *En limpio se escribe la vida* (1988).[8]

What are the general characteristics of this work? Is it, to begin with, a feminist poetry championing demands for equality of women and for a redefinition of female role models, or a woman-centered poetry projected onto a larger sense of national revolutionary unity? In Sandinista policy in general, women's liberation issues and the need to maintain a base of support among a basically Catholic population have not always coincided comfortably (abortion is still de jure illegal, although de facto it is tolerated). On the other hand, it is clear that women's militancy has been crucial to the revolution since its very early stages and that both the pre- and postrevolutionary periods have provided a framework for the liberation of a significant number of women from traditional role models. To mention only some well-known cases: in the Sandinista pantheon Doris Tijerino has a status equal to that of Rugama and Morales; Nora Astorga was appointed ambassador to the United States, and when that was rejected by the State Department, she was appointed Nicaragua's representative to the United Nations. Of the poets of the "Six," Meneses worked on the National Library and then headed the Writers Union within the ASTC; Zamora began as a broadcaster for Radio Sandino during the insurrection and was head of the Literature Section and then vice minister of the Ministry of Culture under Cardenal; Murillo has headed both *Ventana* and the ASTC, and the current Institute of Culture; Najlis worked as head of the immigration office under Tomás Borge in the Ministry of the Interior; and Belli, the best known internationally of the group, has been a sort of free-lance spokesperson and ambassador for the revolution.

In general, these women evolved out of a relatively privileged, upper-class subject position in a process that combined increasing awareness of issues of class in the context of Sandinista militancy with an increasing—though not always explicitly feminist—commitment to women's liberation. Najlis begins as the "little sister" of the Ventana group; Murillo as a mother mourning the loss of her son in the Managua earthquake; Meneses as loving daughter rebelling against her Somocista father; Zamora as the wife who grows with her husband to deep commitments in the FSLN urban underground; Belli as the aggressively erotic lover, equating strike with lovemaking, revolution with orgasm. Thematically, their work expresses the emergence of a "new woman" (in contrast to what they see as the gender-specific connotation of Che Guevara's concept of the New Man) out of the common clay of traditional roles and values. They are in Margaret Randall's expression "Sandino's daughters," projecting a feminine/feminist version of Sandinismo, always wary of the temptation to fall back into traditional roles, of the failures of both male and female *compañeros* to live up to their revolutionary pretensions, of the sometimes suspect appeals to unity in the face of crisis as a justification for postponing women's demands.

In their poetry, the defeat of Somoza is the death of the tyrannical patriarch that unleashes new possibilities of being and feeling for the new woman, who is now "on the cutting edge of the construction of herself." She must show that she is not "quicksand," break with her upper or middle-class background, "want a love with subject / predicate and rifle," identify with the working class and the poor, above all with working-class women. She is "smashing the past to bits, / giving birth to the sun," as she makes her way "along the road of history," ready to "fabricate large, unknown futures," sailing off into a Cardenalian revolutionary cosmos, to make her name her own and "plant it like a flag / in conquered territory. . . / conscious of the portion of history" that belongs to her (we cite here fragments from a number of different women's poems).

The initial models of the Sandinista women poets are Coronel Urtecho, Cardenal, exteriorism in general. Their poetry is experiential, social, directly political, expressing expectation, hope, and faith in the Sandinista future, and anger and outrage over a war that leads to death and destruction, casting doubt over that future. What they add to exteriorism is a thematic of the intimacy, subjectivity and even domesticity marking the "traditional" feminine sphere (Murillo speaks, for example, in a poem dedicated to Belli of "lullabying this different future"). Their intent has been to project an emancipatory conception of female identity without completely negating its origins in the concrete experiences of women as mothers, daughters, lovers in a given time and place.

Does this "feminization" of the formulas of exteriorism also suggest the possibility of its self-transcendence into a new poetic mode? It seems no accident that some of the women poets were in the forefront of the attack on workshop poetry in the name of a more metaphorical and personal poetry. There was also a paradox here, however: they were criticizing not only Cardenal's authoritarianism and his patriarchal status in Nicaraguan poetry, but also a program directed by another woman, Mayra Jiménez, which among other things was empowering large numbers of working-class and peasant women to write poetry for the first time. (Of the "Six," Zamora appears to have been the only one closely involved with Cardenal's project.)

Because of the influence of the church hierarchy, the war, and the collapse of the economy, the revolution has not in fact fulfilled its promises to women, especially working women. Without a continuing transformation of the situation of women, however, there could be no sustained transformation of everyday life and of the values that inform every social institution and project. In this sense, the future of the Sandinista Revolution itself became dependent on how, even in the midst of intense class struggle and enormous economic and military crises, women continued to find ways to advance their own struggle for emancipation and self-development. To the degree that the women poets subsumed during the contra war such women's issues as the right to choose abortion under questions of defense and the "national good"— including population growth and appeasement of the Catholic church— they were consciously falling short of expressing fully the *potential* consciousness of liberated women in the new Nicaragua. Even a woman-centered perspective can run the risk of idealizing aspects of female identity which themselves are ideologically shaped by patriarchy (e.g., the notion that woman's primary identification with the revolutionary process is as mother). But even with these limitations, the Sandinista women poets were and are expressing values and expectations that are on the whole far in advance of the experience of the vast majority of Nicaraguan women. They represent the extent to which at least a certain level of feminist consciousness did have an objective basis in the new social and intellectual conditions created by the revolution, confirming Margaret Randall's assertion early in the reconstruction process that "the process of women's liberation separate from the revolution is not a reality in Nicaragua" (1981).[9]

Nicaraguan Poetry after 1985

The first five years of reconstruction entailed tremendous socioeconomic and political transformations and difficulties, aggravated on one side by the growing opposition to the Sandinistas of the sectors of the bourgeoisie that had joined them in the struggle against Somoza, and on the other by the Reagan administration's determined efforts to isolate and destabilize the revolution, particularly the rapidly escalating contra war. The new conjuncture demanded greater sacrifices and more intense work to maintain and develop international support for the revolution, to keep the internal pro-Sandinista popular bloc more or less intact, and to give ideological animation to the war effort. By 1985, this meant a virtual militarization of cultural work. Cardenal led the way, writing poem after poem about the revolutionary process, including one on the rapidly inflating price of bras. Everybody wrote poems against Eden Pastora. Gioconda Belli wrote an anticontra "Canción de guerra," with a refrain derived from the defense of Madrid in the Spanish Civil War, "No pasarán"—They Shall Not Pass—which Carlos Mejía Godoy put to music. Lizandro Chávez wrote political poems to be used by the ASTC brigades on the border. The slogan of Ventana founder Fernando Gordillo, "Struggle is the highest song," became a virtual watchword defining the duty of poets. Revolutionary vigilance and militancy began to displace and transform even the language of love poetry. Not surprisingly, the politicization of poetry was most extreme among the workshop poets and the activists in the ASTC brigades, many of whom joined the Sandinista army or militias.[10]

Sensing and authorizing the tendency toward politicization, Daniel Ortega reaffirmed the equation between the revolution and poetry in his speech on the fifth anniversary of the revolution in 1984:

> Five years ago songs of roosters and birds proclaimed the triumph, the reign of dreams of hope. Five years ago the bell rang out, the guns and rifles glittered and vibrated announcing the good news, the birth of a free people. All of Nicaragua began to compose the most beautiful poems, with verses on literacy training, on education, culture, health, sports, the nationalization of the banks and exports, the recuperation of the people's riches, the right to work, organize, mobilize, the right to housing and to land, the rights of women and children, the young and old. But these verses broke the snoring of Goliath, the Goliath who for so long had held our homeland in chains, the Goliath who thought he had killed off David when he murdered Sandino. . . . Goliath once more unleashed his fury . . . against the heroic people of Nicaragua. The war drums pound again, the same aggressor as before has launched his pawns to kill, to rape, to torture, to destroy—to try and reimpose the reign of death on Nicaragua. (In Zimmerman 1985: 299)

As the precarious phase of the war between 1984 and 1986 passed, however, other cultural tendencies began to emerge. New comprehensive editions of older poets like Darío, Alfonso Cortés, Azarías Pallais, and Joaquín Pasos were published. On the occasion of the publication of a revised edition of his anthology of Nicaraguan political poetry—which had been one of the central documents of literary Sandinismo during the insurrection—Francisco de Asís Fernández warned against falling into the trap of what he called "Sandinista realism." As the poetry workshops waned, the *Ventana* call for creative diversity and cosmopolitanism seemed to become more dominant. Editorial Nueva Nicaragua published collections by young writers like Alvaro Urtecho and Juan Chow that were not overtly political. New work by Belli and Murillo appeared, also less directly political than might have been expected. (In a group of poems published in *Nuevo Amanecer Cultural* in July 1989, Murillo even explored her conflicts with her *compañero*, Daniel Ortega.)

As a consequence of the ongoing pressure of economic *compactación*, Murillo dissolved the ASTC in 1988 on her own initiative, replacing it with a state-sponsored Institute of Arts and Culture, in effect reconstituting, now under her direction and in a more modestly conceived form, the old Ministry of Culture. Her action provoked an intense debate with Belli and other figures in the Sandinista literary establishment, who criticized not only the loss of the revolution's remaining mass organization for cultural work, but also what they regarded as Murillo's high-handed abuse of authority (everybody agrees the ASTC had serious problems; but there was no formal discussion or debate of the dissolution among the membership of the various unions that made up the ASTC, even though Murillo's action implied transferring the activities of what had been an autonomous—albeit admittedly pro-Sandinista—mass organization directly to the state sector).

Since the disbanding of the Ministry of Culture, Cardenal himself has tended to spend more and more time in his Solentiname retreat, returning to his concerns with pre-Columbian culture and universal cosmology. Though he remains a spokesperson of the revolution and cultural Sandinismo, there is no question that he was personally disappointed and embittered about the attack on the poetry workshops and their eventual dissolution. His recent books indicate a shift away from a poetry of revolutionary activism and immediacy to a vision of human destiny sub specie aeternitas: *Quetzalcoatl* (1986) and *Cántico cósmico* (1989)—the last a six-hundred-page "epic-scientific-mystical-revolutionary" poem reflecting Cardenal's lifelong fascination with scientific theory, something like a *De rerum natura* of the Nicaraguan Revolution.

What is the future of Nicaraguan poetry? This, of course, is in part a question of the future of the revolutionary process itself. To the degree that poetry both anticipates and follows upon social change, we should expect it not to remain the same. Would this mean an end to exteriorism? Not for some time to come. But the work of the women poets already implies a movement away from the specific practice of exteriorism embodied in the workshop poets and Cardenal's great "documentary poems" in the direction of more intellectualized and personal styles.

There has been a tendency, particularly among the writers associated most closely with *Ventana,* toward engaging with some of the concerns and techniques represented by surrealism, which, because of the "objectivist" turn the vanguardists took in the 1930s, were never fully incorporated into Nicaraguan poetry.

There may also be, however, a change in the position of poetry within the overall system of Nicaraguan culture. Poetry will always be an important component of Nicaraguan culture for the reasons we have outlined. But the intensity of its function as a hegemonic expression of national-popular ideology has begun to wane since the early 1980s and will continue to do so. As a harbinger of things to come, perhaps the most interesting new development in Nicaraguan literature has been Alan Bolt's Matagalpa-based Nixtayolero theater collective, which has developed performances critical of various aspects of Sandinista policy and leadership from a position "within the revolution." The problems of poetry are not just a function of the difficult period the revolution is passing through. Cardenal and Jiménez's workshop poetry project was essentially an effort to keep alive—by attempting to democratize it—a certain ideology and practice of poetry that has its roots ultimately in the oligarchical stage of Nicaraguan culture. We are far from thinking that cultural forms have an essential class location or connotation, as our discussion in the previous chapter of the ideological mutations of vanguardism suggests. Still, the results of the project were ambiguous. On the other hand, it is not at all clear that the model represented by Murillo and *Ventana* was a better alternative, among other things because it lacked the antielitist, participatory thrust that, in potential at least, the workshops represented. In some ways its victory meant a partial reinscription within postrevolutionary Nicaragua of the traditional sociocultural line of division between the intelligentsia and the people that had begun to be effaced in the intense mobilizations of the insurrection and early reconstruction years.

Postscript

The unanticipated defeat of the Sandinistas in the elections of February 1990 coincided with our final revision of the manuscript of this book, and leaves us with the difficult task of having to change the ending of our story. We by no means think that the defeat represents the end of the revolutionary process as such in Nicaragua. As in Mexico in the 1920s and 1930s, the ethos of the revolution still remains strong ideologically (the vote for UNO did not represent the victory of a different conception of the national-popular, but either disillusion with Sandinista leadership or a pragmatic sense that there was no other alternative to continued military and economic aggression by the United States). Many of the social gains of the revolution have been constitutionally institutional-ized and will be surrendered only with great struggle. The FSLN remains the largest and best-organized political force in the country. While UNO represents basically a reactivation of Nicaraguan bourgeois parties like the Liberals and Conservatives, several of the deputies elected for that coalition are from parties actually to the left of the Frente like the PSN. Even if the UNO deputies vote as a bloc, they lack the two-thirds majority necessary to amend the constitution in any significant way. As the economy begins to improve slightly and UNO inherits the still intractable problems of running it, it is possible that there may be a polarization to the left again. So the Sandinista project still retains considerable force and room for maneuver.

Nevertheless, the perspective we adopted in our presentation of this chapter—that the revolutionary process was irreversible, despite prob-lems and setbacks—clearly has been deeply problematized. It may be that the revolution will go forward; on the other hand, we may well be witnessing the first stage of a more long-lasting restoration. We had hypothesized in chapters 1 and 2 that one of the key roles of literature in the revolutionary process in Central America generally was to consti-tute a discursive space in which the possibilities of alliance between popular sectors and a basically middle- and upper-class revolutionary vanguard could be pragmatically negotiated around a shared sense of the national-popular. But this had to be, we also suggested, a dynamic process in which the terms of this relationship and the nature and role of literary culture itself were constantly being transformed, as in fact they were in the decade between 1975 and 1985 in Nicaragua.

One of the problems revealed by the elections was precisely that the identification achieved in the period of insurrection and reconstruction between a radicalized intelligentsia—represented by the FSLN leader-ship and upper and middle cadre—and the popular sectors has, at least in part, broken down. The Sandinistas not only failed to maintain the allegiance of sectors of the middle class and bourgeoisie that had previously supported or tolerated them, they also lost support among the urban working class and working poor, among youth and women (mainly because of the draft issue), and in rural towns and cities. As in the case of Guatemala, the spread of Protestant fundamentalism has been a harbinger of ideological demobilization among the poorer sectors of the population (it is estimated that the number of Protestants has gone from some 7 or 8 percent before the revolution to over 20 percent today).

In large part, the breakdown of this identification stems from the fact that from 1985 onward the Sandinistas felt they had to adopt policies to respond to the contra war that often affected the popular sectors directly,

imposing immediate hardships on them and forcing the postponement
or abandonment of long-term plans for economic development and
democratization. The IMF-style *compactación* of 1987–1989 slowed the
rate of inflation, but at the expense of a tremendous loss of purchasing
power and subsidized services by those sectors of the population least
able to bear this. As people struggled to make ends meet, they moved out
of the public sphere of revolutionary mobilizations and participation in
mass organizations back into private life and the family, further inten-
sifying the tendency toward deradicalization and disillusion. Paradoxically, the focus on national elections after 1984 also drained energy and
enthusiasm from the fledgling institutions of participatory democracy.
In this sense, the Sandinista electoral loss represents a victory for the
strategy of low-intensity warfare adopted by the United States to contain
or roll back the Nicaraguan Revolution.

We noted above the effects of the war and *compactación* on Sandinista
literary politics: for example, the decision to close down the poetry
workshops, and the growing ascendancy of the position represented by
Rosario Murillo and *Ventana*, particularly as the Sandinistas sought to
project a pluralistic and cosmopolitan image to gain support abroad and
to prevent polarization internally. In retrospect, our caveat about the
implications of Murillo's project in the cultural sphere seems prophetic.
But was there another alternative? Under the circumstances, it is a
tribute to the resilience and tenacity of the Sandinistas that they were
able to survive at all under tremendous pressure. Cardenal's grass-roots
poetry workshop project seems no less utopian after the Sandinista
defeat, and it is by no means clear that it was ever a genuinely "popular"
initiative. But it could be argued that something like continued radicalization and democratization at the cultural level *might* have produced a
stronger bond between the revolution and the popular sectors, and that
this, in turn, might have offset some of the ideological damage caused by
the economic crisis and the war. We stress very much the conditionality
of this possibility; we do not think there were or are any easy solutions
available to the FSLN.

The boom in Nicaraguan literature since 1979 has depended on the
interaction of an expanded and highly motivated reading public with the
editorial activity of the two state-subsidized publishing houses created
by the revolution: Editorial Nueva Nicaragua and the Frente's own
Editorial Vanguardia. What will happen to these houses under the
control of the UNO government is not at all clear at the moment, nor can
we anticipate the new directions the work of the writers closely identified with the revolution we have profiled here will take. What is clear
to us, however, is that the possibility of reactivation of the revolutionary
process in Nicaragua will both require and bring to the fore cultural

forms quite different from the institution of "good writing" represented by poetry in Nicaragua. The revolution has already passed the point where literature can continue to be its privileged discursive form.

Notes

1. Cardenal's open letter generated or rekindled a debate about the legitimacy of armed struggle in Liberation Theology circles. It was answered by Daniel Berrigan in a piece titled "Guns Don't Count"; see "Conversation between Brothers," *Movement* (Dublin) (1978), 3–4; "To Berrigan I Say, 'Arms Give Life'," *National Catholic Reporter*, September 14, 1979.

2. Their records include *La nueva milpa* and *El son nuestro de cada día* (1978), *Amando en tiempo de guerra* (1980), *Un son para mi pueblo*, and *La tapisca* (1985). Important in developing relations between the Liberation Theology–inspired Popular church and the Sandinistas after the revolution would be Carlos Mejía Godoy's *La misa campesina nicaragüense* (written with Pablo Martínez), a musical resetting of the sections of the traditional Catholic mass with texts—including one in Miskito—celebrating the revolution and Nicaraguan working people.

3. See Tünnerman's "El sandinismo, factor de cultura," in Arrién 1982; Ramírez's "La Revolución: El hecho cultural más importante de nuestra historia," in Zamora (1982); and Cardenal's manifesto, *La democratización de la cultura* (Cardenal 1982). Zamora (1982) is a useful anthology of essays on cultural policy by major Sandinista leaders. For overviews of Nicaragua's "cultural revolution," see, besides the chapter in Vilas 1986 cited above, Girardi (1983); Dore (1985); Mattelhart (1986); Lancaster (1988); Whisnant (1988); and, especially, Craven (1989).

4. The main anthologies of workshop poetry—all edited by Mayra Jiménez—include: *Fogata en la oscuridad: los talleres de la poesía en la alfabetización* (1985a) and *Poesía de las fuerzas armadas* (1985b)—both published by the Ministry of Culture; and *Poesía de la nueva Nicaragua: talleres populares de poesía* (1983). In English see Johnson (1985) and Zimmerman (1985).

5. While most Sandinista-identified writers publish in both *Ventana* and *Nuevo Amanecer*, generally speaking the latter has been a bastion of exteriorism, while the former seems to favor a more metaphorically complex and surrealistic poetry (and is quite cosmopolitan in its cultural interests, covering, e.g., new foreign films or developments in international popular music).

6. For an account and documentation of the debate over the poetry workshops, see White (1986: 100–105), Johnson (1985), Cardenal's talk "Talleres de poesía: socialización de los medios de producción poéticos" (1981b), and Wellings (1989).

7. For a critique centered on a comparison between Cardenal's previctory and postvictory poetry as examples of strong and weak political poetry, see Gibbons (1987). Gibbons argues that Cardenal's recent work is flawed by simplification and "service to a political position enforcing idealization," but this is, of course, to argue from a particular ideology of the aesthetic.

8. Zamora is preparing an anthology, *La mujer nicaragüense en la poesía*,

which will represent the work of these and a significant generation of younger women poets.

9. For an examination of the situation of women in the Nicaraguan revolutionary process, see M. Molyneux, "Women," in Walker (1985: 163–182). For a carefully argued presentation of the role of women writers in national liberation movements and the dangers of transposing "First World" feminist theory and demands directly to Third World situations, in deference to women's actual struggles in those situations, see Harlow (1987: 180–194).

10. A sense of the spirit of the time may be gotten from the following testimony by an ASTC *brigadista* working in the mountains near a zone of contra activity:

> Martí said: "Poetry is durable when it is the work of every one." Those who understand such work are as much the authors as those who create it. In the mountains, this message is encouraging. It provides orientation to artistic and literary work, because it obliges us, it commits us to our people. . . . The historical challenge set before us is to be capable of producing an art of quality that satisfies the people's taste, at the same time that it elevates their cultural level, an art rooted in the most beautiful of popular tradition and creation. And this art has its integral content, because by arriving in the mountains with our songs, poems, dances and paintings, we entered into the struggle against ideological diversionism in the terrain of art responding with firmness and with the development of an art that has to be better, that has to be more beautiful than whatever art produced by the bourgeoisie. And the point is that they cannot produce an art better than ours, because they have nothing new to say, or express in their decadent art. Our slogan of love in the mountains was all of our art for the poetry of life, against aggression and death. (Leyva 1983)

5. Salvadoran Revolutionary Poetry

Our aim in this chapter will be to trace the development of poetry in El Salvador as it becomes involved in the major conjunctures of that country's recent social history. Our underlying theme is that this poetry was and continues to be instrumental in the ideological formation of those groups that made up the insurrectional bloc of the 1970s and 1980s. As we have seen, what such a function entailed in Sandinista poetry was the elaboration of a popular and collective national myth through a constellation of various literary modes—lyric, epic and dramatic, descriptive, satirical, ironic, fictional, documentary, and testimonial—in an open transformational form able to plot a fragmented and discontinuous but ultimately unifiable narrative of national history and possibility. In Fonseca's prose manifestos, in Cardenal's exteriorism and its elaboration by the Frente Ventana writers, in Rugama and the movement in women's poetry represented by the "Six," the Sandinistas could construct such a narrative around the figure of Sandino himself, which, variously interpreted or inflected, would come to constitute a national-popular signifier interpellating the diverse groups and social strata required for the insurrection.

Salvadoran culture lacks an equivalent multiclass signifier of the national-popular. The character of the political struggle (and of the parties and organizations of the left) has taken instead the more conventionally Marxist form of a conflict between bourgeoisie and working class, and capitalist and socialist models of national development. This has, in part, to do with the more thorough implantation of an agro-export plantation economy in El Salvador and, in consequence, the more extensive proletarianization of both rural and urban populations. El Salvador's rural population has undergone a much deeper process of proletarianization than Nicaragua's; San Salvador is larger and more urbanized than Managua. Farabundo Martí belongs more to the sectarian hagiography of the Comintern's Third Period than the populist and romantic Sandino, who can be read politically a number of different ways. The Salvadoran Communist party (PCS) developed early, bid for power and lost in 1932, and, despite the tremendous repression directed against it, remained a significant force in Salvadoran life. Even with its recent approximation to Liberation Theology and Christian activism and the formation after 1979 of the Frente Democrático Revolucionario (FDR), the core of the Salvadoran revolutionary movement represented by the Frente Farabundo Martí de Liberación Nacional (FMLN) has nothing like the FSLN's ability to contain within itself different strategic tendencies and ideological stances. It is instead a coalition of parties and their related military and popular organizations whose vision and internal structure have been more or less Leninist. In comparison with Nicaragua or Guatemala, it is fair to say that Salvadoran left political culture is more secular and urbane, but also much more sectarian.

One question we might pose, then, in taking up the ideological problematic of Salvadoran poetry is whether under certain conditions an overtly left or Marxist political culture may be less successful than non-class-specific interpellations in constituting the national-popular. This is, of course, a variant of the classic nationalism versus Marxism debate in anti-imperialist movements, which in Central America pitted Farabundo Martí against Sandino. At first glance, it might appear that modern Salvadoran literature, particularly of the generation represented by Roque Dalton, is too urban, too intellectualized and ironic, too much centered on left sectarianism, too "petit bourgeois"—to use a term Salvadoran revolutionaries are apt to invoke in such matters—to constitute a discourse representing the shared aspirations of broad social sectors. On the other hand, given the very early and relatively deep implantation of Communist ideas, the relatively small (after 1932) demographic weight of indigenous groups, the brutal tenacity of the agro-export oligarchy, and the degree of combativity of the organized working class, it may well be that Marxist-Leninist sectarianism has itself become a component of the Salvadoran national-popular.

Nevertheless, Salvadoran left literature represents at least a *search* for a broader unity. Hence its efforts (always treated ironically and questioned, however) to achieve a national narrative, to establish a line of progressive heroes (the Indian rebel Aquino, Morazán, Farabundo Martí, Monseñor Romero), to adumbrate a roughly linear historical process leading to some kind of socialist salvation. Hence too the effort—most notably in the recent work of Manlio Argueta, Claribel Alegría, José Roberto Cea, and the rank-and-file poets of the revolutionary organizations—to redirect a primarily urban (and intensely secular and male-centered) poetic instrument in the direction of more rural (and religious and female-centered) concerns. The irony of the Salvadoran left has been that, while its theoretical and literary discourses, including poetry, are primarily articulated in the city, the revolutionary process itself has fared far better in the countryside. This fact suggests how poetry continues to function as a minority discourse in the national culture as a whole, and how far it may actually stand from totalizing the revolutionary process.

This last point connects with a related issue in this chapter: the relationship of El Salvador's politicized literary system to the general question of postmodernism in Latin America we raised in the preface. Though this system has a long prehistory, which we will sketch here, for our purposes it is constituted primarily during the period of the boom by writers involved in the same sort of aesthetic-ideological problematic. At the same time, it represents a break with certain postulates of the boom toward not only a more explicit political content but also a series of new testimonial lyric and narrative forms. Pointing to the "insistence on practice and performative act, on the personal-in-the-collective, on a non-instrumental rationality, on solidarity, non-mimetic representation and on identification" in this literature, Salvadoran critic George Yúdice argues that it is an expression of resistance to the sort of literary postmodernism represented by the boom and its "collusion with capitalist logic in the penetration of Third World cultures" (1985a). Our own perspective is that—particularly in the work of its central figure, Roque Dalton—it should be seen as a "refunctioning" (itself a postmodernist term) of vanguardist and boom strategies around a series of new concerns: the problem of representing adequately in literature popular or subaltern voices; the ambition to develop metahistorical narratives; the related sense of the national as fundamentally discontinuous, heterogeneous, and contradictory; the problem of what Uruguayan critic Mario Benedetti called "writing *from* the revolution" (i.e., from a position of rank and file militancy); the influence of feminism and women's writing; the critique of the category of the subject in structuralism and poststructuralism; the challenges posed by parafictional forms like exteriorist narrative collage and testimonio. These are concerns that clearly mark a new phase of Latin American literature that comes out of the boom but is not reducible to it. As Hugo Achugar has observed, Salvadoran poetry of the past twenty years is the product of a new "situation of enunciation" that transforms both the conception of poetic discourse that had been dominant in Latin America since the vanguardist movements of the 1920s and the accompanying "canon of modernity" proposed by poet-critics like Octavio Paz and Guillermo Sucre (Achugar 1988: 651–662). With all the provisionality such categorizations merit, therefore, we would posit Salvadoran revolutionary literature not as an alternative to the boom or postmodernism in general but rather as one of the richest developments of what has come to be called in contemporary discussions of cultural politics a "postmodernism of resistance."

From Gavidia to the Grupo Seis

For poet/scholar José Roberto Cea, Salvadoran poetry has been a "poetry of underdevelopment, of people dependent on the cultural expressions of other people." What is valid in it takes place around a "search for the national." By this Cea does not mean *costumbrista* local color, but "the spirit that discovers our peculiar manner of seeing and feeling the historical period it befell us to live." The important poets are those "who sought to capture our reality, with all the variants that every development necessarily involves, and . . . with all the diverse sensibilities needed to detect the distinct aspects of a given situation, of a given people at a given time and place." The best Salvadoran poets, he concludes, "have contemplated our national landscape and wondered about human destiny on the geographic parcel that corresponds to us" (1971: 7–9).

There does not appear to have been much literature produced in what is now El Salvador during the colony, and what we know of it tends to represent the *peninsulares* more than the emerging Creole and mestizo groups. In the nineteenth century, there was an extensive production of romantic poetry and drama associated with the relatively strong Liberal oligarchy by figures like Francisco Esteban Galindo. Until fairly recently, the novel made little headway in El Salvador, and the *modernista* renovation of poetry represented by Darío was only partially taken up, leaving for good or bad its poetic system relatively underdeveloped, dominated by romantic sentimentalism and *costumbrismo*. As Paul Borgeson notes, "popular taste still tends to gravitate to the major poets of the nineteenth century and to those of the twentieth that owe them an artistic debt." For whatever reasons, El Salvador was at the turn of the century "a country with a respectable amount of writing but with little real literature, and even less that could properly be called its own" (in Foster 1987: 519, 521).

The Salvadoran writer who most approximates the position of Darío in Nicaraguan literature is Francisco Gavidia. His long life (1863–1955) spanned the period from the formation of the coffee oligarchy to the development of the modern military state and the faint beginnings of the contemporary revolutionary movement. His work in a variety of literary genres dominated the Salvadoran literary scene in the first part of the century, and he is often considered the first genuinely "national" writer. Like Darío, he has been the subject of some debate in recent Salvadoran criticism connected to his role as such.[1]

Gavidia was a friend of Darío, but resisted *modernista* aestheticism, preferring instead to cultivate the older style rhetorical civic poetry of Liberal romanticism. Paradoxically, by being far less open to innovative currents than his fellow poets elsewhere in Central America, Gavidia anticipated in some ways the developments that led away from *modernismo* toward vanguardism and certain aspects of protest poetry in the 1920s. Gavidia's genuine, although class-bound, liberalism is to be found in his reiterated theme of the unity of science and humanism as the basis for a culture that would bring progress while protecting and projecting "justice and liberty." Within this framework, he expressed increasing concern over the force of "tyranny" in national life and the situation of the poor and oppressed. Above all, Gavidia aimed in his work at establishing the forms of a national literature that could be used pedagogically as an instrument of democratization and reform. Behind this project was the conviction that, as Cea puts it, "to stimulate the creative imagination of a people is to create conditions so that all have access to true culture, and all have the chance to be full humans—poets even if they are not the writers of poems" (1971: 8).

The major Salvadoran writer after Gavidia is Salarrué (a pseudonym of Salvador Salazar Arrué), whose work was mainly concentrated in the short story and the novel, and thus falls somewhat outside the scope of our study. We need to mention him because he was the first significant portrayer of rural peasant and working-class life, using elements of the very rich Salvadoran vernacular. He is considered—for example, by Sergio Ramírez—the first modern Central American writer to develop a major narrative voice. The manner he created, usually designated as *regionalismo*, comes to dominate the short story and to strongly influence poetry in Central America up to the impact of the boom.

Salarrué's work has been appropriated by all major sectors of the Salvadoran political spectrum (Roque Dalton was an admirer and borrowed, in the form of contemporary urban slang, Salarrué's penchant for using the vernacular). The officially consecrated poet of the oligarchy was, however, Alfredo Espino, who wrote on rural themes in a modernized version of the quietistic mode of *costumbrismo*. Though he died well before the imposition of the Martínez dictatorship and the 1932 massacre, Espino's work has come to represent one ideological pole of Salvadoran poetic production; it became the model for the apologistic and official poetry of the military regimes in the 1940s and 1950s, the sort of thing writers like Dalton, Cea, and Argueta were forced to read in grade school.

Salarrué's and Espino's major contemporaries—Alberto Guerra Trigueros and Claudia Lars—represent extensions of Gavidia's democratic humanism, now in connection with the first stirrings of socialist ideas in the country and the rapidly growing movement created by Farabundo Martí's Regional Federation of Salvadoran Workers (FRTS), which began in 1920 to organize both rural and urban workers. An important journalist, Guerra Trigueros was involved in a number of muckraking campaigns against privilege and exploitation. Argueta sees him as the first overtly anti-imperialist writer in El Salvador and the most direct precursor of the political poetry that will emerge after 1932.

Claudia Lars was the first modern Central American woman writer to achieve a substantive body of work. After 1932, she became an opponent of the dictatorship and a protector of younger militant writers. She cultivated a slightly politicized *regionalismo*. In her last years, after the "Soccer War," she began to write and circulate poems that were increasingly oppositional. Especially noteworthy were a series of epigrams she called "Migajas" (Crumbs) collected in her *Poesía última*, published in 1974, the year of her death. With the shift toward a more testimonial, woman-centered voice in recent Salvadoran literature we discuss below, her role as a predecessor has become more prominent.

The turning point in modern Salvadoran history was 1932, which represented both the high point of the left militancy that had incubated throughout the 1920s and its decisive defeat. In 1930, after his split with Sandino, Farabundo Martí returned to El Salvador and together with a group of FRTS leaders founded the Salvadoran Communist party (PCS). The collapse of commodity prices caused by the depression brought massive unemployment and precipitated a crisis of hegemony for the oligarchy in El Salvador as elsewhere in Central America. In 1931, in the midst of intense agitation in the cities and countryside, a reform candidate supported by the labor movement, Arturo Araújo, was elected president in what is sometimes described as the only free election in modern Salvadoran history. As the economic situation worsened, the oligarchy engineered a coup installing as dictator Araújo's vice president and minister of defense, Maximiliano Hernández Martínez—theosophist, amateur theater buff, admirer of Mussolini. In a subsequent round of local elections, Communist candidates won a number of positions. Martínez refused to allow their representatives to take their seats and began a campaign to exterminate the party. In response, Martí and the PCS planned a general uprising for January 22, 1932, counting in particular on their support in the northern highlands of Chalatenango and Morazán provinces. The plan was discovered; Martí and the other leaders were arrested and shot. Leaderless and badly coordinated, the revolt was crushed by the army after several days. Then began the event Salvadorans call La Matanza, the massacre. Troops and vigilante groups armed by local landowners were sent into the regions most affected by the uprising. Somewhere between twenty and thirty thousand peasants and rural farm workers were killed—close to 4 percent of the population of the country. Many Indian communities were destroyed outright, and Indian dress and customs were prohibited. The PCS and the FRTS were decimated; a whole generation of liberal and progressive intellectuals was forced into exile or silence.

Already in the 1920s, some *regionalistas* like Francisco Herrera Velado served as early poet-champions of Salvadoran socialism. But the writer who most corresponds with the 1932 rebellion is a figure who has been all but forgotten in subsequent years: Gilberto González y Contreras. A rhetorical, agit-prop poet who came to maturity in the 1930s, González elaborated a kind of sui generis mixture of vanguardism, social realism, and Leninism. His work touches virtually every theme that will be significant in subsequent Salvadoran political poetry: the importance of the Indian heritage, the dispossession and proletarianization of the peasantry, the central role of women, the need for a revolutionary vanguard, the international dimension of the national liberation struggle, seen through the prism of Lenin's *Imperialism*. There is even a quasi-testimonial impulse to dramatize aspects of the national history through constructed voices of the oppressed.

González could be considered in some ways the literary counterpart of Farabundo Martí's own Third Period Comintern politics. The reasons for his relative neglect in subsequent Salvadoran literature may have to do with this fact. Perhaps his poetry was too directly identified with the PCS and the disaster of 1932 to survive in the repressive cultural environment created by the dictatorship. Some protest poetry might be tolerated, particularly if it lacked an explicit political referent, but not an explicitly *communist* protest poetry. González himself went into exile after 1932 and thus was out of touch with the younger poets who were just beginning their careers. Whatever the case, rather than González, two of these new writers, Pedro Geoffroy Rivas and Oswaldo Escobar Velado, are usually considered the founders of modern Salvadoran protest poetry.

Geoffroy Rivas and Escobar Velado

Cea characterizes the two poets as follows:

> Geoffroy Rivas and Escobar Velado are dominated by a kind of Tolstoyan messianism, a mystic system animated by this new tendency of the Catholic Church to take Christ's doctrine to its ultimate humanistic consequences. [They] understand that the task of the intelligentsia is criticism, scrutiny, judgment, in tune with a world view that accords with the national interests of the

people; they give poetry a militant character and were themselves militant, rebellious, nonconformist—given to using violent language against the passivity of the official word, against the hypocrisy of their fellow men of letters. (1971: 14)

As Cea suggests, Geoffroy Rivas and Escobar, like Cardenal in Nicaragua, anticipated in their literary-ideological trajectory some aspects of Liberation Theology. Geoffroy Rivas generated a new, sardonic, socially aware tone in Salvadoran poetry, rooted in an antibourgeois bohemianism (which also made it difficult for him to form part of any organized political opposition—he has a position equivalent to that of Carlos Martínez Rivas in Nicaraguan poetry). His iconoclastic stance strongly influenced Dalton, who took a phrase from one of Rivas's most self-lacerating poems, "pobrecito poeta que era yo," as the title of his autobiographical novel. Although Geoffroy Rivas was among the first to promote Dalton and his generation, he did not follow them in their radicalization in the 1960s, ultimately siding, it is sometimes said, with the government against the revolutionary movement.

Escobar Velado is the most famous member of a group of poets called Grupo Seis, which began publishing in the literary section of San Salvador's *Diario Latino* in 1940. The escalating and ultimately successful struggle to unseat Martínez between 1941 and 1944 formed the immediate context for their literary activity. Escobar's own development paralleled that of the group as a whole, evolving from a neo-Catholic subjectivism similar to that of Cardenal's early work—*Poemas con los ojos cerrados*—to a deepening identification with the struggle of the common people and revolutionary vision in, for example, *10 sonetos por mil y más obreros* (1950), *Volcán en el tiempo* (1955), and *Cristoamérica* (1959). His most influential poem, "Patria exacta," is a lacerating vision of El Salvador under the rule of the oligarchy ("esta es mi patria: 14 explotadores / y millones que mueren sin sangre en las entrañas"). Escobar's personal efforts to become involved in politics as a voice for reform appear to have been off the mark (the military governments often succeeded in using him as a dupe to support one or another of their candidates); but, for the generation of young intellectuals coming of age in the late 1950s, he represented in poetry the pole opposite Espino's conformist rural bucolics.

The Committed Generation

Though the country was still dominated by the alliance between the army and the oligarchy represented by a succession of civilian-military juntas, the years after Martínez through the 1950s were a time of relative prosperity (coffee revenues quadrupled), economic diversification, and relative liberalization of public and intellectual life in El Salvador. This was the context for the emergence of the group of writers who would come to be the dominant political and cultural force in contemporary Salvadoran life: the Committed Generation. Though it was nurtured by poets like Lars, Escobar, and Geoffroy Rivas, and by a revival of Marxist activity, the line of development of this generation also involves the impact of new social and cultural processes.

In El Salvador as elsewhere in Latin America in the immediate post–World War II period, pressures for literary-cultural renovation paralleled middle sector demands for social and political reform generated by the economic prosperity and growth of these years. In prose, renovation meant the experiments in narrative ("magic realism," Asturias, Borges, Carpentier, Rulfo) that would crystallize in the boom. In poetry, Octavio Paz and Pablo Neruda represented stylistically and to some extent politically opposite poles of a common vanguardist model; but younger poets turned increasingly toward a plainer, antideclamatory style that came to be known as conversational poetry. Modeled partly on the work of the Peruvian Communist poet César Vallejo in the 1920s and 1930s and on the "anti-poetry" of the Chilean Nicanor Parra in the early 1950s, the new tendency involved among others Juan Gelman (Argentina), Mario Benedetti (Uruguay), Jaime Sabines (Mexico), Roberto Fernández Retamar and the new Cuban poets of the 1960s, and Cardenal and the Nicaraguan exteriorists. The new kind of lyric they espoused—antimetaphorical, colloquial, flat, self-conscious, youthful, sometimes brittle with anger or irony, sometimes suffused with a fraternal tenderness—would provide the model for the poetry of revolutionary militancy that began to be produced in Latin America in the wake of the Cuban Revolution.[2]

The impact of the new tendencies in literature entered El Salvador, in part at least, through the mediation of the Guatemalan October Revolution of 1944–1954. Guatemalan literature of the 1930s had also been largely defined by its relationship to dictatorship. The primary response was the kind of left-liberalism typified by the country's dominant writer, Miguel Angel Asturias. As the Arévalo and then Arbenz governments fostered policies favoring more popular and/or politicized cultural work, younger writers elaborated increasingly radical orientations toward the role of poetry. After the CIA-sponsored coup of 1954, Otto René Castillo, a young Communist poet and organizer who was a product of these new tendencies, went into exile in El Salvador. There he joined with a group of Salvadoran writers meeting around something called the Círculo Literario Universitario. One of the founders of the Círculo was Roque Dalton.

We discuss Castillo at greater length in our chapter on Guatemalan poetry. Here we need only note that he brought to his colleagues in the Círculo not only a tremendously influential personal example of direct political activism on the part of writers and intellectuals, but also a sense of how to combine the new mode of conversational poetry with an explicitly Marxist thematics connected to the emergence of popular armed struggle as a strategic line in the Latin American left.

The writers around Castillo—all born like him in the 1930s—coalesced as a formal group in 1956 at a meeting held in the library of the Escuela Normal de Maestras de España in San Salvador. At first, they called themselves Grupo Octubre in honor of the Guatemalan Revolution, then, definitively, Generación Comprometida (Committed Generation). The initial members included Waldo Chávez Velasco, Italo López Vallecillos, Eugenio Martínez Orantes, Orlando Fresedo, and Alvaro Menéndez Leal. They were joined later by Tirso Canales, Ricardo Bogrand, Mauricio de la Selva, Alfonso Quijada Urías, Dalton, Roberto Armijo, Manlio Argueta, and José Roberto Cea. Though not formally part of the group, Claribel Alegría, Mercedes Durand, and Rafael Góchez Sosa came to correspond to it in spirit.

The Committed Generation represented a section of the university-based intelligentsia that had grown impatient with the possibilities for peaceful economic and political reform in the late 1950s, and, like its Nicaraguan counterpart, Frente Ventana, had been very much stimulated by the Cuban Revolution. The 1960s began in El Salvador with a promising, although ultimately frustrated, attempt to take power by a group of progressive younger officers who invited prominent university figures to join them. In its wake, the National University, which was funded and granted autonomy under the developmentalist policies of the recently formed Central American Common Market, became a major training center for militant left intellectuals (see our remarks on university modernization in chap. 2). The Committed Generation operated in and around the university and the education system, producing a cosmopolitan and highly politicized literary counterculture that spread with expanding enrollments in higher education, increased publication, and circulation of books and magazines, and growth of the salaried technical-professional work force (e.g., secondary school teachers, who have played a fundamental role in the Salvadoran revolutionary left).

In one of their earliest manifestos—an editorial in the journal *Hoja* in April 1956 attributed to Roque Dalton—the Committed Generation writers made a clear statement of their perspective:

For us literature is essentially a social function. Thus our effort is to help improve the society in which we live, to establish an order by means of which human beings change their social condition, at the same time modifying the ideas they have of themselves. . . . We understand that our highest mission in these moments of crisis is to bring faith and enthusiasm to the forces of intelligence. The "Committed Generation" knows that the work of art necessarily has to perform a service, has to be useful to society, to today's humanity. (Cited in Hernández Aguirre 1961: 87)

The Committed Generation and younger writers who were close to the group later like Rafael Mendoza, Mauricio Marquina, José María Cuéllar, Alfonso Hernández, Jaime Suárez Quemain, and Eduardo Castañeda (a protégé of Dalton's who is now the FMLN *comandante* Fermín Cienfuegos) consolidated themselves as the dominant force in Salvadoran literature in the course of the 1960s and early 1970s. Comparing the group with Geoffroy Rivas and Escobar Velado, Cea notes that "the Committed Generation of 1956 is more incisive, more consistently committed, both as professional writers and militants. They take up the arms abandoned by their predecessors, turning poetry into a weapon against official silence and bureaucratic stultification" (1971: 14). There are differences of perspective within the group: some, like Dalton, became cadre members in the Communist party or the left organizations that resulted from the PCS split in the early 1970s; others took the role of fellow travelers or independent intellectuals. Primarily self-identified as poets, they also worked in a variety of other forms including journalism, theater, and the essay. Though they have not solved the problem of the uneven development of the novel in Salvadoran literature, Dalton, Argueta, Cea, and—independent of the group—Claribel Alegría have made some important experiments in narrative. Armijo, López Vallecillos, Argueta, and Cea in their later work have concentrated in the fashion of *regionalismo* on portraying rural and suburban areas; Menéndez Leal and above all Dalton maintained a strong urban perspective. In the ups and downs of censorship and repression in the 1960s, many members of the group—even those less directly involved in revolutionary politics than Dalton—ended up in exile in Costa Rica, Cuba, or Mexico.

Roque Dalton (1935–1975)

The most compelling poet of the Committed Generation and the central figure in modern Salvadoran literature is clearly Dalton. He writes as a Marxist-Leninist from within the ideological and organizational boundaries of the sectarian left in El Salvador. Though he shares with Cardenal a concern with producing a syncretic historical image of his country, his tone differs markedly from the religiously inflected high seriousness of exteriorism. Partly derived from Brecht, Nazim Hikmet,

Castillo, and Nicanor Parra's cynical "antipoems," partly from Geoffroy Rivas and Escobar, his poetry is both self-absorbed and self-mocking, secular, antiprophetic, aphoristic, didactic. In his short career he experimented with a wide range of forms besides poetry, including political essays, history, autobiographical novel, testimonio, and the collage-poem of Salvadoran history that is perhaps his most ambitious and original work, *Las historias prohibidas del pulgarcito* (1974).

Dalton belongs to an informal pantheon of guerrilla poets in Latin America—Otto René Castillo, Ricardo Morales, Leonel Rugama, Roberto Obregón, Monica Ertl, Argimiro Gabaldón, Rita Valdivia, Ibero Gutiérrez, Javier Heraud, Víctor Jara, Francisco Urondo, Jacques Viau are some of the others—whose work and life were directly connected with the armed struggle movements of the 1960s. Mario Benedetti—who anthologized their production in *Poesía trunca* (Truncated poems)—spoke of them as poets who no longer wrote *for* but rather *from* the people ("el poeta ya no escribe para sino desde el pueblo") (Benedetti 1977: 2–6). They are the voices of Latin America's New Left in the period between the Cuban Revolution and the Sandinista victory of July 1979. As Benedetti's title indicates, the event that often sealed the poet's work and stamped its influence on posterity was a premature martyrdom in the guerrilla *foco* or urban underground.

The particular tragedy of Dalton's death was that it came not at the hands of the death squads or counterinsurgency "special forces" that the Alliance for Progress sowed throughout the region, but rather from his own comrades. The child of a North American father (apparently a descendant of the Dalton brothers of western bandit fame) and a Salvadoran mother, Dalton had what seems a normal urban upper-middle-class upbringing, including private schools and a stint at the Jesuit-run Catholic University of Chile in the early 1950s. In Chile, he was to claim later, "yo llegué a la revolución por la vía de la poesía" (I arrived at the revolution by way of poetry), referring to his contact with Neruda's work (in Zepeda 1988: 6). On his return to El Salvador, ostensibly to study for a law degree, he became involved in the Círculo Literario. He traveled to the Soviet Union as a delegate to a youth congress in 1957. Around this time, he joined the PCS, sharing in the next decade the usual misfortunes—jail, torture, death threats, exile—with the patience and irony that are expected of a good cadre member. (His autobiographical novel *Pobrecito poeta que era yo* is a fictionalized account of this experience.) In the 1960s, he lived for several years in Cuba, working in various capacities with the Casa de las Américas cultural center and the new postrevolutionary generation of Cuban poets and artists. A long period of exile in Czechoslovakia from 1965 to 1967 led to what is generally considered his best collection of poems, *Taberna y otros lugares,* which won the Casa de las Américas poetry prize in 1969.

Throughout these years, Dalton was in and out of El Salvador doing underground work for the PCS. Between 1969 and 1972, the party split under the impact of the new generational and ideological tendencies that argued the necessity of armed struggle on the Cuban model against the cautious Popular Front reformism of the dominant faction. In 1970, the then secretary general of the PCS, Salvador Cayetano Carpio, led a group out of the party to found the Fuerzas Populares de Liberación–Farabundo Martí (FPL), with a Vietnamese-inspired strategy of a "prolonged popular war" based in the countryside. In 1972, the PCS, the Social-Democratic MNR, and the Christian Democrats formed an electoral coalition, UNO, around the presidential candidacy of José Napoleón Duarte, then the popular mayor of the capital city. UNO was crushed in a massive and blatant electoral fraud, Duarte beaten up and exiled, and a wave of repression launched against the UNO parties and the trade unions. The bubble of an electoral challenge to the power of the army and the oligarchy had burst. This was the context for the emergence of armed struggle in the 1970s.

Sympathetic to the new strategic direction because of his identification with the Cuban experience, Dalton traveled to Vietnam for military training in 1973.[3] Though he was closer politically in some ways to Cayetano's FPL, Dalton joined the Ejército Revolucionario del Pueblo (ERP, Revolutionary Army of the People), founded in 1972 by radicalized middle-class university students and Christian Democrat activists. As an alternative to the "people's war" conception of the FPL, the ERP pursued a Guevarist approach to armed struggle, counting on successful "actions" to incite a broad popular insurrection. After some initial successes, the organization got badly bogged down by 1974. Dalton and a faction of the organization close to him argued the need to supplement what came to be called *militarismo* with the development of legal mass organizations. In the sectarian hothouse of Salvadoran politics, and in a very down period for the Latin American left in general (by 1971 the Guatemalan guerrilla had all but collapsed; Allende's Unidad Popular and the Uruguayan Popular Front and Tupamaros were defeated in 1973), the debate turned bitter. Dalton's opponents in the ERP accused him of revisionism. He persisted in his critique of their strategy, only to find himself charged with treason. Along with several of his allies, he was summarily tried and executed by the ERP leadership, who then spread the rumor that he had been working for the CIA. His assassination provoked a split in the ERP, out of which emerged a new guerrilla organization, Resistencia Nacional.

There is a way in which life imitates art in Dalton's case that he might have appreciated, given his penchant for irony.[4] The persona he liked to project in his poetry is the idealist beginning to rise on the wings of song only to crash suddenly into the brutal philistinism of everyday life in the backyard of the American Empire: the ugly but lovable Marxist Cantinflas, national—Salvadoran—in his very imperfection. Behind the pose and the self-mocking humor, though, is a deadly seriousness and a life put on the line in the face of one of the most violently repressive regimes in Latin American history. The traumatic political unconscious of Dalton and the Committed Generation was the failure of the 1932 uprising and the *matanza*. "We were all born half dead in 1932," Dalton wrote in one of his most famous poems, "We survive only half alive" ("Todos"). There is a harsh lesson to be learned from this:

> There have been good people in this country
> ready to die for the revolution
> But the revolution everywhere needs people
> who are ready not only to die
> but also to kill for it
>
> ("Old Communists and Guerrillas")

Dalton's literary persona—poised somewhere between nice guy and terrorist—merges here with the terms of the great debate on the Central and South American left over the strategic wisdom or necessity of armed struggle. Dalton's position is clear: the "peaceful road to socialism" represented by Allende in Chile is the lyrical illusion, the temptation based on the very feelings of love, humanity, tolerance, and justice that the revolution stands for. Softness—Dalton feels a great softness inside himself—is a danger to oneself and to the movement. A passion for beauty and justice denied turns into hatred, hatred into militancy, militancy into revolutionary violence.

Dalton will insist on a poetry of "ugly words," *palabras feas*: "worm-eaten scream," "asphyxiating skin," "face of bread out of ovens," "hell of quicklime," "eyes and ears pierced with needles." There is an urgency to wound, and then to reject consolation, to keep the wound from healing too quickly. To the poet as the patriarchal seer of the national liberation struggle in the fashion of Neruda or Cardenal, Dalton counterposes in his manifesto *Poesía y militancia en América Latina* "the poet as a scrutiniser of his own time . . . because, like it or not, by insisting too much on what will come we lose at some level our immediate perspective, and we run the risk of not being understood by all the people who find themselves immersed in everyday life." The problem is how to raise "to the category of poetic material the contradictions, disasters, defects, customs, and struggles of our present society," a task Dalton admits, "involving a great deal of destructive activity." Only after the work of destruction is finished "is it possible to begin constructing, without major obstacles, the prospectus of the future"—a thesis Dalton holds to be valid "in the preparatory stage, the insurrectional stage and the triumphal stage of any Latin American revolution" (1981: 9–28).

The concept of poetry as a "destructive activity" is where Dalton's work as a writer dovetails with his defense of and involvement in armed struggle in El Salvador. The unremitting mocking/self-mocking that composes the verbal texture of his style is meant as a tactic of personal disenchantment addressed to his contemporaries who are the potential constituency of the new revolutionary organizations. Its function is to deconstruct the mendacious humanism of the official history, to tell the other side of the story.

But Dalton's poetry is not just directed against the oligarchy; it is also concerned with redefining the sense of Marxism-Leninism and revolutionary militancy in order to bring them closer to the sensibility of the new generation emerging in El Salvador on the heels of the Cuban Revolution. Dalton creates what James Iffland calls a "pedagogy of laughter," using this to attack pomposity, dogmatism, sclerosis of political thought. Humor provides the distance effect necessary to revive a Marxism that has become official and officious, allowing space for the more skeptical, antidogmatic spirit of the New Left movements of the 1960s. The effort is to define socialism, the national reality, poetry itself as based on exploration and invention, rather than formulas or preestablished truths. Even as Dalton's bitter wit incites cynicism, it produces a recoil effect affirming the existence of a lyrical–utopian value world. Dalton's strongest moments come when his irony contains his greatest anger at what has happened to his country in a precarious balance (Iffland 1985: 112–157).

Dalton's audience is generationally specific, and many of his poems, like "Old Communists and Guerrillas" above, carry generational markers. The persona he elaborates is a model for a new kind of revolutionary subjectivity: the self-ironic or nonheroic hero. Entwined and alternating with the different aspects of this persona, whether in his poetry or narrative prose, is an almost continuous dialogue between new and old lefts meant to bridge both sectarian and generational schisms in Salvadoran and Latin American left culture (we will return to this issue in our remarks on Dalton's testimonial narrative *Miguel Mármol* in chap. 7).

There are some problems: Dalton's persona depends in part on activating—albeit self-critically—the image of the charming but sentimentally unreliable revolutionary Don Juan. The dominant mood is a sort of hip machismo directed against that tenderness the poet is afraid will reassert itself, take his anger away, make him a dupe and a victim. In a machista sense, there is something peculiarly and intimately Salvadoran about this interplay of toughness and sentimentality. For all his posing as a lady-killer, Dalton is someone for whom the imperfect fraternity of the guerrilla organization and the imagined equality of communist society are both, in the end, utopias of male bonding. In writing about other men, Dalton sometimes lets his vulnerability show through and harmonize with the pose of the revolutionary punk.

Women, on the other hand, enter his writing usually in the conflictive zone of domesticity. A long poem called "Para un mejor amor" (For a better love/sex) proposes ambitiously to develop Kate Millett's feminist slogan that "Sex is a political category." But this involves principally evoking the struggle of women "in the rearguard of household work / in the strategy and tactics of the kitchen"—not the sort of thing calculated to address the schoolteacher, or the nurse, or the *compañera* who has just become head of her union local.

We touch here on the very real and difficult problem of sexism in Latin American revolutionary culture. It would be a kind of idealism to abandon machismo as an ideological signifier to the political right and the death squads, because it has been a concept closely bound up with both male and female ideas of personal integrity and militancy. Dalton's particular brand of sophisticated, self-ironic machismo was undoubtedly a factor in establishing his poetry's political impact. But it also underplays the changing role of women in Central American social and economic life, thus producing a devaluation and inhibition of women's potential self-actualization in revolutionary struggle.

Although one of the strengths of Dalton's poetry is its ironic oscillation between difficult and divisive alternatives—macho and feminist, bohemian and commissar, old and new lefts, Marxist dialectics and the Salvadoran colloquial voice—there is also a sense in which it stays within this specular dialectic. Dalton's audience was people much like himself, college-educated intellectuals of petit bourgeois background. Given our previous remarks about the formation of a revolutionary intelligentsia, this is an important, perhaps decisive, audience for a Marxist poetry in Central America, but it is not the "people." Dalton was finally the poet, as well as the victim, of the micropolitics of revolutionary cadre.

Las historias prohibidas *and the New National Narrative.* There is a notable tension in Dalton's work between the cultivation of a personal voice in small lyric or satirical forms and an impulse toward narrative. Dalton's problem, which he was still struggling with at the time of his death and which is related to the sectarian, encapsulated character of the Salvadoran left itself, was to find a way to synthesize the dialectically complex persona of the poems with large-scale narrative forms that would express a collective, transindividual vision of class struggle and

Salvadoran national history. In chapter 7, we deal with his two major efforts in prose narrative along these lines: *Miguel Mármol* and *Pobrecito poeta que era yo*. Here we need to look at his collage-history of El Salvador from the conquest to the 1969 Soccer War with Honduras, *Las historias prohibidas del pulgarcito* (1974) (*pulgarcito* or little thumb, because that was the name Chilean poet Gabriela Mistral gave El Salvador when she compared the five republics of Central America to the fingers of a hand). This is clearly the work—or "poem-object" to use Dalton's own term—that most fully brings together his poetry, his practical and theoretical involvement in revolutionary politics, and his concerns with historical and fictional, individual and collective narratives.

Dalton pioneered the collage-narrative technique of *Las historias* in a project called *Un libro rojo para Lenin*, which he worked on between 1970 and his residence in Hanoi in 1973 and then apparently abandoned. (Reconstructed from his personal papers, it was published in Managua by Editorial Nueva Nicaragua in 1986.) The text is an attempt to achieve what Dalton calls a "vivificación poética" of the figure of Lenin in relation to the immediate Latin America and Salvadoran revolutionary perspectives problematized by the death of Che Guevara and the crisis of the guerrilla strategy he represented. Divided into ninety-three short sections, it mixes didactic poems and fragments of political essays by Dalton with a collage of passages from Lenin's works and from Georg Lukács's 1924 essay *Lenin* (one of the classics of what came to be known as ultraleftism), adding secondary materials on Lenin and Leninism from Mayakovsky, Gramsci, Ho Chi-Minh, Kim Il-Sung, Che Guevara, Fidel and Raúl Castro, Regis Debray, Harry Magdoff, testimonios by Salvadoran peasants, and so forth.

Dalton conceived of *Un libro rojo* as a response to a question posed by Brecht: Why couldn't a political-ideological text also be poetic? In an influential discussion of the interaction of ideology and form in the bourgeois novel, Fredric Jameson (1981) has noted that any given literary text, however generically unified it may seem, must be seen as involving a complex tension between several, often contradictory, generic modes or strands. What Dalton does in *Un libro rojo* is make this contradictory heterogeneity explicit, producing a kind of flexible, undogmatic, open-ended Leninism that necessarily has to resolve itself in concrete revolutionary practice rather than theoretical correctness. He describes the text in the prologue as "un poema inconcluso, en correspondencia con la revolución latinoamericana, como proceso de desarrollo" (an incomplete poem, corresponding to the developmental process of Latin American revolution), and again at the end as "poema inconcluso—mientras viva el autor" (incomplete poem—while the author is alive).

Las historias is a more ambitious and successful articulation of this compositional strategy. The text is an excavation of the Salvadoran national-popular, a great cut-and-paste job of documents, poems in good and bad taste by Dalton and others (among other things, it contains a mini-anthology of Salvadoran poetry), dirty jokes from vernacular culture (*bombas*), speeches, sayings, journalistic material, false or erroneous citations, and testimonios (including sections from Dalton's own *Miguel Mármol*). The central line of the narrative traces the main conjunctures of Salvadoran history (Dalton had written a short history of El Salvador for Casa de las Américas in 1965). But *Las historias*, as the plural suggests, also makes fun of the effort to construct a monolithic national narrative. "Badly" made, ungainly, incoherent, it is an example of the fragmentation and silences of the national culture it seeks to represent, a world of unexpected contradictions and combinations, of multiple codes and temporalities. The narrative design of Liberal historicism, based on a linear conception of historical progress, is cut across by anachronisms that decenter even if they do not completely abolish it. The standpoint of the omniscient narrator and the emphasis on individual subjectivity (in Dalton's own early poetry) is overwhelmed by the integration of multiple contradictory subjectivities; fragments of testimonial narratives from widely different sociohistorical moments combine in one complex collective narrative. *Las historias* retains something of the orthodox Communist party stage theory of Latin American development, which assigns a progressive function to Liberal modernizers like Morazán and Creole bourgeois culture as a whole. But Morazán is counterposed by accounts of the anti-Liberal Indian-mestizo rebellion led by Anastasio Aquino. Passages from chronicles of Indian resistance to the conquest are positioned as narrative anticipations of the mobile guerrilla "war of the ants" of the 1960s and 1970s. Dalton sets up but also lends irony to the official pantheon of left heroes, including Farabundo Martí, looking for a more direct identification with his country's dispossessed popular sectors (see in particular his beautiful and irreverent "Poema de amor" to the Salvadoran—male—working class and lumpenproletariat). *Las historias* is a sort of Marxist *Inferno*, but there is also in it a confidence that the hell it paints is provisional, that beyond the official history of El Salvador and even the sanctioned forms of progressive opposition, there is another history awaiting its time.

Las historias, like Cardenal's "documentary poems," is a form of collage-narrative. If, as we suggested in chapter 1, boom narrative corresponds to the modernizing projects in Latin America that gestated in the 1950s and are encouraged by U.S. policy in the region in response to the Cuban Revolution, testimonio emerges as a counterhegemonic project of subaltern discourse generated and promoted by the Cubans and other left cultural fronts in Latin America.[5] However, if the relatively linear chronological narrative of testimonio represented a break with boom fiction, collage marked a continuity, a technique bequeathed by the boom to other nonhegemonic discursive forms for use in the 1970s. Collage was pioneered by the European avant garde in the 1920s and 1930s, and adapted into Latin American literature mainly through the influence of surrealism. The characteristics of Latin American combined and uneven development—the fragmented nature of its national histories, the force of foreign intervention and economic dependency, the constant migrations, the processes of *mestizaje* and transculturation, the simultaneous presence and interaction of several modes of production and their corresponding superstructures—made its literary culture especially open to collage. If conversational poetry implied a change in poetic systems away from the grand historical design and the patriarchal tone of Neruda's *Canto general* toward the sort of slender lyric of revolutionary commitment developed by Otto René Castillo, both Cardenal and Dalton represent the effort to reintegrate history and narrative with the new subjectivism and radical moralism such a poetry was concerned with responding to and defining. Cardenal stays within poetry, attempting its "prosification" or "depoetization." (This is one of the continuities between his exteriorism and the vanguardist attack on *modernismo*.) In *Hora 0* or the great Sandinista long poems of the 1970s like *Oráculo sobre Managua*, linear narrative schemes are crisscrossed by varying modes of collage. The element, tone, and overall design are different from those in *Un libro rojo* and *Las historias*, but what results is the same lyrical, satirical, polemical, testimonial, deeply heterogeneous text in which multiplicity and disjunction become a form of political indoctrination.[6]

It is not accidental that both these efforts appear at a time of crisis for the future of Latin American national liberation movements signaled by the general collapse of *foco* strategies after 1969, Allende's defeat in Chile, and—in Central America—the effects of the Soccer War and the repression of the UNO electoral coalition in El Salvador and the earthquake in Nicaragua. *Las historias* is written in response to and in a sense *on* the fault line of left fragmentation and debate over theory and strategy in this conjuncture. As such, it sets the frame for all forms of subsequent left and even reformist cultural practice in El Salvador: slogans sprayed on walls, agit-prop street theater, dance, the rhetoric of revolutionary speeches and communiques, work in popular song, radio, film, and video, as well as developments in literature proper.

Un libro rojo and *Las historias* are incomplete or—to use Dalton's own term—"intervened" narratives, because the conditions for their resolution cannot be given in the literary text itself, and require the action of other social practices. While the ideal of political and cultural unity becomes a key theme of the revolutionary left after the extreme sectarianism of the early 1970s, it is not something that is automatically or easily achieved, even when revolutionary organizations or writers have come together to work out bases of collective work. The Salvadoran revolution has yet to find even the contradictory unity achieved by the FSLN under the populist banner of Sandino, but Dalton's work is certainly the most ambitious attempt in that direction. After the great turning point of 1979, however, the Salvadoran literary system undergoes a series of new transformations that both build on and lead away from his achievement.

Poetry and Civil War after 1979: The Shift to Testimonial Forms

In October 1979, on the heels of the Sandinista victory, a group of young officers calling itself Juventud Militar staged a coup and took power in El Salvador. Led by the charismatic Colonel Adolfo Majano, and influenced by the antioligarchical reformist and technocratic currents of the 1970s, the new junta invited the Christian Democrats and the electoral left parties (the MNR and PCS) to join it in a new civilian-military junta. The revolutionary groups, initially suspicious of the coup, generally adopted a wait-and-see position when the new government announced an ambitious program of nationalization, agrarian reform, and democratization, provoking the departure to Miami and Guatemala of the more reactionary sectors of the oligarchy.

Under pressure from both the right and left, the junta soon disintegrated. In January 1980 its civilian members resigned, charging the military with failing to begin the process of structural reform. In a rightward power shift, the junta was reconstituted as an alliance of the Christian Democrats led by Duarte and a group of military hard-liners advocating destruction of the armed left. In response, the guerrillas and the popular organizations resumed their activity. The archbishop of San Salvador, Oscar Romero, called for "preserving the liberation process" and denounced stepped-up U.S. aid to the junta; he was assassinated on March 24 while celebrating Mass by a right-wing death squad. In the same month, the electoral left parties coalesced with the revolutionary groups in the Democratic Revolutionary Front (FDR). In May, the entire left wing of the Christian Democrats left the junta, joining the FDR. On May 14, six hundred peasants trying to flee fighting between the army and the guerrillas were massacred along the Sumpul River by Salvadoran and Honduran troops. Around the same time, the guerrilla groups placed their activities under the control of a single directorate, the DRU, which would evolve by the end of the year into the command structure of a unified "people's army": the Farabundo Martí National Liberation Front (FMLN). The brutal civil war that continues today, at a cost of more than seventy thousand lives, had begun.

More or less in tandem with the efforts to unify the left and broaden its base of support in the face of the intense repression of popular forces unleashed between 1979 and 1985, the central tendency in Salvadoran revolutionary literature of the 1980s has been toward testimonial forms in both poetry and prose narrative. To an extent, this is a move away from Dalton's sophisticated modernism, although his own work clearly anticipates the shift.[7] The new mood is less self-consciously literary and less politically sectarian, more diverse in its enunciation of class and party, less male-centered, less urban and secular, more open to perspectives stemming from Liberation Theology and from both contemporary and pre-Columbian Indian cultures, and, in the face of very dangerous and often painful situations of personal commitment generated by the war in the countryside and the death squads, more testimonial and popular.

In the years since Dalton's death, his closest comrades from the Círculo Literario—José Roberto Cea, Manlio Argueta, and Alfonso Quijada Arias—and related figures like Roberto Armijo, Tirso Canales, Ricardo Castrorrivas, and Rafael Góchez Sosa, have continued to develop his vein of a sardonic poetry centered on the nation's fate. Of these figures, Cea is the one who most clearly qualifies as Dalton's direct successor in style and subject matter. The trajectory of his work may be charted from two Dalton-style "poem-objects" of the late 1970s: the ludic, erotic *Mester de picardía*, and—in his own words—the "magical-religious-Catholic-pagan-fetishistic-totemic, etcetera, etcetera" collage *Misa-Mitín* (including "orations, spells, sermons, rites, psalms, invocations, placards, photos"), both published in 1977. In 1981, more or less in tandem with the FMLN Final Offensive, Cea published a collection of historical and testimonial poetry, *Los herederos de Farabundo*, which won Nicaragua's Rubén Darío Prize in poetry; in the same vein was *Los pies sobre la tierra* (1985) and a testimonial pamphlet portraying the war in the Guazapa area, *Corral no, corral de los desplazados* (1986).[8]

Cea's project is to emulate and extend Dalton's "intervened" narrative of El Salvador's past and present history, mixing colloquial, satirical, documentary, and testimonial elements. However, in the greater emphasis he gives to the testimonial voice and historical anecdote, his avoidance of Dalton's specific party commitments, his interest in pre-Columbian culture, his attempt to shift thematic focus from the city to the Salvadoran countryside, he seems also to be trying to overcome the intellectual elitism inscribed in the earlier phases of left literary discourse, sensing perhaps a growing split between the range and concerns of Salvadoran literature and the practice of the revolutionary movement itself.

The 1980s witness the emergence of a new generation of writers born in the 1940s and 1950s. It includes a significant number of writers affiliated with groups or journals: Rafael Mendoza and Ricardo Castro-rrivas of *Piedra y siglo*; the members or associates of *La Cebolla Púrpura* (The red onion), founded in the late 1970s by Jaime Suárez Quemain, with Rigoberto Góngora, David Hernández, Eduardo Salvador Carcoma, and José Luis Valle; Mauricio Marquina, Roberto Monterroza, and Manuel Sorto of *La Masacuata*; a group around the journal *El Papo* led by Miguel Hueso Mixco, with Nelson Brizuela, Horacio Castellanos Moya, Roger Lindo, and Roberto Quesada; and a number of poet-*comandantes* of the FMLN itself (Carlos Aragón, Luis Díaz, Lil Milagro Ramírez, Dalton's protégé Eduardo Sancho Castañeda).

In general terms, these writers are struggling with the same question as Cea: how to relate their work to the conditions created by the war, particularly the staggering levels of repression against any form of leftist activism in the early 1980s, which forced the revolutionary movement back to its base in the liberated zones and prioritized the need to overcome sectarianism and anchor the revolutionary project deeper in the life of the people. According to Keith Ellis, who has studied the new production closely (in Yanes et al. 1985: 1–13), Salvadoran poetry goes through a virtual sea change as the war begins to dominate consciousness. Many of the new poets are active militants in the FMLN and its urban or international support networks. Their work "conveys a firm will to implement a vision of a new society," reflecting a sense of "the deep involvement of literature" in the attempt to rectify national life. They are "inclined to employ expressive forms notable for their simplicity. They capture the rhythms and diction of popular speech, and their imagery is rooted in the experiences and way of life of the people." They tend to use a testimonial, first-person narrator, a device that "gives a documentary character to the writings." They write from the situation of the body, so to speak, "poems of terror, absurdity and desperate armed reaction, of bizarre and extreme states of consciousness."

Manlio Argueta's effort to ruralize and feminize the national voice, bringing in the dimension of Indian patterns of life and culture in his poetry and above all in his novels *Un día en la vida* (1980) and *Cuzcatlán* (1986) (which we discuss in chap. 7), was a major indication of the new orientation in literary and ideological production. Also important in defining the shift toward testimonial forms and a woman-centered thematics were Alfonso Hernández's anthology of poems, testimonios, and documents from the armed struggle and the liberated zones, *León de piedra* (1982), and a similar collection by Claribel Alegría and Darwin Flakoll, *El Salvador en armas* (1984, 1989b). But at the same time—and in this, recent Salvadoran poetry parallels the evolution of Nicaraguan poetry after 1975—women themselves begin to assume a greater presence and militancy in the literary system.

The New Women's Poetry and Combat Poetry

Prior to Claudia Lars, there are no women poets in El Salvador, or at least none whose work became part of the official literary canon. González y Contreras wrote about *la mujer india* or *la mujer proletaria*. But on the whole, like Dalton, most progressive male writers (which is to say, most writers before the 1970s) succumbed to and/or struggled with a machismo that was not only inscribed in the culture, but given a kind of new legitimacy in the early constructions of revolutionary selfhood associated with the Cuban Revolution and the celebration of guerrilla struggle.

Of the few women in the prewar years able to follow Lars's lead, Grupo Seis member Matilde Elena López and Liliam Jiménez, a PCS militant imprisoned and exiled in Mexico for many years, were the most prominent. Contemporary with the male poets of the Committed Generation is Mercedes Durand, whose poems dealing with the years 1979–1981 are one of the most vivid testimonial portraits of this critical period.

In the process of feminization of Salvadoran literature, however, Claribel Alegría has been perhaps the most representative figure. Born in Estelí, Nicaragua, of an upper-class family, but personally identified with El Salvador, she has been one of the most versatile contemporary Central American writers. The center of her work is a deeply subjective evocation of the small world of life in a Central American rural town, partly a reconstruction from childhood memories, partly, like García Márquez's Macondo, an imaginary allegory of place. Alegría is not a people's poet; in fact, she began her career as a protégé of the leading representative of Spanish "poesía pura" (pure poetry), Juan Ramón Jiménez. But she has managed in a way parallel to but very different in tone from Dalton to synthesize a point of view centered on the tensions of her own intimate value world with the emerging forces of popular struggle in her adopted country. She combines the sensibility of the upper class *poetisa* with the immediacy of political and testimonial poetry, plotting through her poetry how even a woman with ties to the oligarchy can be transformed by the conditions of Latin American history.

Alegría and her husband and collaborator, Darwin Flakoll, published in 1966 a semiautobiographical coming-of-age novel, *Cenizas de Izalco*. In the 1980s, she returned to this interest in narrative, producing among other things a chronological account of the Nicaraguan Revolution (again with her husband), and two texts that we discuss in chapter 7: a testimonio of the armed struggle in El Salvador, *No me agarrán viva*, and an autobiographical poem/novel/fable, *Luisa in Realityland*. In terms of the new tendencies in Salvadoran poetry, however, her major contribution has been the elaboration of a poetized testimonio in which the transcribed oral accounts of witness-participants in the war, in many cases peasant women, are edited and rearranged in verse form. "La mujer del Río Sumpul," which reconstructs in a series of voices the famous massacre of 1980, is her most powerful and influential effort in this vein.

We use Alegría to highlight a group of women writers who work in and around the new mode of testimonial poetry. It includes figures from previous literary generations like Claudia Lars (in the more denunciatory style she developed in her last poems), Matilde López, Liliam Jiménez, and Mercedes Durand, but overwhelmingly young women who write from a situation of militancy like Marta Benavides, Martivón Galindo, Sara Martínez, Eva Margarita Ortiz, Ana del Carmen, Lil Milagro Ramírez, Jacinta Escudos, Reyna Hernández, Mirna Martínez, Sonia Civallero, Sonia Herrera, Gabriela Yanes, and Bernadina Guevara Corvera.[9]

This list of proper names is misleading in a way it would not be for the Committed Generation. One of the characteristics of the new poetry is precisely its insistence on the relative anonymity or selflessness of the poetic voice, the sense that it speaks from and in the name of a collective experience. In the liberated zones still under the control of the FMLN, a good deal of cultural work has now been collectivized through the activities of the Salvadoran Cultural Front (FCES).[10]

As in the relatively more elaborate Sandinista women's poetry, it is difficult to separate what in this poetry represents women joining in a national-popular voice and what is specifically centered on questions of women's liberation as such. The distinction is somewhat academic in any case, since the revolution has been the context in which a women's movement of any sort at all has developed in El Salvador. Most of these women are from middle- or upper-class backgrounds, but have abandoned that situation of privilege to become involved with the FMLN at one level or another. Lil Milagro was a *comandante* in the FARN at the time of her capture and disappearance in 1976; Vázquez, Ortiz, and Mirna Martínez participate actively in the Salvadoran Association of Workers in Art and Culture (ASTAC), with Martínez coordinating that organization's cultural journal; Sara Martínez, who spent 1982–1983 as a political prisoner, now lives in exile in the United States; Hernández served in the FMLN guerrilla component and is now in exile in Sweden; Escudos has been living in exile in the United States.

Alegría and Flakoll's anthology includes a section of semianonymous poems by people who came to poetry as they took on revolutionary consciousness and responsibilities: Lety and Ruth, political educators; Carmela and Haydé, literacy teachers; Karla, a literacy teacher and health worker; Nino, a security unit lieutenant; Jacobo, a guerrilla detachment captain; Julio, a guerrilla combatant; Haroldo, an FMLN propagandist; and so on. Bernadina Guevara and a young woman named simply "Pastora" (Partnoy 1988: 180–183) represent a testimonial poetry from the refugee camps created by the war. Guevara was nine years old when, in a refugee camp in Honduras in 1981, she presented her poems, cursing Reagan and praising the *guerrillero* Federico, on little bits of paper in a match box to Alfonso Hernández who included them in *León de piedra*. "Pastora" learned to read in another Honduran refugee camp, after her family had been killed by the army, and then became a literacy teacher for other refugees, writing poems about her experiences and her hopes.

This is what Salvadorans call "combat poetry" (*poesía de combate*), written under conditions of struggle and repression that make it very difficult to sustain normal literary production, dissemination, and discussion. Combat poetry tends to short poems of direct personal testimony that speak to readers with a sense of urgency. ("Some of us write poems on scraps of paper from supermarkets, in prisons and refugee camps," notes one of the anonymous writers—Anglesey 1987: 147.) In Michael Schneider's characterization, it is not concerned with "personal sensibility straining for nobility in the face of a high-tech, materialist culture . . . existential aloneness, the scars of wounded psyches, 'confessional' self-analysis or personal sexual politics." It seeks clarity and avoids allusion, ambiguity, irony, complex syntax, "unresolved tensions." Its documentary quality reflects a rejection of bohemianism, the mythic or archetypal, philosophical idealism, in favor of a public poetics of physical participation and solidarity, stressing concreteness and orality (Schneider 1985). These features are the products of writers seeking to reach a larger audience, to connect more closely to the lived experiences, hopes, and sufferings of those they try to represent. Many of the writers have been imprisoned, tortured, or exiled; some— Dalton, Rigoberto Góngora, Delfy Góchez, Jaime Suárez Quemain, Lil Milagros, Carlos Aragón, Alejandro Coti, José María Cuéllar, Luis Díaz, Roberto Saballos—have been among the thousands killed or "disappeared" in the process of the war.[11]

The new testimonial poetry involves a recuperation of the initial inspiration of conversational poetry and the sort of portable militant lyric that Otto René Castillo pioneered in Central America. Gone from it is Dalton's ambition to create a plural, complex, polyphonic, metahistorical narrative and along with it the privileged position the "great" writer occupied in the national culture. In its place is the more informal and democratic proliferation of many actual voices.

Current Perspectives

The new stance in poetry reflects directly or implicitly both the FDR-FMLN's increasing internal pluralism and the strategic and political shift represented by its new program—*Gobierno de Amplia Participación*—drafted in the wake of a dramatic sectarian fight in the ranks of the FPL-BPR over the direction of the armed struggle. (In what seemed like a tragic repetition of the circumstances of Roque Dalton's death, the debate resulted in the murder of FPL leader Mélida Anaya Montes—"Ana María"—and the suicide of her rival, Salvador Cayetano Carpio, in Managua.) Issued in January 1984 in anticipation of the U.S.-mandated March 1984 elections, the new program aimed at establishing a coalition government "in which no single force predominates." Abandoning Cayetano Carpio's strategic line of a prolonged people's war, it assumed a military equivalence of the FMLN and government forces that obliged both sides to enter into a "national dialogue." It advanced along these lines a number of proposals for a cease-fire and truce leading to the formation of an interim government to end the war and to prepare a transition to elections. To placate potentially sympathetic sectors of the middle class and bourgeoisie, it dropped previous demands for extensive nationalization and economic planning, and moderated its agrarian reform proposals (see Dunkerley 1988: 407–408).

Duarte's election in 1984 and the partial liberalization of public life that followed have posed a new series of challenges to the left, in particular how to combine working within the framework of the limited and precarious (particularly with the reappearance of the death squads under the new ARENA government) democratic space that has appeared with its previous strategy of armed struggle. In terms of cultural production, perhaps something like Mao Tse-tung's principle of "walking on two legs" has resulted. If the early 1980s marked, as we noted, a shift to a more rural perspective as a consequence of the revolutionary movement's retrenchment to the liberated zones, the post-1984 period has witnessed a return to urban concerns, now, however, articulated in close relation to the development of the Salvadoran labor movement and the popular organizations, which have become the principal force of the nonmilitary left. The testimonial tendency we have profiled above—closely connected to the circumstances of the armed struggle—continues (the FMLN recently issued a striking account of life in the liberated zones by a Flemish woman, *El quinto piso de la alegría*, which we describe in chap. 7). At the same time, a new kind of broadly based cultural activism, no longer centered so much in literature, has emerged, in the collective work of groups like the Association of Salvadoran Cultural Workers (ASTAC) or the Salvadoran Movement for Art and Cultural Identity (MAICES). ASTAC in particular conceives of itself as a "counterministry" to the official Ministry of Culture, which under both Duarte and now the ARENA party has given over cultural matters pretty much to private sponsorship. ASTAC bases its practice on Paolo Freire's pedagogic principle of *conscientización*, arguing for a self-reflective, participatory insertion of artistic activity in the daily life and struggles of the people. In these terms, it seeks to work directly with popular organizations like religious base communities, farm cooperatives, slum dweller committees, and trade unions, contributing—with very limited resources—performances to strikes, demonstrations, rallies, congresses, *fiestas*, and the like. Poetry and testimonio continue to be important cultural forms: very close to the raw political edge of Dalton's best poetry, for example, is the work of the young poet Otoniel Guevara collected in *El violento hormiguero* (1988) and Rafael Menjívar Ochoa's novel *Historia del traidor* (1985). But against the hegemony of written literature as a left cultural form, ASTAC emphasizes the need to develop and combine a wide variety of other arts, closer perhaps to the tastes and concerns of the popular audiences it wants to reach: folk music, mime, dance, puppetry, mural painting, video, and graffiti.[12]

Given the difficult circumstances faced by the Salvadoran revolutionary movement in the last years, we see this new cultural activism as tuned to the more cautious and defensive strategy of resistance the FDR-FMLN evolved in response to the counterinsurgency war. Optimism about the possibilities of revolutionary victory in a direct confrontation with the government and the oligarchy has faded, and there is a real danger of entering into a period of protracted stalemate. But the Salvadoran left has accumulated the greatest experience of struggle in both urban and rural contexts of any movement in Central and perhaps Latin America today, so its potential for action is still considerable. The key to its future lies perhaps in its ability to radicalize the power represented by the rapidly growing Salvadoran labor movement and combine it with the rural base of support consolidated by the FMLN in now almost two decades of armed struggle. In accomplishing this, the work of groups like ASTAC and the new generation of revolutionary writers will be crucial.

Notes

1. Manlio Argueta characterizes him as "a man of the library. Without answers for our world, he remains silent before the injustice that is felt every day and at every hour, but that he couldn't perceive, given his tendency to enclose-

ment" (1983b: 10–11). For Cea, on the other hand, Gavidia is "the first to be concerned with our nationality. He became aware that without tradition there could be no culture or a true poetry. Therefore he dedicated himself to search for our being. He historicized his work and by so doing established the bases for a later development" (1971: 8).

2. For a discussion of the new tendency that is itself one of the important critical manifestos of Latin American political poetry, see Fernández Retamar's 1968 essay "Antipoesía y poesía conversacional en Hispanoamérica" (in Fernández Retamar 1984: 85–114).

3. Dalton had already become involved in problems of armed struggle theory and strategy while he was in Cuba. See, for example, his critique of Debray and *foquismo, ¿Revolución en la revolución? y la crítica de derecha*, originally published by Casa de las Américas (Dalton 1970), and *Un libro rojo para Lenin*, which we discuss below.

4. In Dalton's autobiographical novel *Pobrecito poeta que era yo*, there is a scene where a CIA agent working with the Salvadoran army tries to get the main character to betray his comrades by threatening to spread the word that he has sold out to the CIA.

5. We anticipate here and in our account of post-1979 poetry (which follows in the next section) a number of questions about the nature of testimonial forms, about which we go into in some detail in the first part of chapter 7. Some readers might want to jump ahead to that discussion.

6. On the political implications of avant garde collage technique in general, see Bürger (1984: 55–82). On collage in Latin American boom narrative and poetry, see N. Jitrik and F. Alegría in Fernández Moreno (1978: 219–258).

7. *Miguel Mármol* is constructed on the same tensions as *Las historias*, but as a coherent, single-voiced historical-autobiographical narrative. In his final poems of 1974–1975 (*Poemas clandestinos*), Dalton attempted other narratives of national history without the recourse to the self-ironic intertexuality of *Las historias*. The change reflects perhaps the precarious nature of his personal situation in the guerrilla underground, and his involvement in the difficult strategic, tactical, and theoretical questions that led to his fatal split with the ERP leadership.

8. An extremely prolific writer, Cea has also published the anthology of Salvadoran poetry we cite at the beginning of this chapter; a sociohistorical study of Salvadoran painting; a collection of short stories, *De la guanaxia irredenta*; a novel on the armed struggle, *Niñel se fue a la guerra*; and an anthology of his own testimonial poetry, *Pocos y buenos* (1986).

9. For a representative selection of the new testimonial poetry, see Angelsey (1987), Yanes (1985), Zimmerman (1988a), and Alegría and Flakoll (1989b).

10. For cultural work in the liberated zones, including examples of poetry and song, see, for example, Pearce (1986), Lievens (1989), and Alegría and Flakoll (1989b). On the Frente Cultural, see "Manifesto I. Frente Cultural de El Salvador," and Mario Conti (1984).

11. Delfy Góchez Sosa's poem, "Con gusto, moriré," which anticipates her death in combat, has become one of the classic statements of Salvadoran guerrilla martyrology. There is a translation in Alegría and Flakoll (1989b: 24–27) and (along with a commentary poem by her father) in Zimmerman (1988a:

260, 266–268).

12. Among other things, ASTAC has given attention to the development of children's literature. On MAICES, ASTAC, and current FDR-FMLN cultural policy see José Luis Guzmán and Roberto Herrera, "Sobre el papel del trabajador del arte y la cultura en el momento actual salvadoreño" (1987); and the essays in the first issue of ASTAC's new theoretical journal, *Vereda* (San Salvador) 1:1 (January–February 1989). Our thanks to Todd Jailer of South End Press for bringing this material to our attention.

6. Guatemalan Revolutionary Poetry

Poetry has been less significant as a literary medium in Guatemala than in Nicaragua and El Salvador. The administrative seat of Spain's Central American colonial rule, Guatemala dominated the region until the end of the nineteenth century. Among the upper strata of Spanish speakers, an extensive literary system developed after independence that was centered on European models. Varying kinds of poetry by José Batres Montúfar and others were just one aspect of a literary system that included historical and *costumbrista* plays, narratives, and essays by the likes of Antonio José de Irrisari and José Milla. Prose was the main language of Liberal/Conservative polemics, of policy and policy debate, of official ideology and ideological struggle; poetry tended to be reserved to social commentary and personal experience—a situation that still persists. Darío made Nicaragua the regional center for poetry early in this century; Guatemala's most important *modernista*, Rafael Arévalo Martínez, was best known for his fantastic fiction and his *Ecce Péricles*. Most famous Guatemalan writers have written poetry, but they are best known for their prose.

The evolution of Guatemalan prose shows the marks first of Spanish/ Creole, and then of Conservative and Liberal ladino hegemony. Only gradually, in the face of the Estrada Cabrera and Ubico dictatorships, and perhaps swayed by the Mexican Revolution, does an anti-imperialist and at times *indigenista* prose emerge, primarily among the most "progressive" writers of the so-called Generations of 1920 (Asturias and Cardoza y Aragón) and 1930 (Galich and Monteforte Toledo). The left-liberal reformist ideological project emerging from the Ubico years reached hegemony in the 1944 Revolution. The writers of Grupo Acento generated the first wave of directly political poetry in Guatemala. Then the Grupo Saker-ti poets took increasingly radicalized positions as they associated with Guatemala's Communist party (the PGT, or Partido Guatemalteco de Trabajo). But their project could not maintain its hegemony in the wake of the CIA-inspired coup of 1954. In the ensuing years, younger poets, sometimes identified as the "Generación Comprometida," emerged; but only with the leftist crisis of the late 1960s did they join together, mainly in the Grupo Nuevo Signo (but also in Moira and other groups) to stand, somewhat like Nicaragua's Frente Ventana, as an oppositional cultural vanguard that, in spite of repression and changes, continues to this day.

Each group of new political poets contributed to the radicalization of ladino middle sectors willing to take on the dictatorship and project reformist and then—with the formation of the Guatemalan guerrilla component in 1962—revolutionary alternatives. Their poetry in turn fed off this process of radicalization, which expanded their audience and impact, bridging traditional social and cultural divisions in a movement toward the creation of a Guatemalan popular subject. But even at its point of greatest intensity in the work of Otto René Castillo, Guatemalan revolutionary poetry never achieves the national epic represented by the work of Cardenal or Dalton.

This difference has to do in some measure with the relative dominance of prose in Guatemala's literary system we noted above, which has given testimonial or quasi-testimonial narrative a special prominence in the last decades (see our remarks on Guatemalan testimonio in chap. 7). It also responds, however, to the limitations of Guatemalan literature itself as a vehicle of national-popular expression, limitations imposed by the fact that a majority or close to a majority of the population of Guatemala is made up of non-Spanish-speaking Indian peoples. Before moving on to discuss the specific poets and groups associated with the revolutionary movement, we need, therefore, to say a few words about this problem, which influences both the general context and the concerns of Guatemalan literature.

Literature and the Ethnic Question

What has happened to the Indian population of Guatemala and what its future role might be constitute the major factors distinguishing that country from the rest of Central America, where the population is overwhelmingly mestizo. Since colonial times, Guatemala's political economy has rested essentially on coercive control of Indian land and labor in one form or another. Despised, superexploited, and dispossessed, subject to a continuous process of cultural despoliation, repeatedly attacked by military regimes that have dominated this century, seriously considered on the level of national policy only during the reform period of 1944–1954, the indigenous communities have a long tradition of resistance and survival strategies.

What has been the relation of Guatemalan literature to what is usually termed the "Indian question"? Is there some larger totality—a specifically Guatemalan national-popular—of which ladino and Mayan language communities, *letrado* print culture, and oral tradition are a part? These questions are more than simply literary. With the crisis of the late 1970s, the Indian population became for the first time also a major force in Guatemala's revolutionary movement and a potential key to its future survival and victory. Ladino-Indian political unity has been one of the most crucial strategic goals of this movement, but also one of the most difficult to achieve and maintain in practice.

We have noted that in Central America in general to speak of literature as a "national" cultural form is problematic; in the case of Guatemala, this is doubly so. Only some 25 percent of the Indian population speaks Spanish, and a much smaller percentage reads or writes it. There are at least twenty-two Indian languages spoken, so that many indigenous groups do not understand one another's languages well; very few of them read or write their own languages, let alone Spanish. Even under the most benevolent auspices, they have resisted ladino efforts to modernize their education. So for all practical purposes, literature as a cultural form is all but completely alien, not to say hostile, to their experience.

Until fairly recently, Guatemalan writers have almost invariably come from ladino sectors with at least minimal Spanish language literacy and formal education. (For someone from an indigenous background to be a writer or teacher is already a mark of separation from the ethnic community or group from which he or she comes.) While they may consider the native cultures as basic to their national cultural identity, and seek to bring elements of these into their work, they may be unable to do so in any deeply authentic way. Moreover, the model of literary "transculturation" that has tended to underlie their efforts in this direction (in which pre-Columbian elements are supposed to be blended with the sophisticated poetic and narrative techniques of modern literature) presents a number of problems from a cultural-ideological point of view.[1] We cannot go into them in detail here, but just to mention two: (1) the model is linked to the larger ideology of *mestizaje* as the basis for Latin American racial identity, an ideology that does not necessarily take into account the ethnic claims of Afro-American or indigenous groups as such; (2) in privileging literature, it still presumes print culture in Spanish as the hegemonic site of cultural representation and synthesis.

Finally, and most crucially, there has not been a unity of views on the "Indian question" on the part of the Guatemalan left and progressive intelligentsia itself. Reflecting its strong trade union base, the PGT traditionally looked to ladino field-workers and the urban working class as the basis for its support. CP-related intellectuals like Cardoza y Aragón or Severo Martínez Peláez in his *La patria del criollo* argued that the separation of an Indian and ladino peasantry was largely a colonial inheritance, a survival of feudal arrangements implanted by the Spanish and reinforced by agro-export dependency, and that therefore the indigenous communities must become—through a process of acculturation—part of a modern multiethnic proletariat that struggles for its rights and emancipation as such. The idea of Indian-ladino *mestizaje* or synthesis suggested by Asturias and other left-liberal writers associated with the October Revolution was replicated in the thesis of the "ladinization" of the Indian population developed within the framework of modernization theory assumptions by North American social scientist Richard N. Adams in the 1950s. Influenced by dependency theory and the emerging critique of Eurocentrism and modernization assumptions in the social sciences, however, Guatemalan New Left intellectuals of the 1970s like Carlos Guzmán Böckler and Arturo Arias argued for an "ethnicist" perspective that emphasized indigenous cultural specificity and difference, arguing that the "Indian question" could not be reduced to class categories and rejecting modernization and/or transculturation models. The new perspective had a strong influence on the strategy of the armed struggle in the late 1970s.[2]

The most thorough discussion of the relation of Guatemalan literature to the "Indian question" is by José Luis Balcárcel (1981). Balcárcel starts with the problem of the submergence, domination, and marginalization of peoples and groups in the general socioeconomic processes producing both class and state formation in Guatemala. From this perspective, he tends to see the Indian population in relation to its insertion in the structure of dependency as a whole, rejecting, like Martínez, an analysis based primarily on cultural difference, as if each group configured an autarkic cultural unit:

> It is a matter of social formations which are insufficiently structured due to their economic, social and political marginalization to constitute particular cultures or supports of national culture. Thus, to speak of popular cultures or nationalities parallel to an imposed ladino national culture makes no more sense than it does to speak of national culture without taking Indian dimensions into account. ... Thus, clearly, for much of the colonial period and deep into our own century, there are varying oral currents, but only one Guatemalan literary tradition, with little Indian input from the seventeenth century to the emergence of modern testimonial literature. (P. 20)

For Balcárcel, however, it is not simply a question of recognizing class differences, class domination, and oppression—matters that affect cultural production in all dependent capitalist countries experiencing the effects of imperialism and neocolonialism. The important issue is how these relate to the specificities of a given country. In Guatemala, many of the Indian communities exist at or close to a subsistence level. The insertion of the country in the international market via expansion and modernization of the agro-export sector produces pressure against the lands held by these communities, partial proletarianization of their members, their superexploitation as agricultural wage labor, and the imposition of military regimes to counter resulting resistance. Transnational imperialist and neocolonial culture introduces into the country heterogeneous elements and demands, reordering and remaking native cultural forms and practices (among other things, transforming Indian crafts into commodities). The results include "confused deformations of popular arts," but also a ladino literary system that is a "sad distorted image of colonial models, representing the ideological confusions of a dependent bourgeoisie." Thus, for Balcárcel, there is no Guatemalan national culture as such, only "a partial and fragementary culture" (p. 21).

In the struggle against this situation, Guatemalan cultural workers have tried to overcome division, manipulation, and alienation, and to forge something like a unitary sense of a national-popular. But sympathizing with such a goal does not mean being blind to the difficulties they face—difficulties that are particularly acute with respect to the conditions for literary culture in Guatemala. Writers, including poets, have a very narrow audience for their work; and in the sphere available to them, they have to deal with serious problems of censorship and repression and at the same time compete with an imported transnational commercial literature.

Even in the most difficult circumstances, under Ubico, Castillo Armas, Lucas, or Ríos-Montt, however, progressive and revolutionary writers have continued working inside Guatemala or in exile; and, in varying degrees, they have had an impact on the creation of a ladino left public sphere. From Cardoza's *Revista de Guatemala* of the reform years, through such oppositional cultural journals as *Lanzas y Letras, Presencia, Alero,* and *Cuadernos Universitarios,* the literary supplements of newspapers, and small university-based presses that have been able to count on the relative academic freedom sometimes afforded even under dictatorship, they have kept alive at least modest means for the publication and distribution of their work.

Balcárcel points out that the drama was one medium where literature could at least begin to connect with a wider—albeit still predominantly ladino—audience. Unlike Nicaragua and El Salvador, Guatemala has had a relatively strong theatrical tradition, part of the heritage of Spanish Golden Age culture it received in the colonial period. During the October Revolution, theater was a vehicle through which (given relatively low ticket prices, subsidized performances, etc.) significant intellectuals like Rafael Martínez Arévalo, Asturias, and Manuel Galich could get their work before a broad middle-sector audience and even sectors (frequently the student-children) of the ladino urban working class. Among radicalized student and intellectual circles in the 1960s, the avant garde experimental political theater represented by foreign writers like Bertolt Brecht and Peter Weiss became fashionable. For the ladino working class there was a popular theater dealing often satirically with work and everyday life problems. Sometimes avant garde and popular perspectives came together to create a potentially effective political theater, similar to the *teatro de creación colectiva* of the sort that developed elsewhere in Latin America in the 1960s. A number of the major Guatemalan revolutionary poets of these years (e.g., Otto René Castillo, José Manuel Arce, and Marco Antonio Flores) worked also in theater and film.

But in general the forces acting against Guatemalan literature have been great. Writers living in the country have had to practice self-censorship to be published or to avoid the sometimes more terrible consequences of having escaped the censor's eye. Given the weight of cultural and ideological domination, and well-learned fears of brutal and sometimes capricious repression, to the degree that Guatemalan writers have expressed openly dissident or radical perspectives they have often been forced into clandestinity or exile. Those who have spent years abroad have been freer to write as they choose, but almost in direct relation to the subversive character of their work, their dissemination and impact within Guatemala have been limited.

The problem Balcárcel describes for Guatemalan literature in general applies particularly to the progressive and revolutionary poets whose work we profile here. At least in principle, they have committed themselves to breaking down the separation between literature and the people. Poetry as conveyor of popular messages has passed in recent years from the schools and literary forums to large public arenas and workplaces, and with the guerrilla from the city to the countryside. The situation of a writer like Asturias as—to use Gramsci's category—a "traditional intellectual" gives way to the cadre/poet as "organic intellectual" of the revolutionary movement. A number of poets have been disappeared and killed (among the best-known: Alaíde Foppa, Otto René Castillo, Roberto Obregón, Arturo Oscar Palencia, and Luis de Lión); many others have suffered discrimination, prison, torture, death threats, and exile. They continue developing an oppositional discourse in the dangerous and uncertain circumstances of Guatemalan cultural production; but because of these circumstances, their work has not been as effective in generating revolutionary ideological mobilization as Nicaraguan and Salvadoran committed poetry. As in earlier stages of Guatemalan literary history, narrative—the social novel and in the last decade the testimonio—remains decisive. But even in the case of narrative, the fault line that separates Guatemalan literature as such and Indian cultural forms is still very much there. Perhaps José Carlos Mariátegui's judgment in his *Siete ensayos* on a similar impasse in Andean culture in the 1920s that "an indigenous literature will come into being only when the Indian peoples themselves are in a postion to produce it" still holds some truth.

If not an achieved unity, however, there has been, particularly in the testimonial orientations of recent Guatemalan literature, an accommodation and approximation between ladino and Indian elements that has become increasingly a two-way process (before, it was the ladino writer "transculturizing" the Indian) and that suggests future possible articulations adequate to meeting the sociopolitical and cultural agendas of the Indian peoples in their own struggle for survival and liberation. In tandem with this process has been a feminization of the literary system similar to the one we have observed in recent Nicaraguan and Salvadoran poetry.

Asturias and the Generations of 1920 and 1930

The "Indian question" was crucial for the "Generations" of 1920 and 1930—including Guatemala's first explicitly left-wing writers: vanguardists Miguel Angel Asturias and Luis Cardoza y Aragón; and Grupo Tepeus "fellow travelers," Mario Monteforte Toledo and Manuel Galich. The Estrada Cabrera dictatorship, the failed democratic experiments that followed, and then the Depression-period Ubico military regime provided the context for the development of these writers.

As in Nicaragua and El Salvador, the 1929 crisis revealed the fragility of the traditional system of agro-export dependency and fractured the forms of its corresponding Liberal-Conservative ideological hegemony. In literature this meant rejecting the dominant models of *costumbrismo* and *modernismo.* Asturias and Cardoza shared with the Nicaraguan vanguardists both an interest in the new avant garde literary movements of Europe and the Americas and a desire to make literature a place to define a new sense of national identity no longer centered in the project of the Creole elite. Unlike their Nicaraguan cousins, however, the Guatemalan vanguardists tended politically to the sort of center-left progressivism represented by the October Revolution itself.

Influenced variously by Marxism, Pan-Americanism (*mundonovismo*), Mexican *indigenismo*, and French surrealism's literary mobilization of the unconscious and the myth-world represented by Third World pre-Christian cultures, the Guatemalan vanguardists launched what Roberto Armijo calls "a redefinition of the Indian majorities in a new poetry and new national vision.... Guatemalan Vanguard poetry meant an intense cultural mestizaje in function of a growing consciousness of national identity and above all, of *indigenismo* seen as a source for spiritual revitalization in the face of years of dictatorship, of economic debilities, and strong class, caste and ethnic divisons" (Armijo and Paredes 1983: 8).

Indigenista orientations also dominated the more regionalist writers in and around Grupo Tepeus. But, perhaps because of poetry's secondary status in Guatemala's literary system, the writers of the left of both generations are best known for their work in other media: Cardoza, the greatest poet, for his brilliant essays on Guatemalan culture and history—especially *Guatemala, las líneas de su mano*, a classic text of Latin American national liberation literature; Galich for his testimonial journalism and theater (he has been a major force in developing Latin American political theater in the wake of the Cuban Revolution); and Asturias and Monteforte Toledo for their novels and stories. A Nobel Prize winner, Asturias is clearly the most famous figure.

Like so many other Latin American literary intellectuals, Asturias began his career living abroad in Paris in the 1920s, as both a student of pre-Columbian culture and a budding poet in the fashionable avant garde styles of the day. The key to his work was the way in which he was able to combine these two dimensions. His first book, *Leyendas de Guatemala* (1930), was a retelling of mythic narratives from the *Popol Vuh* and other Mayan chronicles. By learning how to project these materials onto social themes of modern Guatemalan life, he was able to explore the interactions between a ceremonial Indian-peasant world and a secular ladino world represented by the repressive dictatorships of his youth and adult life. His *Hombres de maiz* (1949) was a formative text of what came to be known as "magic realism"—the immediate precursor of Latin American boom narrative of the 1960s.[3]

Asturias's ideological project was based on his notion of a core Mayan/ladino identity for the Guatemalan people; his artistic problem was the forging of a literary mode able to both express and embody the transculturation process that the achievement of such an identity required. To be sure, the solutions he posed were generally putative and symbolic. Despite his anti-imperialism, he was never fully convinced of or involved in the various Marxisms of his day. Lacking a specific vision of social transformation, he tends to leave his reader encapsulated in an ultimately self-referential world of the fantastic and "magically real" text, without the breakthrough to actual revolutionary militancy projected by the new writers of the post-1954 generations, such as Otto René Castillo. The younger writers complained of Asturias's idealization of pre-Columbian myth, seeing it as a form of literary exoticism; but the difficulties of finding an effective revolutionary strategy based on ladino-Indian unity may also give his work a continuing ideological relevance today. There is, in any case, hardly any attempt to deal with the problem of representing Indian life and culture in contemporary Guatemalan (or even Central American) poetry or prose that does not have his work as an explicit or implicit reference point, even when, as has often been the case, his specific political judgments have been contested.

Involved in the same problematic of fashioning a national-popular synthesis of ladino and Indian cultures as Asturias—but with a more orthodox Marxist perspective on matters of class and ethnicity (see our remarks above on differences on the "Indian question" among intellectuals of the Guatemalan left) and a more politically militant stance that would lead him for a time into the PGT—was novelist/sociologist Mario Monteforte Toledo, author of an influential group of social realist novels of Guatemalan Indian life that appeared during the October Revolution.

The Reform Years and Saker-ti

The October Revolution put on the agenda of national politics what had only been a literary idea in Asturias and his fellow writers of the left. The progressives who had protagonized Guatemalan literary life from the 1920s on would reach their apogee in the 1944–1954 decade, only to meet a historical limit with the fall of Arbenz. Among the younger writers who launched their careers during the October Revolution years, more explicitly Marxist and social realist tendencies appeared, in tandem with the ebb and flow of political radicalization and polarization produced within the reform process.

The rupture of structures represented by the October Revolution generated a literature alive to the moment. In 1943, in the context of the political mobilization against the Ubico regime, a group of young poets led by Enrique Juárez Toledo, Raúl Leiva, and Otto Raúl González began writing an aggressively oppositional poetry as members of Grupo Acento. They would be the major poets associated ideologically with the October Revolution.[4] Asturias continued to develop the motifs of myth and fantasy found in his early work, now integrated with a depiction reminiscent of the social realist novels of the 1930s of the impact of North American imperialism on Guatemalan society and culture, particularly in his three-volume Banana Trilogy: *Viento fuerte* (1949), *El Papa*

Verde (1950), and *Los ojos de los enterrados* (1954). Galich became minister of culture under Arévalo. Cardoza edited the cultural journal *Revista de Guatemala* and began work on his book-length essay, *Guatemala, las líneas de su mano*, a text whose passionate critique of the neocolonial situation of Guatemala was ultimately framed by the 1954 coup.

In accord with its social policies, most particularly the Agrarian Reform, the October Revolution sought to dynamize cultural production and quickly moved to create a wide range of cultural centers, journals, book publishing and distribution houses, programs of competition for the arts, fellowships, grants, and subsidies. A cultural front was formed, the AGEAR (Asociación Guatemalteca de Escritores y Artistas Revolucionarios), to support work along these lines. Some critics on the left pointed to the reformist character of the Arévalo and Arbenz measures, arguing that the new art programs and works they promoted primarily benefited the urban petite bourgeoisie. Nevertheless, there is no doubt that, as Arias puts it, "during this period, more books and journals were edited, more expositions, concerts and theater presentions were held and there was more cultural activity, than during the entire century before" (1979: 286). Experimental projects attempting to address the question of a satisfactory cultural program for the indigenous communities and peasant ladino sectors were launched for the first time.

Of all the literary projects emerging in the 1944–1954 period, Saker-ti (Quiché for "dawn") was the most important and representative. Comprising mainly young students and cultural workers, it issued a manifesto in 1950—"Siete afirmaciones"—defining itself as a literary-cultural vanguard linked directly to the policies and political dynamism of these years. In particular, it aimed to create a "democratic, nationalist and realist art" that would maintain and further radicalize the impulse of the October Revolution. The signers included a group of then relatively unknown writers (Miguel Angel Vázquez, Julio Fausto Aguilera, Rafael Sosa, Olga Martínez Torres, Melvin René Barahona, José María López, Roberto Paz y Paz, Huberto Alvarado), as well as established figures like Raúl Leiva, Enrique Juárez Toledo, Augusto Monterroso, and Carlos Illescas who had been involved in the anti-Ubico campaign.

Saker-ti brought together various sectors and ideological tendencies among Guatemala's progressive intellectuals: competing forms of Marxism, left Catholicism, anarchism, *indigenismo*, feminism—in accord, perhaps, only over the need to change as rapidly as possible all anachronistic institutions and ways of thought that kept Guatemala in a state of backwardness and social injustice. Among its other activities (which included running a journal and a press), the group convoked an

Assembly of Young Artists and Writers, the first such meeting in Guatemala's history, and a direct forerunner of the cultural assemblies that were to occur in Sandinista Nicaragua. The assembly called for Guatemalan artists to "forge a new type of culture, which, responding to the needs of the people, would act in support of the young Guatemalan democracy," and would be "national, scientific and democratic," at the service of the country's "great popular majority." They should seek to appropriate what was "positive" in the nation's cultural tradition, at the same time respecting ethnic diversity and rejecting "superstition, ignorance and bigotry" (in Rodríguez Mojón 1973: 17).

The group's youthful radicalism and diversity contributed to its chaotic but energized evolution beyond the reformist ethos dominating the October Revolution. Saker-ti marked the beginning of a new, explicitly revolutionary, stage in Guatemala's literary history. That the group's major limitation—the fact that its iconoclasm and enthusiasm for rapid social and cultural change were potentially at odds with its own sense of engagement with the "Indian question"—never became a major issue was due perhaps only to its extinction. With the 1954 coup, Saker-ti saw its work cut short. The writers and artists who had lived years of creative freedom and revolutionary euphoria were silenced or forced into exile.[5]

Otto René Castillo: 1936–1967

> It is beautiful to love the world
> with the eyes
> of those who have not yet been born.
>
> —Otto René Castillo

Arias makes the following overall judgment of the cultural and literary projects of the October Revolution:

Before 1944, literary production was almost exclusively artisanal. Industrial modernization and the realization of its attendant ideological projects prior to 1944 created the need for a mode of cultural production closer to the existing capitalist model in hegemonic societies. From this need came (during the October Revolution) the creation of a cultural infrastructure which involved new circuits of production, distribution and consumption. This meant the provision of materials, instruments, and techniques of production, as well as the product itself. . . . These external conditions could not but encourage the constitution of literary texts. An infrastructure of apparatuses was created for the circulation and consumption of certain kinds of cultural products. . . . (Those) most conforming to reform year norms succeeded. With the counterrrevolution of 1954, this petty bourgeois project would collapse, and a new more revolutionary mode of writing would come to the fore. (1979: 287)

Arias refers here to the emergence of a new generation of writers born in the late 1930s and early 1940s, which shared a childhood shaped by the years of the October Revolution. It includes Manuel José Arce (1935), Luis Alfredo Arango (1935), Otto René Castillo (1936), Marco Antonio Flores (1937), Luis de Lión (1939), Francisco Morales Santos (1940), Roberto Obregón (1940), José Ovalle Arévalo (1942), and Arqueles Morales (1943). Although their common reference point was a feeling of outrage and loss over the 1954 coup, these writers also began to question the liberal-left unity that had been part of the political consensus represented by the October Revolution governments and programs.

Symptomatic of their new ideological protagonism was their repudiation of Asturias. The immediate pretext was the novelist's decision, after initially denouncing the coup (among other places in a novel, *Weekend in Guatemala*), to accept a post as ambassador to France from the new regime. But there were deeper issues. Among particularly the Communist party and sectors of the Marxist left, there had been a sense that Arbenz should have attempted to arm the people against Castillo Armas in 1954, that his failure to do so showed finally the limits of his middle-class reformist perspective. According to this analysis, a resurgence of the impulse represented by the October Revolution would have to be more firmly anchored in the masses and in specifically Marxist ideology and organizations.

The younger Guatemalan writers generally shared this view. Many of them, like Fonseca in Nicaragua or Roque Dalton in El Salvador, were beginning to come into direct contact with the Soviet Union and the socialist countries as scholarship students or delegates to youth congresses. Inside Guatemala, the PGT with its extensive clandestine apparatus and a strong presence in the trade union movement represented the best organized and most militant opposition force. The institutionalization of a militarized reactionary state apparatus after Castillo Armas suggested the necessity of moving from the PGT's Popular Front electoral strategy to some form or other of armed struggle. By the late 1950s, a new political reference point had appeared for this: Fidel Castro's 26 of July Movement in Cuba. In 1960, a Castro-style revolt led by young officers at the Zacapa barracks was put down with U.S. assistance. The leaders of this revolt—Marco Antonio Yon Sosa and Luis Turcios Lima—went into exile to organize small guerrilla groups.

In 1961, after an intense debate, the PGT also shifted to a strategy of armed struggle. The main guerrilla group of the 1960s, the PGT-related FAR (Fuerzas Armadas Rebeldes) was formed at the end of 1962.

At the same time that the new writers signaled their break with the past by denouncing what they saw as Asturias's sellout to the regime, they also took as their own his motto "El poeta es una conducta moral" (the poet is a form of moral behavior), arguing for a combination of literary work and direct political militancy. In practice, this meant becoming either cadre members or fellow travelers of the PGT and/or the various guerrilla groups that appeared after 1960. Hence the sobriquet they s⊦ are in subsequent Central American literary history with Roque Dalton and his contemporaries in El Salvador: La Generación Comprometida, the Committed Generation.

The most representative and important figure of this group in the years between 1954 and 1967 was Otto René Castillo, his poem "Intelectuales apolíticos"—one of the best known in Latin American political poetry— perhaps the closest thing to its poetic manifesto.[6] As in the case of other poet-martyrs of the Central American armed struggle we have looked at (Dalton, Rugama, Morales Avíles), his life and work have become to some extent inseparable.

Born in Quezaltenango of a middle-class ladino family in 1936, Castillo became a student activist in his teens, and eventually a youth leader in the PGT. He was eighteen at the time of the 1954 coup, which forced him into the first of many periods of exile, in this case to El Salvador, where—with a highly developed sense of internationalism— he promptly joined the Salvadoran Communist party (it is said that he carried out a number of clandestine missions for the party). He also began university studies, meeting and deeply influencing Dalton and the Círculo Literario Universitario, as we noted in chapter 5.

In 1958 Castillo returned to Guatemala, registering in the law faculty of the University of San Carlos, one of the few surviving pockets of university resistance. Already a prominent poet (in 1955 he shared the Central American Poetry Prize with Dalton; in 1957 he won the Poetry Prize of the World Festival of Youth in Budapest), he helped launch a cultural journal, *Lanzas y Letras*, which would become a platform for most of the important dissident voices in the country. Awarded a scholarship by the Asociación de Estudiantes Universitarios de Guatemala, he went to East Germany to continue his law studies at the University of Leipzig in 1959.

In 1962, Castillo abandoned his studies in Germany to join the documentary film brigade led by Dutch director Joris Ivens, which was seeking to represent the revolutionary struggle emerging throughout Latin America on the heels of the Cuban triumph. The experience implied his further involvement in the problems of guerrilla struggle and began to affect the imagery, technique, and orientation of his poetry.

Castillo returned to Guatemala in 1964, again entering into intense cultural/political work (among other things, he was the director of an experimental theater group in Guatemala City). Around this time, he started to become active in the FAR. His most important collection, *Vámonos patria a caminar* (1965), registers his new involvement in armed struggle. In 1965, he was arrested while making a documentary of FAR's guerrilla activity and was deported. As a sort of informal ambassador for the guerrilla movement, he traveled in East Germany, Algeria, Hungary, Austria, and Cuba, eventually returning to Guatemala where he was named the head of propaganda of FAR's eastern region. In 1967, he was wounded in combat and was captured by the government's antiguerrilla forces; along with his *compañera* Nora Paíz, he was taken to the Zacapa military base, where he was tortured to death.

In his prologue to Castillo's collected poems, Roque Dalton (1971) argued that Castillo represented for his generation "the passage to a new revolutionary militancy which corresponds to the new stage of Central American history centrally marked by popular armed struggle." This entailed both in his life and his work "the highest level of responsibility of the revolutionary intellectual, of the revolutionary creator, in the unity of theory and practice." Dalton noted that Castillo initiated his public activity at the final phase of the Guatemalan democratic process and in the heart of the PGT. His direct contact with revolutionary theory and literature and with the socialist countries gave him an advantage over other Central American intellectuals of his generation, which accounts in part for the regional influence he exercised in the late 1950s and early 1960s. In Guatemala, Castillo's generation was the first one not tied to petit bourgeois or bourgeois political parties. In this context, his membership in the PGT gave him a certain prestige, because the party was seen, Dalton suggests, "as the only political force which under reactionary terror tried to organize clandestine resistance, and because the commitment of those young people was with the Revolution . . . as an abstraction, without precise dimensions and without specific concrete modes of operating, motor forces, character or given forms of struggle." At the same time, Castillo pointed beyond the limits of the dominant perspectives of the Latin American CPs in the 1950s toward the new revolutionary possibilities signaled by the Cuban Revolution. He was, Dalton concluded, one of the few members of his generation with access to the central problem of "political line of the revolutionary organization, the line that had produced defeat, the line that . . . could potentially lead to a correct resolution in the future."

Castillo's poetry seems at first glance to belie the intense political involvement Dalton's tribute suggests. It shows a predilection for simple metrical forms and emotionally direct language and images. It is less narrative and historical, more lyrical and metaphorical, than Dalton's own work or that of Cardenal in Nicaragua, his two peers in Central American revolutionary poetry. This is in part the effect of a literary system in which, as we have noted, poetry tended to be reserved for private introspection. It is also an effect of Castillo's reaction against the grand Nerudian mode of political poetry and his appropriation of the more fraternal/sororial mode of conversational poetry that marked the Latin American literary ambience in the years after the Cuban Revolution. The proportion of Castillo's poems that deal with love and other seemingly nonpolitical themes in fact is quite large, and one suspects that many of his party comrades must have spoken condescendingly about them, mocking their sentimentalism and wide-eyed idealism.

What Castillo was fashioning, however, was a new kind of political poetry, a committed but also intensely personal lyric form designed to appeal to the idealism of young people facing difficult problems of choice and commitment in both their emotional and political lives, to represent their process of ideological transformation as they moved toward more militant positions. Though it stems in part from the intimism of Guatemala's poetic tradition, for Castillo the theme of love is not simply a private question, detached from politics. It embodies a sense of how the personal self is related to something larger than itself, a reaffirmation of life that can be counterposed to experiences of injustice, sadness, and death, which has to be there for the imaginative leap of faith that the armed struggle represents and for the very dangerous and difficult work that it involves (Castillo would have subscribed to Che Guevara's remark that a revolutionary must be guided by great feelings of love). This accounts too for the persistent theme of death in his poetry, including what Alfonso Chase calls his "prevision"—his premonition and acceptance of his own death as part of the process leading to socialist transformation (among other places, in the short poem "Viudo del mundo," where Castillo in effect wrote his own epitaph). Like Rugama in Nicaragua, the combination of his poetry and his martyrdom in the guerrilla was to make of Castillo a powerful symbol of the many young people in Central America willing to risk their lives for the sake of the future. (For the current generation of Central American intellectuals, he is perhaps also a symbol of the misguided romanticism that was so much a part of the *foquista* period of guerrilla struggle.)

The rejection of irony and complexity on the one hand and of historical narrative on the other means that Castillo's poems—"Apolitical Intellectuals" is characteristic in this sense—tend to be very closely keyed to questions of moral choice and authenticity. But these questions are always placed in relation to the problem of the nation as a whole, a sense of the need for social and political commitment: "Vámonos patria a caminar, yo te acompaño" (get up and walk, country, and I'll go with you). Chase speaks of how Castillo's poems involve the dialectic of "a poet who craves to express a personal truth, in order to also incarnate a collective soul," describing them aptly as "ceremonies of discovery" in which readers are led through past assumptions and prejudices to recover an unviolated, pristine innocence that leads to new possibilities of understanding and empathy (1982: 411–419). Where there is an explicit political vision, it tends to revolve schematically around the polarities of Guatemala and an overidealized socialist world represented by Castillo's experiences in East Germany, heaven and hell, development and underdevelopment.

One of these new possibilities that breaks with Castillo's simplistic East/West ideological schema has to do with his approach to the "Indian question." Against the traditional CP focus on the ladino working class (but without embracing the sort of "magic realist" *indigenismo* represented by Asturias), Castillo sees the Mayan *campesino* and the elements of Guatemalan nature itself as the basic embodiments of the national-popular (see, e.g., his "Oración por el alma de la patria," which begins with a quotation from the *Popol Vuh*, or the long poem "Octubre," which is the closest thing to a "national epic" in his work).

Castillo also anticipated in a limited way the process of feminization of Central American revolutionary culture we have noted in Nicaragua and El Salvador. Many of his poems entail conventional expressions of romantic and physical love for women, whose image the poet's "revolutionary" male persona will take with him to the struggle (e.g., "Uno es así de extraño"). But the persona is also a figure of tenderness and sensitivity; at times it is difficult to determine whether the person addressed is in fact a woman or an aspect of Castillo's own self, as if he were constructing a dialogue with himself (see, e.g., "Sabor a luto"). There is a pronouncedly less machista tone than in Dalton, and, infrequently, a new image of woman as *compañera*, coequal in the struggle for political and personal liberation. What this intimates in Castillo's poetry is a mode of revolutionary subjectivity inflected by a series of new factors: the stronger presence of indigenous culture in Guatemala (tending to be less machista than mestizo or ladino ones); the greater involvement of women in education and political and cultural activity; the emerging theoretical discourse of socialist feminism; and the new definitions of gender role that begin to occur in the communal life of the guerrilla organizations and the urban underground.

Nuevo Signo

Building on the work of Castillo, but also differentiating themselves from it, were the writers who emerged under the auspices of Nuevo Signo in 1968. The group initially consisted of six poets—two figures from Castillo's generation, Luis Alfredo Arango and Francisco Morales Santos, three older writers, Antonio Brañas, Julio Fausto Aguilera, and José Luis Villatoro, and one younger writer, Delia Quiñonez. In its first year, Roberto Obregón joined, and many other writers of divergent ideological positions have been identified with it (e.g., Iván Barrera, Ligia Bernal, Luis de Lión, Romelia Alarcón, Mario Payeras, and Isabel María de los Angeles Ruano.[7]

The group first gained prominence in 1970 with the publication of an anthology of their poetry, *Las plumas de la serpiente.* The main vehicle for their ongoing work was the university journal *Alero.* The generative experience of the Nuevo Signo poets was the crisis of individual and national conscience in the face of a deeply divided and militarized society, marked by extremes of poverty, degradation, violence, and exploitation. So their poetry has in part a testimonial and denunciatory function. But they were also looking for forms of a syncretic national expression that might point to alternatives to the impasse faced by the Guatemalan left in the early 1970s. Possessed with a strong colloquial verve, their major contribution was to make, somewhat in the fashion of Nicaraguan exteriorism, poetry of materials considered unpoetic, bringing in language and themes related to the life of the country's rural population.

Several members of the group came from poor—presumably ladino—rural backgrounds, and tended to focus on *campesino* themes. Luis Alfredo Arango, for example, was from the village of Totonicapán. A rural schoolteacher, he had direct ties with the Indian communities of his area and gave expression to their experience and their values in a series of collections appearing from 1959 into the 1980s. But Nuevo Signo's heightened concern with rural issues was also in part a response to the lack of substantial Indian involvement in the Guatemalan guerrilla movement of the 1960s. In place of what they called Asturias's "lyric exaltation" of the Indian and pre-Columbian myth, which they regarded as a kind of exoticism without serious political implications, and of Castillo's relatively synthetic and allegorical celebration of the Mayan roots of Guatemalan culture, the Nuevo Signo writers wanted to create a poetry that would represent the actual situation of the Indian communities and ladino poor peasants. To use the title of perhaps their most representative volume, Villatoro's *Pedro a secas*, the subject they were looking for was the Guatemalan man of the people "just-as-he-is" (*a secas*:

i.e., straight, without elaboration).

Roberto Obregón was the poet of the group who most veered toward the "committed" stance represented by Castillo. The title of his major collection, *Poesía de barro* (Clay poetry), suggests allusively the *campesino* focus of Arango or Villatoro, but Obregón's poetry is much more deeply—almost hermetically—personal. Perhaps the best known of the Nuevo Signo poets, he began to publish in his teens, when, like Castillo, he got involved in the PGT and was sent to study in Moscow. During his years in the Soviet Union, he mastered Russian and translated Russian poetry into Spanish. (A Russian edition of his own poetry appeared in the Soviet Union in 1968.) In 1970, working with the guerrillas, he was captured on the border between Guatemala and El Salvador by units of the Salvadoran army and "disappeared."

Several other members of the group besides Obregón were closely involved in the armed struggle; but in general Nuevo Signo writers showed a tendency to avoid an explicitly partisan poetry. While they cultivated the protest poem as an aspect of their work, their main impetus was for a broader exploration of the forces operating in Guatemalan society. Recalling a distinction we invoked in chapter 1, we could say that the group's collective project was more "ideological" than "political": in a conjuncture marked by the crisis of the sectarian Marxist left in Guatemala, it saw as its purpose to create new modes of cultural opposition deeply rooted in the Guatemalan national-popular. José Mejía observes in this regard of *Pedro a secas*

> [Villatoro's book] breaks . . . with the conventionalism of the
> "socialist poets" who eternally sing of themselves, and see them-
> selves as victims. Because it is time to end this rhetoric of imagi-
> nary rifles, bread, flags, . . . and proletarian girlfriends; so that we
> conquer the obscure side of national identity with which Villatoro
> confronts us: the Indian. But not the inoffensive Tecún Umán of
> the statues, nor the falsely lyrical Tecún Umán of the verses of bad
> patriots, but rather the other, the real Indian of every day, "Pedro as
> he is," day worker, peon who makes for our comforts and over
> whose sadness we raise our precarious and fictitious liberty. (In
> Villatoro, *Pedro a secas*: 3)

The door that Nuevo Signo's work opened was toward a more broadly cultural and popular, and less explicitly militant, lyric than Castillo's (which Mejía seems to allude to in his remarks above about a "rhetoric of imaginary rifles"). In part, this was a reaction against the sectarianism and revolutionary romanticism that dominated the left, and a conscious or unconscious retrenchment in the face of the collapse of the *foquista* guerrilla groups in the early 1970s. In part, it also represented Nuevo Signo's interest in the colloquial and the everyday, and its desire to explore more complex states of subjectivity than Castillo's model permitted. But if Nuevo Signo marks a certain distance from Castillo, it also continued the implicit assumption in his poetry that the exploration of subjectivity itself somehow incarnates the national problematic, that, as the generic 1960s slogan had it, "the personal is the political." In this aspect of its work, Nuevo Signo anticipated and connected with emerging feminist and socialist-feminist tendencies in Guatemalan poetry.

The New Women's Poetry and Other Trends

The youngest member of Nuevo Signo and the only woman among its founders, Delia Quiñónez revealed a strong lyric gift in her early work (1968), with only faintly political allusions. Her subsequent writing, however, would place her at the forefront of an emerging movement of Guatemalan women's poetry, which included, besides her, Alaíde Foppa, Margarita Carrera, Ana María Rodas and Luz Méndez from Grupo Moira, Lucinda Rivas, and a host of younger writers in recent years.[8]

There are some antecedents for a militant women's poetry in Guatemalan literary history: in the nineteenth century, Pepita García Granados, whose work broke religious and sexual taboos; Luz Valle (1896–1971), publisher of a women's literary journal, *Nosotras*; Amanda Montenegro y Montenegro, a writer prominently involved in the struggle against the Estrada Cabrera regime; Magdelena Spinola and Romelia Alarcón de Folgar. But generally Guatemalan women's poetry had been in the quietistic "feminine as opposed to feminist" mode of the upper-class *poetisa* we have already noted in Nicaraguan and Salvadoran literature. Like the "Six" in Nicaragua, the Guatemalan women poets of the 1970s would change that identification dramatically.

Foppa was born in Barcelona and was raised in Italy. She married Guatemalan politician Alfonso Solórzano and went into exile with him in Mexico after the 1954 coup. During her years of exile, she became a feminist, helping to edit a major Latin American woman's journal, *FEM*, hosting a "Foro de la mujer" program for Mexican radio, and involving herself in the development of the Guatemalan women's movement. Her major publications in a feminist vein are *Elogio de mi cuerpo* (1970) and *Las palabras y el tiempo* (1979). Kidnapped and presumably murdered by members of the judicial police on her return to Guatemala in December 1980, she has become a symbol of women's participation in Guatemalan resistance, and her poems—though they are not always explicitly political—are frequently reproduced in movement publications (one of the major contemporary leftist cultural groups in Guatemala is named after her).

The first woman graduate in literature from the Universidad de San Carlos, Margarita Carrera wrote criticism as well as poetry. Her important collection, *Del noveno círculo*, written after the earthquake of 1976, creates a powerful literary image—modeled on Dante's *Inferno*—of Guatemalan reality on the eve of the crisis of the late 1970s. Luz Méndez began publishing in the early 1950s in the literary supplement of *Diario de Centro América* as a member of Grupo Moira, headed by Manuel José Arce and Carlos Zipfel. Like Carrera a literature PhD and editor of the cultural supplement *La Hora*, she would come to write several pioneering volumes of Guatemalan feminist criticism. Under the pseudonym of Lina Marques, she cultivated an erotic and politically iconoclastic poetry. In the same spirit was Ana María Rodas's aptly named *Poemas de la izquierda erótica* (1973), which rebukes the machismo of the male revolutionary left and declares itself in favor of a "Che Guevara not so much of the countryside but of love." Less well known today than these figures is Lucinda Rivas, whose *Cantar para vivir* (1967) contains a series of testimonial poems dealing with the emergence and evolution of the armed struggle in the early 1960s.

In tandem with Nuevo Signo and the new feminist poetry, a few other figures came to the fore in the 1970s. A founder of Grupo Moira, Manuel José Arce was an important force in maintaining and reconstructing oppositional perspectives in Guatemala. His earlier poetry collections show him to be a major voice, in an existentialist version of the intimist lyric mode consecrated by Guatemalan literary tradition; for much of his career, his politically significant work was mainly in his daring experimental plays and testimonial journalism. Just prior to his death in 1985, however, Arce produced a remarkable body of directly political poems, some of which appeared posthumously in the new journal *Tzolkin*. Luis de Lión, an only partially ladinized Indian, emerged as one of the first poets who could present Indian perspectives in his work firsthand. Oscar Arturo Palencia wrote a strident denunciatory political poetry, reminiscent of the Saker-ti poets and Otto René Castillo.

The closest follower of Castillo's project of attempting to create a poetic mode that would unite national and personal perspectives was, however, Marco Antonio Flores. Like Castillo and Arce, he also worked in experimental theater. His work has explored themes of alienation, conquest, subjugation, and rebellion, attempting sometimes in the fashion of Asturias's "magic realism" to link a reenactment of the pre-Columbian world and its resistance to Spanish domination to the immediacy of contemporary guerrilla struggle (see, e.g., his "El guerrero Kekchí," which begins "Cuando el rito fue la razón de vivir"—when ritual was the reason for living—and ends "Esta noche los *beatles* cantan *help*"—tonight the Beatles are singing "Help"). Gradually disillusioned with the left in the late 1960s, Flores turned from poetry toward the acidic, disenchanted prose fiction represented by his novel *Los compañeros*.

Along with the writers of Nuevo Signo, these figures may be seen as transitional ones in the evolution of contemporary oppositional literature in Guatemala, anticipating the heightened relation between poetry and testimonio that would develop in the late 1970s and 1980s. We turn our attention now to this dramatic period, which embraces the rise and eventual defeat of Guatemala's third major revolutionary upsurge in the last half-century.

1978–1988

The period was initiated by the military-backed expansion of the agri-business sector into previously uncontested Indian lands in the 1970s, under the pressure of the Central American Common Market competition. As lands were appropriated and village life was threatened, the indigenous communities most affected began to develop both nonviolent and armed forms of resistance and to seek help from and alliances with existing ladino radical church and peasant organizations. These developments were countered by army pacification measures, producing an interacting spiral of Indian political mobilization on the one hand, assassinations, "disappearances," resettlements, and massacres on the other. In this context, the ladino guerrilla groups that had been suffocated in the early 1970s began to reassert themselves, slowly at first but then with increasing force and tenacity. For the first time they were able to secure the general support of at least certain of the Indian groups and to recruit extensively from them. A very rapid process of radicalization ensued.

The Committee of Campesino Unity (CUC) was formed as an organization uniting both ladino and Indian peasants and rural workers in 1978, the same year as the Panzós massacre of over one hundred Indians by the army and landowner paramilitary groups. By 1980, the confrontations had spread from the highlands throughout the country. In January of that year some forty Quiché activists involved in the protest occupation of the Spanish embassy were massacred by the police in a widely reported incident. In February–March, a huge farmworkers' strike organized by the CUC paralyzed the agro-export sector of the economy. In October, the main guerrilla organizations—Ejército Guerrillero de los Pobres (EGP), Fuerzas Armadas Rebeldes (FAR), Organización del Pueblo en Armas (ORPA), and the Partido Guatemalteco de

Trabajo (PGT)—agreed to form a unified military-political command subsequently known as the URNG (Unión Revolucionaria Nacional Guatemalteca). One of their first objectives was a campaign aimed at keeping the Guatemalan army from intervening in El Salvador against the FMLN "Final Offensive" in January 1981.

In response, a succession of generals—Lucas-García (1976–1981), Ríos Montt (1981–1983), Mejía Victores (1983–1985)—oversaw what surely must be counted as one of the most brutal and effective counterinsurgency wars of modern history, directed particularly against the indigenous peoples of the northwestern and north central highlands, the major rural base of the guerrilla movement. By the Guatemalan army's own estimates, it destroyed over four hundred villages in the *altiplano*. Some fifty thousand people were killed, and perhaps close to one million Indians—about a quarter of the total nonladino population of the country—were forcibly resettled into Vietnam War–style "strategic hamlets" or refugee camps in the south of Mexico. Civil Defense Patrols (PACs) designed to spy on and keep guerrillas out of civilian areas drafted all males between the ages of fifteen and sixty. Particularly under Ríos Montt, proselytization campaigns financed and organized by U.S. fundamentalist sects came to represent the cultural arm of the war, threatening the very basis of Indian community and belief structures. Although the guerrilla groups were able to retrench and survive, by 1983 the liberated zones they had established in the highlands once again came under military control.

By the mid-1980s, with the guerrilla threat temporarily at bay and faced with a deepening economic recession that required more direct U.S. aid, the military moved to reduce Guatemala's international isolation by providing for elections and a return to formal democratic rule. In January 1986 Vinicio Cerezo took office as the country's first democratically elected president since 1970. Cerezo promised to end human rights abuses and military violence, but it soon became clear that the military had only ceded the presidency and was determined to protect its own interests. While a semblance of democratic normality returned to the country (which included a revival of literary activity), the degree to which Guatemalans could organize and express themselves freely and openly depended on the military's own assessment of what it took (diplomacy, democracy, or force) to maintain its hegemony. In the last instance, the military made the rules, so it was never easy to know exactly what they were. Yet the price for breaking them could be terrible. After the failed coup attempt of mid-1987, it seemed that Cerezo's modest reform program was declining and that both military repression, civil disorder, and armed popular resistance were coming to the fore again.

The years of maximum revolutionary mobilization and struggle between 1978 and 1982 were characterized by three major, closely interrelated, cultural-ideological developments: (1) the emergence of Liberation Theology perspectives, and the related radicalization of traditional Mayan and Christian belief structures and practices; (2) the merging of religious, community, trade union, and political groups as they confronted problems that they increasingly saw as common, most dramatically, perhaps, in the evolution of the CUC ; (3) the appearance of new syncretic literary expressions bringing together Marxist, mythic, Christian, and Indian perspectives in varying presentational modes, including theatrical skits, poems, songs, and adaptations of both Christian and Mayan liturgies. The most important of these expressions—representing in both their form and content the process of cultural-political unification produced by the new revolutionary upsurge—are the Guatemalan testimonios of the armed struggle and Indian resistance that we discuss in chapter 7, and among these particularly Rigoberta Menchú's *Me llamo Rigoberta Menchú, y así me nació la conciencia* and Mario Payeras's *Días de la selva*.

In poetry, the dominant emphasis in these years was on a *poesía de combate* of the sort we have seen in Salvadoran literature of the same period: fairly impersonal testimonial or sloganeering "performative" texts that could be declaimed on buses or in meetings, passed out on the streets, spray-painted on walls, put to music and sung. Inevitably, the direct linkage of political and literary work invited a crackdown on writer-militants and increased censorship of cultural production in general on the part of the military regime. Foppa's murder in 1980 had a particularly chilling effect on the legal literary left represented by Nuevo Signo and the women's poetry movement (in those years, we should recall, it was not uncommon for even Christian Democrats and Social Democrats to be assassinated or "disappeared" as subversives).

Under the extremely repressive conditions of the Ríos Montt dictatorship, several writers of varying political tendencies joined together in a kind of literary popular front to keep alive a public sphere in which writing and publishing activities could be maintained. Taking on the name of Grupo Literario Editorial RIN-78, the project included many of the figures associated with Nuevo Signo and the new feminist poetry, as well as younger writers. The term RIN is said to come from a Japanese ideogram that the group's founders took to mean unity and development stemming from the toleration and fostering of diversity. Luz Méndez has pointed to the group's disavowal of the attempt to articulate any particular political ideology or cultural program of the sort represented by the previous political-literary groups we have looked at. She insists that the RIN-78's goals are simply "divulgativo-culturales," and she points with pride at the number of titles (thirty-six, including fifteen of poetry) it has been able to publish.⁹ Nevertheless, it is clear that RIN-78 very broadly is representative of the positions of at least a significant part of the Guatemalan cultural left and center-left today—in a period of retrenchment—and that much if not all of the new work we outline below owes its existence to the group's activities.

Formally the Cerezo opening meant a liberalization of literary production in Guatemala, as the new government attempted to encourage prodemocratic if not radical cultural activity. Its efforts in this direction included the sponsorship of the progressive literary journal *Tzolkin* by the Ministry of Culture and Sports, initially edited by Marco Vinicio Mejía Dávila.¹⁰ Many of the writers in exile like Otto Rául González returned, and there was (and is) again an open and extensive production of political poetry in Guatemala (although many writers and artists persist in the tactics of self-censorship and indirection inculcated during the hard years of overt dictatorship). Something like a renewed literary bohemia took shape around a working-class bar in Guatemala City, the "Cofradía de Godot," which became a meeting place for writers, artists, actors, and critics during the Cerezo years. Alongside RIN-78 a new center-left writers' group—the Comunidad Guatemalteca de Escritores—was formed in 1988, involving, among others, Francisco Morales Santos, Ana María Rodas, Max Araújo, Arturo Arias, Otto Raúl González, and Dante Liano.

But despite the renewal of literary activity under Cerezo, no figure has emerged to take the place of Castillo in the 1960s literary-political system, and in the recent work of some of the Nuevo Signo and feminist writers there has been a postpolitical note of exhaustion and metaphysical despair (e.g., Margarita Carrera's *Siglo veinte*, which came out just before the Cerezo transition). Nor is RIN-78 anything like a new literary-ideological tendency on the order of the Committed Generation or Nuevo Signo. It seems as if the frustration of the revolutionary impulse of the late 1970s and early 1980s has also meant a frustration of the movement toward new popular-democratic literary forms opened up by the dramatic political events of those years. The work of RIN-78 in this sense represents a tendency to move away from "party literature" and testimonio—even Nuevo Signo's nonsectarian exploration of the Guatemalan national-popular—toward a rearticulation of "high culture" literary experimentalism in traditional forms like the short story.

Nevertheless, some of the writers coming to maturity in the 1980s and specifically in the Cerezo years show both a continuation of the tradition of Guatemalan militant poetry and some interesting new possibilities. As a consequence of the Cerezo government's decision to reorganize *Tzolkin* under more conservative auspices after the failed coup of 1987, a new group emerged calling itself playfully "La Rial Academia" (i.e., the royal/real/rail academy), which has dedicated itself to attacking RIN-78's stance of both literary and political retrenchment, critiquing the group as, in effect, a new literary-ideological establishment. Its members include René Leiva, Juan Antonio Canel, Eduardo Villagrín, Marco Augusto Quiroa, Carlos René García Escobar, and Mejía Dávila, the editor of *Tzoltzin* replaced in 1987. Among the male Guatemalan writers who write political poetry in a Saker-ti–Generación Comprometida–Nuevo Signo vein are Armando Bedaña and Mario Payeras—both better known for their work in testimonial narrative— Arqueles Morales, Rafael Gutiérrez, and Rafael Piñeda Reyes. Among the women, Quiñónez, Ruano, and RIN-78 poets Carrera, Méndez, and Rodas have continued to work in a strongly feminist vein, together with a series of younger women who have joined or published with the group. Two important political voices to emerge are Alenka Bermúdez and Julia Esquivel.[11]

A new theme evident in the work of many of these writers is the destruction of the national ecology—making thematically and ideologically explicit something that has been latent in the tendency in Guatemala literature from Asturias on to allegorize the state of nature as a political force against the depredations of an imperialist "civilization." The most significant new development of the 1980s has been, however, the appearance of a Mayan testimonial poetry. The more formally "literary" expression of this poetry is represented by the work of one of the initial members of RIN-78, Enrique Luis Sam Colop: *Versos sin refugio* (1978) and *La copa y la raíz* (1979). Sam Colop is the only major contemporary Guatemalan poet of predominantly Quiché background, a fact that attests to both the deeply entrenched character of the split betwen ladino and indigenous cultures and the complexity of his own position on both sides of this split. He writes his poems in Spanish, claiming they are "translations" from the Quiché, but Luz Méndez has noted that it would be more accurate to speak of "a tonality which partakes of the pain for the oppression of his race Colop feels" than a Quiché poetry as such. She adds, however, that "the intent to write verse in Quiché, . . . even if the poems are initially thought in Spanish, is nevertheless worthy in its own right," given the fact that Quiché has been virtually made mute as a formal literary language since the conquest (Méndez 1986).

Sam Colop and Luis de Lión are, however, exceptions; in general, the new Mayan poetry represents versifications of testimonial experiences composed by people who are not professional writers. Together with *Me llamo Rigoberta Menchú*, the emergence of this almost anonymous poetry is probably the most striking new dimension in the Guatemalan literary system, because it addresses directly the impasse in Guatemalan literature and politics to which Balcárcel drew attention. Many such testimonial poems must exist in Indian languages outside the range of what gets registered as literature. Those that we have access to are poems written in or translated to Spanish that have been clearly encouraged and mediated by middle-sector ladina radicals and solidarity workers. As in the prose testimonio, their intention is to address a ladino and perhaps an international audience, not to create a poetry for internal consumption of the Indian communities themselves. In general, they are the products of women who, like Rigoberta Menchú, have become organic intellectuals of the Indian resistance movements. In this sense, this is not exactly a people's poetry, although that seems the best existing rubric to put it under. It does share in style, content, and form many features with Nicaraguan *poesía de taller*. Most important, its appearance represents the intrusion into the sphere of the dominant culture of a new, nonladino, woman-centered Indian intelligentsia— itself at least in part also related to the development of the Guatemalan women's movement. The figure who perhaps best represents the new testimonial Indian poetry is Caly Domitila Cane'k. A Maya Cakchikel, whose pen name may well be a literary construct alluding to the Bolivian activist of testimonio fame, Caly Domitila was working as a literacy teacher and, like Rigoberta Menchú, a lay catechist, during a time when over one hundred of her fellow workers were killed. Forced to flee from her village after her three brothers were killed and she had received a death threat, she became active as an exile in refugee and sanctuary work, and drafted an unpublished manuscript of testimonial poems based on her experiences. The examples that have appeared (Anglesey 1987: 47–51) are a narration of the atrocities against her family she was forced to witness, embellished with reflections on Mayan and Christian culture and history. While they speak of and to her own community, they also reach out in a search for solidarity. "Today only poetry tells the story / of our lives," she writes.

> Lit candles
> light new candles
> Extinguished candles
> still will light new candles
> This is struggle
> candles that light
> and fade.
>
> (Translated by R. Kereger in Partnoy 1988: 221)

With these words, Caly Domitila speaks to the uses of literature in passing along the possibilities of liberation struggle even in conditions of frustration and defeat, even as old literary formulas are replaced by new ones. The question for the future is whether Guatemala can move again from the struggles of particular sectors, groups, and communities to that of a people sufficiently united to appropiate its own history, to move from individual protest and testimonio to the totalizing popular epic narrative of a succesful transformation of social life. As we have seen, that possibility will depend to an important degree on what is happening now in the ideological laboratory of Guatemalan literature.

Notes

1. Angel Rama (1982) has most prominently suggested "transculturation" as a model for Latin American literature in equation with a left-oriented moderni-zation process.

2. See, for example, the theses of the EGP, "The Indian People and the Guatemalan Revolution," in Fried et al. (1983: 278–284). Carol Smith (1987) gives what we regard as a well-balanced summary and of the class/ethnicity discussion in Guatemala. Arias (in Camacho and Menjívar 1985: 118) agrees that the indigenous population has become crucial to the future of the revolutionary movement, but warns that an overemphasis on ethnic identity and separatism— representing the interests of rich and middle Indian producers and encouraged by anthropologists and by agencies and programs linked in the last instance to U.S. counterinsurgency policy—may constitute also a danger to the revolutionary movement, as in the case of the CIA's manipulation of the Misquito autonomy movement in Nicaragua. Smith, on the other hand, notes that "if Marxism is to become truly the theory of liberation in Latin America it must break free of the dogmatism that reduces age-old cultures of resistance and ethnic identity to mere epiphenomena [of] objectivized class categories" (p. 217).

The literature on the "Indian question" includes Richard Adams's *La ladinización en Guatemala;* Humberto Flores Alvarado's critique, *El adamscismo y la sociedad guatemalteca;* Ciro F. S. Cardoso, "Severo Martínez Peláez y el carácter del régimen colonial," in ESC 1; Arias's critique of the CP position in *Ideologías, literatura y sociedad durante la revolución guatemalteca;* and Carlos Guzmán Böckler's *Guatemala: una interpretación histórico-social, Colonialismo y revolución,* especially pp. 256–257, and *Donde enmudecen las conciencias: crepúsculo y aurora en Guatemala.*

3. Perhaps his best known work, though, is *El señor presidente,* written in the 1930s in the experimental *estridentista* style popular in those years, but not published until 1946 after Ubico's fall. Dealing with life under a dictatorship modeled on both Estrada Cabrera and Ubico, the novel begins in the ladino/urban ambience of a capital city apparently surrounded by barbarism: the jungle and Indian tribes (a classic dichotomy of Latin American Liberal narrative). Gradually, as the story progresses, the Indian world comes to the fore and reveals the real barbarism to be the closed and perverted world of the dictator, built precisely on the fear and repression of the Indian and nature.

4. The Grupo Acento poets all continued to write after the 1954 coup, but representative of their work specifically in the context of the October Revolution process are Leiva's *Cuatro danzas para Cuauhtémoc* (1955); Juárez's *Pueblo y poesía* (1944) and *Dianas para la vida* (1956); and González's *Voz y voto del geranio* (1943), *A fuego lento* (1946), *Sombras era* (1948), *Viento claro* (1953), and *El maíz y la noche* (1959).

5. Alvarado (1967) is perhaps the definitive work on the group. See also his *Por un arte nacional* (1953) and the collection of statements by Saker-ti writers he edited, *El artista y los problemas de nuestro tiempo* (1947). Not everyone in the current generation of Guatemalan left intellectuals has a positive view of the group, however. Julio Fausto Aguilera and other writers associated with Nuevo Signo (see below) have complained about the sectarian leftism of its program. At an opposite extreme, Arias (1979) sees Saker-ti as bound up with the October Revolution's own petit bourgeois reformism.

6. It begins: "One day / the apolitical / intellectuals / of my country / will be interrogated / by the ordinary / men and women / of our people."

7. For an introduction to and representative anthology of Nuevo Signo poetry, see *Poetas de Guatemala / Poeti di Guatemala*, edited by Dante Liano.

8. For a representative selection of recent Guatemalan women's poetry, in English, see Anglesey (1987: 35–143) and Partnoy (1988: 180–235). Our account of it here is based in part on the research of Andrea Barrientos at the University of Illinois at Chicago.

9. See the introduction to her anthology *La poesía del Grupo RIN-78* (Méndez 1986). RIN-78's titles include a reissue of poetry by Julio Fausto Aguilera and new poetry collections by Max Araújo, Amable Sánchez Torres, Hugo Estrada, Ana María Riccica, Ligia Escriba, María Belém, Ana María Rodas, Luz Méndez, Carmen Matute, and the Quiché poet Luis Sam Colop, whom we discuss below.

10. Our remarks on poetry during the Cerezo period owe a great deal to the unpublished research of Rául Rojas at the University of Illinois at Chicago.

11. A Chilean by birth, Bermúdez married a Guatemalan and has taken on a strong Guatemalan identification in the diction as well as the content of her poetry. (She lost one of her children in the armed struggle.) Working in exile in Nicaragua, she has published a small number of militant poems on the necessity and difficulties of armed struggle. Coming from a strong religious background, Esquivel has served as director of the Evangelical Institute of Latin America. She published three volumes of poetry during the 1980s, very much bound up with Liberation Theology perspectives and activism.

7. Testimonial Narrative

Barbara Harlow has drawn attention to the ways in which the social transformations produced by national liberation struggles also transform the narrative paradigms that reconstruct these struggles as stories of individual and collective change. "While poetry and the poems of organized resistance movements struggle to preserve and even to redefine for the given historical moment the cultural images which underwrite collective action, military as well as ideological," she writes, ". . . narrative by contrast analyzes the past, including the symbolic heritage, in order to open up possibilities for the future" (Harlow 1987: 82). One of these new paradigms that has become perhaps the dominant contemporary form of narrative in Central America, displacing or transforming both lyric poetry and the novel and story, is the *testimonio*—testimonial narrative. In previous chapters, we have spoken of the influence of the testimonial impulse on Central American political poetry. Here in our final chapter we turn our attention to a consideration of the testimonio as such. The Nicaraguan critic Ileana Rodríguez has argued that Central American testimonial literature is an important component of the study of popular insurgency in the region. She points to its value in revealing the "hidden secrets of popular tradition in relation to questions of resistance," providing access to situations and forms of thought unknown or poorly understood by officially sanctioned culture. In her view, testimonio is not only a form of representation of popular ideologies and cultural forms; it is also a means of popular-democratic cultural practice, closely bound up with the same motivations that produce insurgency at the economic and political levels (Rodríguez 1982: 85–96).

We follow Rodríguez in seeing the origins and evolution of testimonio in Central America as a cultural aspect of the overall struggle for hegemony, linked to the impulse to displace or overthrow both elites and elite cultural modes (including those represented by dominant models in literature) in favor of a more informal and popularly inflected culture.

Inevitably we are led to the assumption that there is a relation between the crystallization of testimonio as a narrative genre and the crisis and corresponding revolutionary upsurge of the 1970s in Central America.

The Nature of Testimonio

What exactly is a testimonio? The general form of the testimonio is a novel or novella-length narrative, told in the first-person by a narrator who is also the actual protagonist or witness of the events she or he recounts. The unit of narration is usually a life or a significant life episode (e.g., the experience of being a prisoner). Since in many cases the narrator is someone who is either functionally illiterate or, if literate, not a professional writer or intellectual, the production of a testimonio generally involves the recording and/or transcription and editing of an oral account by an interlocutor who is a journalist, writer, or social activist.

The word suggests the act of testifying or bearing witness in a legal or religious sense. That connotation is important, because it distinguishes testimonio from simple recorded participant narrative. In René Jara's phrase, testimonio is a "narración de urgencia"—a story that *needs* to be told—involving a problem of repression, poverty, subalternity, exploitation, or simply struggle for survival, which is implicated in the act of narration itself (Vidal and Jara 1986: 3).

For practical purposes, Latin American testimonio coalesces as a clearly defined genre around the decision in 1970 of Cuba's cultural center, Casa de las Américas, to begin awarding a prize in this category in their annual literary contest. But its roots go back to a tradition in previous Latin American literature of nonfictional narrative texts like the colonial *crónicas*, the *costumbrista* essay (*Facundo, Os sertões*), the *diarios de campaña* of, for example, Bolívar or Martí, or the romantic biography—an important genre of Latin American liberalism. This tradition combined with the popularity in the early 1960s of two diffrent kinds of participant narrative texts: the anthropological or sociological life history composed from tape-recorded oral accounts developed by academic social scientists like Oscar Lewis or Ricardo Pozas; and Che Guevara's *Reminiscences of the Cuban Revolutionary War* (*Episodios de la guerra revolucionaria cubana*), whose reception, along with its corresponding manual, *Guerrilla Warfare*, was related to the general impact of the Cuban Revolution in the Americas.

On the model of Che's *Episodios*, a series of direct-participant accounts by combatants in the 26 of July Movement and later in the campaigns against the counterrevolutionary bands in the Escambray mountains and at the Bay of Pigs began to appear in Cuba around the mid-

1960s. The extension of the theory and practice of the guerrilla *foco* lent such accounts a new prestige and urgency. Testimonios centered on participation in guerrilla activity proliferated all over Latin America, in part as a form of propaganda for armed struggle directed toward a progressive general public, in part as a kind of cadre literature internal to the revolutionary organizations themselves.

The first-person narrative form and situation of the testimonio suggest an affinity with the picaresque novel, which was one of the major narrative forms associated with the early stages of Creole liberalism in Mexico and Central America (e.g., *El periquillo sarniento*). But testimonio, even where it approximates in content a kind of neopicaresque, is a very different narrative mode. First, it is not fiction. We are meant to experience both the speaker and the situations and events recounted as real. Second, testimonio is not so much concerned with the life of a "problematic hero," to recall Georg Lukács's characterization of the hero of the novel, as with a problematic collective social situation that the narrator lives with or alongside others. The situation of the narrator in testimonio has to be representative of a social class or group; in the picaresque novel, by contrast, a collective social predicament like unemployment or marginalization is experienced and narrated as a personal destiny. The "I" that speaks to us in the novel is precisely the mark of a difference or antagonism with the community, the subject-form of the self-made man. The narrator in testimonio on the other hand speaks for or in the name of a community or group, approximating in this way the symbolic function of the epic hero, without at the same time assuming his hierarchical and patriarchal status. Another way of putting this would be to define testimonio as a nonfictional, popular-democratic form of epic narrative.

A sense of this aspect of the testimonial voice may be gotten from the opening words of one of the greatest Central American testimonios, which we will discuss in greater detail below, *Me llamo Rigoberta Menchú*:

> My name is Rigoberta Menchú. I am twenty three years old. This is my testimony. I didn't learn it from a book and I didn't learn it alone. I'd like to stress that it's not only my life, it's also the testimony of my people. It's hard for me to remember everything that's happened to me in my life since there have been many bad times but, yes, moments of joy as well. The important thing is that what has happened to me has happened to many other people also: My story is the story of all poor Guatemalans. My personal experience is the reality of a whole people. (Menchú 1984: 1)

Rigoberta Menchú was and is an activist on behalf of her community, so this statement is perhaps more explicit than is usual in a testimonio. But the symbolic function of the testimonial voice she invokes here—its power to stand in for the experience of the community as a whole—is something that is implicit in the form, that is part of its narrative convention. Unlike traditional epic or mythic narration, which depends on the hero's having a higher status than the reader or listener, testimonio is a fundamentally democratic and egalitarian form of narrative in the sense that it implies that *any* life so narrated can have a kind of representativity. Each testimonio evokes an absent polyphony of other voices, other possible lives and experiences. Thus, one common formal variation on the classic first-person-singular testimonio is the polyphonic testimonio made up of accounts by different participants in the same event.

What testimonio does have in common with the picaresque and with autobiography, however, is the powerful textual affirmation of the speaking subject itself. As the passage from *Rigoberta Menchú* suggests, the form's dominant characteristic is that voice which speaks to the reader in the form of an "I" that demands to be recognized, that wants or needs to stake a claim on our attention. This presence of the voice, which we are meant to experience as the voice of a real rather than fictional person, is the mark of a desire not to be silenced or defeated, to impose oneself on an institution of power like literature from the position of the excluded or the marginal. Even though testimonio points to the importance of collectivity, it also insists on the integrity and importance of the individual subject in the face of dehumanizing experiences.

As, generally, a textual representation of actual speech, testimonio implies a challenge to the loss of the authority of orality in the context of processes of cultural modernization that privilege literacy and literature as a norm of expression. It represents the entry into literature of persons who would normally—in those societies where literature is a form of class and/or ethnic privilege—be excluded from direct literary expression, who have had to be represented by professional writers. There is an important difference between having someone like Rigoberta Menchú tell the story of her people and having it told, however well, by Miguel Angel Asturias.

Testimonio involves an erasure or attenuation of the role and thus also of the textual presence of the author, which by contrast is so powerfully present in all major forms of European writing since the Renaissance, so much so that our very notions of literature and the literary are bound up with notions of the author or at least of an authorial intention. In Miguel

Barnet's phrase, the author has been replaced in testimonio by the function of a "compiler" (*compilador*) or "activator" (*gestante*), somewhat on the model of the film producer.[1] Even where there is not an interlocutor and the narrator speaks or writes for him- or herself, the intention is not to achieve the magisterial or omniscient point of view of an author. Implicit in this situation is both a challenge and an alternative to the patriarchal and elitist character of literature in class and sexually and racially divided societies such as those of Central America. It signals, in particular, returning to our theme of the relation between testimonio and popular-democratic mobilization, a shift away from the figure of the "great writer" as culture hero, which was so much a part of the Liberal ideology of Latin American writing from romanticism through the boom.

The erasure of authorial presence in testimonio allows a kind of complicity between narrator and reader different from what is possible in the novel or story, whose fictional character and degree of aesthetic elaboration require a distancing on the part of both novelist and reader from the fate of the protagonist. But just as testimonio implies a new kind of relation between narrator and reader, the contradictions of sex, class, race, and age that frame the narrative's production can also reproduce themselves in the relation of the narrator to this direct interlocutor. This is especially the case when, as in *Rigoberta Menchú*, the narrator is someone who requires an interlocutor with a different ethnic and/or class background in order first to elicit the oral account, then give it textual form as a testimonio, then see to its publication and distribution.[2]

These are important contradictions, which have to do with testimonio's location at the center of the dialectic of oppressor and oppressed in the postcolonial world. Among other things, they represent the possibility for a reactionary or folkloric—*costumbrista*—articulation of the testimonio, or for the manipulation of a genuine popular voice by well-intentioned but repressive notions of political correctness or pertinence.

The relation of narrator and compiler in the production of a testimonio represented by Burgos-Debray and Menchú can also serve, however, as a powerful ideological figure or symbol of the union of a radicalized intelligentsia with the poor and working masses of a country, which has been so decisive in the development of movements for social change in the Third World. Testimonio gives voice in literature to a previously voiceless and anonymous collective popular subject, the *pueblo*, but in such a way that the intellectual or professional, usually of bourgeois or petit bourgeois origin, is interpellated as being part of, and dependent on, this collective subject without at the same time losing his or her identity as an intellectual. Politically, the question in testimonio is not so much the *difference* of the social situations of the direct narrator and the interlocutor as the possibility of their articulation together in a common program or front.[3] In the creation of the testimonial text, control of representation does not just flow one way: someone like Rigoberta Menchú is also in a sense manipulating and exploiting her interlocutor in order to have her story reach an international audience, something which, as a political activist, she sees in quite utilitarian terms.

Testimonio is not, in other words, a reenactment of the function of the colonial or neocolonial "native informant," nor a form of liberal guilt. It suggests as an appropriate ethical and political response the possibility more of solidarity than of charity. Generally speaking, the audience for testimonio, either in the immediate national or regional context or in metropolitan cultural centers, is that reading public which is still a partially class-limited social formation. The complicity a testimonio establishes with this public involves the possibility of its identification with a popular cause normally distant, not to say alien, from its immediate experience. Testimonio in this sense has been extremely important in linking rural and urban contexts of struggle within a given country, and in maintaining and developing the practice of international human rights and solidarity movements in relation to particular struggles. (Rigoberta Menchú now spends much of her time speaking to audiences in the United States and Europe.)

The sense of presence of a real, popular voice in the testimonio is, of course, in part illusory. As in any discursive medium, we are dealing with an effect that has been produced both by the direct narrator who uses devices of an oral storytelling tradition and the compiler who, according to norms of literary form and expression, makes a text out of the material. While it would be easy to deconstruct this illusion of presence, it is also necessary to insist on it to understand the testimonio's peculiar aesthetic-ideological power. Because it is the discourse of a witness who is not a fictional construct, testimonio in some sense or another speaks directly to us, as an actual person might. To subsume testimonio under the category of literary fictionality is to deprive it of its power to engage the reader in the ways indicated, to make of it simply another form of literature.[4] The more interesting question—we will come back to it presently—is how testimonio radically puts into question the existing institution of literature itself as a form of class, gender, and ethnic violence.

Because the authorial function has been mitigated or erased in the testimonio, so has the relationship between authorship and forms of individual and hierarchical power. Testimonio cannot affirm a self-identity that is separate from a group or class situation marked by marginalization, oppression, and struggle. If it does this, it ceases to be testimonio and becomes in effect autobiography, that is, an account of, and also a means of access to, middle- or upper-class status, a sort of documentary Horatio Alger story. (If Rigoberta Menchú had become a writer living in Guatemala City—or Paris—instead of remaining as she has a member of and an activist for her ethnic community, her narration would have been an autobiography.) Even where its subject is a person "of the left," as in, for example, Tomás Borge's memoirs (which we describe below), autobiography is an essentially conservative mode in the sense that it implies that individual triumph over circumstances is possible. Autobiography produces in the reader, who in most Latin American contexts is already either middle or upper class or looking to be, the specular effect of confirming and authorizing his and (less so) her situation of relative social privilege. Testimonio, by contrast, always signifies the need for a general social change in which the stability and complacency of the reader's world must be brought into question.

If the novel and the short story are closed and private narrative forms in the sense that both the story and the subject end with the end of the text, defining that autoreferential self-sufficiency that is the basis of formalist reading practices, in testimonio the distinction between public and private spheres of life has been transgressed. The narrator in testimonio is a real person who continues living and acting in a real social history that also continues. Testimonio implies the importance and power of literature as a form of social action, but also its radical insufficiency. To produce testimonios, for the form to have become more and more popular in recent years, means that there are experiences in the world today that cannot be adequately expressed in forms like the novel, the short story, lyric poetry, or autobiography, in other words, which would be betrayed or misrepresented by literature as we know it.

In principle, testimonio appears therefore as an extraliterary or even antiliterary form of discourse. As we have noted, in Latin America it has represented both a rejection of and an alternative to the sophisticated boom narrative identified with Borges, Carpentier, Donoso, García Márquez, Vargas Llosa, Fuentes, and Cortázar. But testimonio has also been incorporated to some extent within this narrative. In the literature we discuss below we will encounter for example: (1) fictional novels that are pseudotestimonios (Manlio Argueta's *Un día en la vida* and *Cuzcatlán*); (2) the incorporation of testimonial voices in complex boom-style narrative structures (Sergio Ramírez's *¿Te dió miedo la sangre?*); (3) texts that fall somewhere between the authorial novel and/ or autobiography and testimonio as such, like Claribel Alegría's *Luisa in Realityland*, Roque Dalton's *Pobrecito poeta que era yo*, or the recent first volume of Tomás Borge's memoirs, *La paciente impaciencia*.

What happens, however, when testimonio is appropriated by or becomes itself literature? Does this involve a neutralization or attenuation of its peculiar aesthetic effect, which depends on its status outside sanctioned literary forms and norms? As we will see in the case of Nicaragua, this becomes an issue particularly in a postrevolutionary period where the situation of urgency, activism, and collective enthusiasm that informs the testimonio has abated. But if the testimonio comes into being necessarily at the margin of the historically given institution of literature as a sort of antiliterature, it is also clearly in the process of becoming a new, postfictional form of literature, with significant cultural and ideological repercussions as such. It functions in a zone of indeterminacy between these two positions.

Nicaraguan Testimonio

Testimonio begins to flourish in Central America only in the course of the revolutionary process itself, and then to an extent in the 1960s as a Cuban import, through the contacts of Carlos Fonseca, Roque Dalton, and other Central American writers and journalists with Casa de las Américas and the younger Cuban writers. Perhaps the most important link was the North American socialist-feminist writer Margaret Randall, who played a major role in developing the form in Cuba in the 1970s and worked in Nicaragua under the auspices of Cardenal's Ministry of Culture between 1979 and 1985.[5]

Nevertheless, a fairly explicit testimonial tendency has existed in Central American literature, at least since the great insurgencies of the early 1930s, which the Cuban influence could be grafted onto, especially in the tradition of social realist and anti-imperialist novels like Hernán Robleto's *Sangre en el trópico* (1930) in Nicaragua, Luis Carlos Fallas's *Mamita Yunai* (1941) in Costa Rica, or Miguel Angel Asturias's *El señor presidente*.[6] In Nicaragua, a sort of proto-testimonio exists before the emergence of the genre as such. The most important example is *Maldito país* by a writer associated with the vanguardists, José Román.

Maldito país owes its origins to the short-lived alliance between the vanguardists and Sandino. Hoping to publicize his cause, Sandino invited Román, then working as a journalist, to interview him at length between February 25 and March 29, 1933. *Maldito país* is essentially the record of these conversations.[7] The book presents Sandino talking about his life and movement, framed by Román's descriptions of the mountains and jungle of the Segovias region where Sandino had his base. It relives in Sandino's own colloquial voice his childhood experiences, his struggles with his father, his exile in Mexico (and the great influence the Mexican Revolution had on him), the origins and evolution of his campaign against U.S. occupation, his hopes for Nicaragua.

Maldito país is not so much a testimonio as a journalistic interview with a strong testimonial component in the sections based on Sandino's own narrative. Hodges (1986) uses it as a source for his study of Sandino's ideology, and the book has played a role in current debates over the meaning of Sandino's legacy (it can be read as a vindication of a non- or anti-Marxist Sandino—see note 7 above). But how much of the vanguardists' literary and political bias is present in the construction of Sandino it offers, which anticipates the romanticized image of Sandino in Cardenal's *Hora 0*? We will see, however, that Nicaraguan testimonio in general has been closer to poetry and therefore more marked by a mixture of literary and direct narrative elements than its Salvadoran and Guatemalan counterparts.

Though it remained unpublished, *Maldito país* marked not only a critical conjuncture in Nicaragua's modern history—Sandino and Somoza's counterrevolution—but also a major change in its literary system, which until the 1930s had been centered on highly refined and elitist forms of poetry. As we have seen, the transition between Darío and the vanguardists was already a step in the direction of the prosification and historicization of poetry, with figures like Pablo Antonio Cuadra and Coronel Urtecho trying their hand at both journalism and fiction. After the 1930s, prose fiction would begin to occupy a more central place. Even before *Maldito país*, there existed a tradition of fictionalized history centered on the U.S. intervention and Nicaraguan resistance to it: Hernán Robleto's *Sangre en el trópico* (subtitled *novela de la intervención yanqui*) and Pedro Joaquín Chamorro Zelaya's *El último filibustero* (1933) on William Walker are early examples more or less contemporary with the concerns of the vanguardists in poetry. This tradition extends through Robleto's later *Los estrangulados* (1933), Adolfo Calero Orozco's *Sangre santa* (1940), José Román's novel of Nicaraguan rural life, *Cosmapa* (1944), and the emerging work in the 1950s and 1960s of Juan Aburto, Fernando Silva, Fernando Gordillo, Mario Cajina Vega, Lizandro Chávez Alfaro, Sergio Ramírez, and Rosario Aguilar—writers who were more or less the generational contemporaries of Fonseca and the early Sandinistas.

Two writers deserve special mention in this trajectory: Manolo Cuadra, originally a member of the vanguardists, and Emilio Quintana, author of one of the classic works of Central American social realism, *Bananos*. Cuadra had been an infantryman in the campaigns against Sandino launched by the government in 1932. The experience converted him to an admirer of Sandino, and he used it to write a collection of short stories, *Contra Sandino en las montañas*, which became one of the key literary documents of the Sandino legend (it will remind readers of Soviet literature of Isaac Babel's stories of the Russian Revolution).

Cuadra followed *Contra Sandino* in 1944 with *Almidón*, a "grotesque" (his own description) novel written in diary form satirizing the society and institutions created by Somocismo again from the point of view of a witness and participant. But the work of Cuadra that most clearly anticipates testimonio (and that is generally considered his most successful book) comes between these two works of fiction; it is the "prison notebook" of his experiences as a political prisoner on an island off the Atlantic coast, *Itinerario de Little Corn Island*, published in 1937.[8]

Cuadra wrote the preface to the original edition of Quintana's *Bananos*, which appeared in the early 1950s with the descriptive subtitle *La vida de los peones en las bananeras*. *Bananos* is a short, semiautobiographical book written in a spare, sometimes brutally direct style. It consists of twelve scenes or *cuadros de costumbres*, to use the Spanish term, based on the author's own experiences as—like many poor Nicaraguans—an immigrant worker in the Costa Rican plantations of the United Fruit Company. Because Quintana wrote from the point of view of an ordinary worker, Cuadra saw *Bananos* as inaugurating a specifically proletarian literature in Nicaragua: "estamos convencidos de que este libro será el primer estímulo a una literatura social sistemática, desnuda, a muerte. Y que los trabajadores americanos lo recibirán como cosa propia" (we are convinced that this book will be the first stimulus to a direct, uncompromising, systematic social literature. And that American workers will receive it as something of their own) (quoted in Osses 1986: 73).[9]

A bridge between the proto-testimonio of Cuadra and Quintana's generation and the young Sandinistas who appear in the late 1950s is Fonseca's diary of his trip to the Soviet Union, *Un nicaragüense en Moscú*, and his arrangement of the "Carta-testamento" of Rigoberto López Pérez, both of which we described in chapter 2. We have also already noted the ties between Cardenal's exteriorism and the testimonial impulse, in particular in the production of the Solentiname and postrevolutionary poetry workshops, which represents in effect the application of the formula of narrative testimonio to poetry. The tradition of prison testimonio begun by Cuadra would be resumed in the 1950s in Edwin Castro's influential prison poems—like the "Carta-testamento," a product of the Somoza *ajusticiamiento*—and in the 1960s and 1970s in the prison poetry and memoirs of Sandinista cadre like Ricardo Morales-Avilés, Daniel Ortega, Doris Tijerino, Tomás Borge, and Carlos Guadamuz. In the novel, Lizandro Chávez Alfaro and Sergio Ramírez were especially effective in recuperating and revising the Sandino legend for their own generation.

In general the Central American novelists of the 1960s saw the boom as their literary model, rather than the previous tradition of documentary realism represented by Cuadra. Chávez's *Trágame tierra*, which appeared in 1969 at a moment when the FSLN had experienced a series of political and military setbacks and needed to reorient itself ideologically, was the first explicitly Sandinista novel. Written in the polyphonic style of boom narrative, it tells the story of a father and son, Plutarco and Luciano Pineda. Plutarco, born at the end of nineteenth century, represents the failure of the Liberal-Conservative project of national development: he still dreams of a canal through Nicaragua, which will someday make him wealthy (he owns a small estate along the projected route). Luciano, born in the 1930s, rejects his father's illusions, joins the anti-Somocista opposition as it develops in the early 1960s, and is arrested and killed in Managua's infamous Aviación prison. Intersecting with the Pinedas and symbolizing the bourgeoisie allied with the Somoza regime is a second family, the Barrantes, one of whose members becomes an officer in the Guardia. The domestic histories of these two families move backward and foward in time and across different points in the political geography of the country to profile key episodes in Nicaragua's modern history from the downfall of the Zelaya government and the beginnings of U.S. intervention to the emergence of the first *focos* of armed resistance to the dictatorship in the years 1959–1962. Chávez's point is to show the meaning of Sandinismo as deeply lodged in the Nicaraguan national-popular, a sort of centralizing motif among crisscrossing ideological currents that define this history.

But it was Ramírez's *¿Te dió miedo la sangre?* (1983b) that more directly engaged the possibility of testimonio. The novel is an attempt to reconstruct the Nicaragua of the early years of the Somoza dictatorship, which places it in relation to Miguel Angel Asturias's much earlier *El señor presidente* and what has come to be known as the Novel of the Dictator in boom fiction (e.g., Augusto Roa Bastos's *Yo El Supremo*; Alejo Carpentier's *El discurso del método*; Gabriel García Márquez's *El otoño del patriarca*; and Tomás Eloy Martínez's *La novela de Perón*). But Ramírez was also revising this model by refusing to center the narrative introspectively on the figure of the dictator himself and his immediate circles of power. Somoza appears in the novel only as refracted through a complex polyphonic structure of six interlapping stories, which are narrated orally in the first-person as the dreams, monologues, flashbacks, and memories of the characters who make them up. The stories range in time from the 1920s to the resurgence of guerrilla activity in 1958–1959, and are meant to represent the collective consciousness and experience of the Nicaraguan popular sectors. The effect—which because of the number of characters is often quite hard to follow—is as if these sectors were narrating themselves directly, instead of having their experiences "told" by an author. (Not incidentally, one of the major characters is a singer of *corridos* and ballads with a popular trio: Ramírez believes the popular taste for Mexican music was a key form of cultural resistance in Nicaragua during the Somoza period.)

As Barbara Harlow has suggested, Ramírez actualizes in this deliberately decentered quasi-testimonial form of narration the separation and antagonism between a monological narrative voice (of the dictator, of the "author") and the multivoiced, predominantly oral culture of the popular sectors. She notes that the novel exposes the failure of the Somoza regime, as a sealed-off interest group or class fraction, to maintain control over the population, represented by the narrators of the stories. "The authoritarian discourse of the regime is thus revealed as already subverted from within the social order and the disarray of the novel's plots and narrative lines is determined by that very social disorder of Nicaraguan society and the confusion of its members in the decades just preceding organized resistance" (1987: 93–94).

Sandinista Testimonio

Trágame tierra and *¿Te dió miedo la sangre?* incorporate features of the testimonio, but they are both more and less than testimonios proper, still very much products of middle- or upper-class professional authors working at the edge of but still within the high culture mode of the boom novel. The pioneer work of Nicaraguan testimonio as such is probably *Y... "Las casas quedaron llenas de humo,"* by Carlos José Guadamuz, today a Sandinista radio broadcaster. Written in 1970 while Guadamuz was in prison, with a preface from fellow prisoner Daniel Ortega, *Y... "Las casas"* is an inside account of the evolution of the FSLN from its founding in 1961 to what was perhaps the climactic moment of the FSLN's initial *foquista* strategy, the shootout in a Managua suburb between Julio Buitrago and the National Guard on July 15, 1969 (the title comes from Rugama's famous poem on the incident).

Y... "Las casas" portrays the recruitment, training, disputes, travels, actions, and evolution of a number of early FSLN cadre who appear in the text under pseudonyms. Above all, Guadamuz is concerned to reconstruct the figure of Buitrago from memory and suggest the tremendous impact his life and death had on other Sandinistas. Although he mixes his own experiences into the account, it is more a testimonial biography than a testimonio proper, in the sense of a narrative of direct personal experience.

The Frente decided the text should be smuggled out of prison, edited, and published. The preparation of the text was done by another of the Ortega brothers, Camilo (later killed in combat), who was responsible for dividing it into fragmentary chapters introduced by year-by-year historical overviews. Like much Sandinista literature of the insurrectionary period, the initial editions of *Y. . . "Las casas"* were produced in mimeo and hand-distributed (Omar Cabezas was apparently involved in the preparation of the text).[10] Subsequently, it was used in propaganda work with potential recruits and in Sandinista study groups. It was apparently quite popular among women because of the strong portraits of Frente heroines it contained.

One of the Frente cadre portrayed in *Y. . . "Las casas"* was Doris Tijerino who was with Buitrago during the 1969 shootout and subsequently passed through a long period of tortures and imprisonment. Her own testimonio, prepared with Margaret Randall, is *"Somos millones . . .": La vida de Doris María, combatiente nicaragüense* (1977). Again the title stems from Sandinista poetic tradition, in this case from a poem by Tijerino's *compañero*, Ricardo Morales-Avilés. *"Somos milliones"* covers much the same ground as Guadamuz's volume, but represents a more highly elaborated use of the testimonial form. The book plots a movement from the narrator's intimate family history—it features a particularly rich evocation of her childhood years in Matagalpa—to her growing commitment and identification with the national struggle represented by the Frente, which involves a crisis and redefinition of her sense of self. In Barbara Harlow's description, Tijerino

> . . . begins with a recounting of significant moments in her personal development: her "first act of conspiracy," when as a child she smuggled a gun out of town, her "first steps as a militant," or the "first time the guard beat (her)." Soon, however, in the course of the narrative the significant moments become those of the FSLN itself: "the first street demonstrations of the popular liberation movement," on 23 July 1959, and in 1963 the "first 'expropriation' in a Bank of America branch." (1987: 189–190)

In the concluding section, which is built around a litany of names of guerrillas killed in the course of the struggle, Tijerino's personal history has become completely subsumed in the collective project of the Frente, and the form of the narrative shifts to something like a movement report assessing the strategic situation of the FSLN in 1975. The pluralization of the narrative "I," which deepens as the text progresses, is reflected in the paradoxical title, which suggests on the one hand autobiography (*la vida de*) and on the other a collective, transindividual narrative (*somos millones*).

The next important Sandinista testimonio is Tomás Borge's *Carlos, el amanecer ya no es una tentación*, written in prison by Borge after learning of Fonseca's death in combat in 1976. (Borge's evocative title was to become itself a theme for poems, songs, and speeches about

Fonseca.) The text centers on the impact on Borge's consciousness of this news. It tells of Borge's own relations with Fonseca—their childhood together in Matagalpa, their collaboration as PSN militants in the late 1950s, the founding of the Frente, its early actions and setbacks including the defeat in Pancasán in 1967, the long period of reorganization and recovery in the early 1970s—narrated in a series of short passages, vignettes, and flashbacks strung together around a chronological succession of dated sections.

The effect of this form is to suggest the activity of a mind wounded and traumatized, seeking to provide an image of hope in the midst of failure and despair. Although Borge disclaims any special competence as a writer, *Carlos* is marked by his own deep admiration for and involvement with boom writing, particularly the work of García Márquez and Cortázar. (He notes in his introduction, "The writer of these lines is as much an author as García Márquez is a refrigerator salesman. These lines, though, have a different merit: they were written almost entirely in prison, possessed by the god of fury and the devil of tenderness," Borge 1984: 11.) This makes it a hybrid text, part testimonio, part what Margaret Randall calls in her translation a "long biographical prose poem."

Whether pure testimonio or not, *Carlos* and Borge's prestige were important factors in establishing participant narratives by Frente cadre members as a key postrevolutionary literary form. One of these is the book that perhaps more than any other has come to symbolize the Nicaraguan Revolution, *La montaña es algo más que una inmensa estepa verde* by FSLN comandante Omar Cabezas, which won the Casa de las Américas prize for testimonio in 1982.[11]

Like Doris Tijerino's testimonio, *La montaña* loosely follows the model of the first-person *bildungsroman* or coming of age novel; it deals basically with the initiation of a young, middle-class college student into the guerrilla. But this process is also represented as an initiation into Nicaragua itself, into a new sense of the national-popular. The "mountain" that is the space in which the guerrilla *foco* operates is also nature, the Nicaraguan countryside, the peasantry, the historical memory of Sandino, and the tradition of rural struggle that the Frente sought to reactivate.

Cabezas generated the text by tape-recording himself speaking aloud, and then editing a typed transcription. The resulting casual, direct quality of the narration differentiates it from, for example, Guadamuz's and Borge's testimonios and constitutes part of its national-popular character. Coronel Urtecho has argued that Cabezas's oral monologue is "the form of narrating of the Nicaraguan people." *La montaña* "is written in pure Nicaraguan, in the language we all speak," representing as such a new dimension of Nicaraguan literature. The text as a speech-act is the linguistic equivalent of the revolution itself, "the literary birth of a revolutionary Nicaraguan language . . . made of word-things, word-objects, word sensations, word-ideas, word-acts" (Coronel Urtecho 1982: 27).

Juan Duchesne (in Vidal and Jara 1986: 85–137) has also stressed this relationship between (oral-testimonial) style and content (revolutionary apprenticeship) in *La montaña*. Cabezas begins in adolescence describing his experiences as a political organizer in the university (Cabezas was from León). Even as he goes to the mountain to join the guerrilla, the focus of his narrative is still individualistic, petit bourgeois. What gives the book its full life is that the process of birth/maturation to a new collective national and personal identity through the "mountain" experience is replicated in the process of telling the story as the protagonist/narrator finds ways to represent this experience through the spoken word, recuperating possibilities of expression lost or damaged since colonial times.

Cabezas published a sequel to *La montaña* continuing the story of his involvement in the FSLN guerrilla up to the 1979 victory and its immediate aftermath: *Canción de amor para los hombres* (1988). Like *La montaña* it is a book full of anecdotes and details of life in the guerrilla told with considerable verve. But it is interesting to note how the same subject matter and technique of narration produce a very different effect a decade away from the events narrated. What gave *La montaña* its freshness and immediacy was the connection of its stylistic and formal testimonial features with the images of Sandinista insurgency itself, still vivid in the early 1980s. In *Canción*, these same features can at times seem self-conscious, as if Cabezas were parodying himself or striving to reify what had been a direct and spontaneous form of storytelling into a new literary manner (we understand that he wrote instead of spoke the initial narrative material this time).

Canción is connected to the recent development in Nicaraguan literature of what we might call "neo"-testimonio—that is, texts based on testimonial materials, but very much controlled and worked up by an author with explicitly literary goals. Some important examples of this are Chuncho Blandón's *Cuartel general* (1988), Charlotte Baltadono's *No se rompía el silencio* (1988), and Sergio Ramírez's *La marca del Zorro. Hazañas del comandante Francisco Rivera Quintero* (1989). *Cuartel* is an arrangement of testimonial accounts collected by the author that recreates the people of the town of San Rafael del Norte and their interaction with Sandino in the 1920s and 1930s. *No se rompía*—one of the few testimonios besides *"Somos millones"* by a woman—is a very carefully wrought (Baltadono is an artist) and highly regarded memoir of the author's experiences in prison during the struggle against Somoza.

La marca del Zorro, Ramírez's second effort at direct testimonio (see note 8), is an edited version of some seventeen hours of videotaped conversation with an FSLN comandante. It recounts somewhat the same story of guerrilla apprenticeship as Cabezas, but—for better or worse—without Cabezas's insistent personal presence in the narrative. For Ramírez, the importance of the book is to show Rivera as a simple and direct man of the people, whose personal story represents the collective masses for whom and by whom the revolution was waged.

Tomás Borge won the Casa de las Américas prize in testimonio for the first volume of his memoirs, *La paciente impaciencia* (1989). One of the members of the Casa jury praised the book—somewhat overenthusiatically—as "el *Cien años de la soledad* del género testimonio." The comparison, however, also underlines the major problem with the book as testimonio: while it covers much the same ground as *Carlos, el amanecer ya no es una tentación,* it does so as a leisurely and reflective autobiographical memoir, without the pain and urgency of the earlier book. Borge's current situation as a major leader of the revolution and his own literary interests and ambitions, which are very much in evidence in the text, make it difficult to sustain the convention of a direct narrative "from below" essential to testimonio. *La paciente impaciencia* is certainly an important and interesting book, in a mixed genre somewhere between testimonio, revolutionary memoir, standard autobiography, and boom-style narrative; but it is even further from direct testimonio than *Carlos.*

Gioconda Belli has moved from poetry to narrative to tell the story of an upper-class woman's recruitment to the Frente during the insurrection in *La mujer habitada* (1988). Though the book has a testimonial core based on her own involvement in the FSLN urban underground (and in particular the December 1974 hostage taking—see chap. 4), Belli uses here a fairly conventional third-person novel form, combined in the fashion of Asturias's "magic realism" with a parallel story of a Mayan woman in struggle against both the Spanish conquest and the confining female role models of her own culture. Belli is concerned with showing from a feminist point of view vital continuities and possibilities of solidarity in Central American culture, but compared to, say, Rigoberta Menchú's evocation of both contemporary and traditional aspects of a Quiché culture of resistance—existentially rooted in her own life experience—the effect of this sort of device is somewhat contrived (we are meant to understand that the Indian woman's spirit or *nahual* is lodged in an orange tree in the modern woman's yard; the modern woman makes orange juice from the tree, and thus is "inhabited" by the other).

Sergio Ramírez's new novel, *Castigo divino* (1988), is a richly detailed historical and documentary recreation of provincial bourgeois life in the city of León in the 1930s, built around the reconstruction of a bizarre crime. It is another chapter in Ramírez's ongoing narrative archaeology of Nicaraguan history and society since the nineeenth century—surely the most ambitious and sustained project in contemporary Central American fiction; but as an exploration of essentially an upper-class milieu, it is also a step away from the testimonial impulse of the popular voices of *¡Te dió miedo la sangre!* (Ramírez's implicit political aim in the novel may have been double: to give the Nicaraguan Revolution the prestige of a major boom novel and at the same time pillory the narrowness and nastiness of the class predecessors of the Sandinistas' bourgeois opposition.)

Perhaps the most interesting recent Nicaraguan testimonio is *A lo que el viento dijera. Los náufragos de Masachapa* (1989), assembled by Guatemalan journalist Iván Carpio. Armed with Margaret Randall's manual on how to make a testimonio, Carpio went to the Nicaraguan coastal town of Masachapa to interview two fishermen who had been lost at sea for twenty-three days. Around the core of their survival narrative, he added the voices of other people from the town, creating a sort of microcosm of the everyday life of the Nicaraguan popular classes. The context of *A lo que el viento* is postrevolutionary Nicaragua, and the book is certainly "within" the revolution ideologically, but political issues are kept in the background and never become the essential point of the book (one of the fishermen, in fact, was an ex-Guard who had been imprisoned for some time after the victory). A kind of split emerges in Carpio's reconstruction between the narrative and popular force of the story and an epic Sandinista sense of struggle and historical becoming—dimensions that had been merged in the testimonios of the insurrection.

Nicaraguans continue to think of testimonio as the revolution's special contribution to literature, but what is evident in this new narrative from Nicaragua is a problematization of or turning away from the formula of direct testimonio. Whether this is caused by the same deradicalization produced by the war and economic crisis that affected the poetry workshop project or by a lack of suitability of the testimonial form itself to postrevolutionary situations is a matter for speculation. In part, it is a question of just how many more or less unpolished first-person accounts of Sandinista heroics the literary system can sustain; on the other hand, to the extent testimonio becomes a new literary manner or fashion, cultivated by professional writers, it loses the very qualities of sincerity and artlessness that gave it—paradoxically—its artistic freshness and appeal.

Where an authentic testimonial impulse has survived to some extent in postrevolutionary Nicaraguan narrative has been in collections dedicated to accounts of the war with the contras—for example, Carlos

Rincón and Dieter Eich's book of interviews with captured contras, *La contra* (1984); the very moving stories of the mothers of Sandinista soldiers or *brigadistas* killed in the war gathered by Roser Solá and María Pau Trayner, *Ser madre en Nicaragua. Testimonios de una historia no escrita* (1988); Hans Van Heijningen's reconstruction of the murder of peasant leader Alfonso Núñez, *!Que se convierta este dolor en fuerza para seguir luchando!* (1987); or books by international solidarity workers active in the processes of the reconstruction, like Sheryl Hirshon's memoir-diary of her work in the National Literacy Crusade, *And Also Teach Them to Read/Y también enséñeles a leer* (1984). These are certainly not "great" literature and perhaps not literature at all, but in some ways they bring us closer to the texture of popular life and struggle in Nicaragua after the revolution than the more elaborate texts of neo-testimonio. The point we made earlier in this chapter about the relation between testimonio and the urgency of a situation of immediate militancy seems relevant here. Testimonio seems better adapted to express a process of struggle than of revolutionary consolidation or counter-revolutionary destabilization.

Salvadoran Testimonio

As in the case of Nicaragua, there are precedents for the testimonio in some aspects of Salvadoran left vanguardist poetry of the 1930s, particularly the work of Gilberto González Contreras with its fictionalized voices of Indians, peasants, and workers. But the first achieved example of the form—and one of the great narratives of modern Central American literature—is undoubtedly Roque Dalton's *Miguel Mármol*, which appeared initially in 1971. The book had its genesis in a chance encounter: in Prague in 1966, Dalton met Mármol who had been living there in exile. For Dalton, who was then a young Communist party member, Mármol, one of the founders of the party, a survivor of the *Matanza* of 1932, and a veteran of more than half a century of militancy, was a quasi-legendary figure. Dalton proposed that Mármol tell the story of his life—which would also be by extension a slice of the history of the organized working class of El Salvador. The two men worked together over a period of three weeks, with Mármol revising and expanding sections of his account before they parted. The resulting narration covers the period from 1905 to 1954, which they chose as a cutoff point because they feared more recent revelations would endanger current party work.

The book gives a particularly detailed account of the origins of the labor movement and the Communist party in El Salvador, and of the attempted failed uprising and massacre of 1932. Mármol, Dalton says in his introduction, is "the prototypical incarnation of the Latin American communist worker and peasant leader of what is usually called 'the classical period', 'the heroic era', of the parties that, as sections of the Communist International, sprang up and developed in nearly every country on the continent." Dalton's perspective, on the other hand, represents, as we noted in our discussion of his poetry, a generation that comes to maturity in the wake of de-Stalinization, the Cuban Revolution, and the New Left movements of the 1960s. The conflict between the two men—which straddles the question of the relationship of the intelligentsia to the popular classes—is played out at the level of the composition of the testimonio itself: Dalton, who was educated to be a lawyer, notes his "natural tendency to complicate things, which bristles seriously at Mármol's tendency to simplify them" (27–28). In effect, in both form and content the book is a sometimes tense, sometimes fraternal meeting and dialogue between old and new lefts, the heritage of struggle represented by the CPs of the Popular Front period, and the new possibilities for the future suggested by the model of the Cuban Revolution.

These were in fact the basic terms of the debate raging in Latin American Communist parties throughout the 1960s. During the time *Miguel Mármol* was being prepared, the Salvadoran CP split over the issue of armed struggle, and Dalton himself left the party to throw in his lot with the ERP, then in formation. It is this aspect that gave the book its special significance for Salvadoran left culture, because it became a representation of the confrontation and transformation of left traditions and perspectives that would be crucial to the future development of the revolutionary movement.

For Dalton, Mármol's personality and life are ultimately a way of representing for people of his own generation and (petit bourgeois) class background a historical aspect of the Salvadoran national-popular: "the at once communitarian and revolutionary agrarian tradition of peons and day-laborers which had its origins in the early 19th century uprisings led by Anastasio Aquino" (p. 28). Despite their differences, Dalton declares that "more than to argue with Mármol, I feel my duty as a Central American revolutionary is to assume him; just as we assume, in order to see the face of the future, our terrible national history" (p. 23). At the same time, he makes explicit his own priorities, which favor a strategy of armed struggle. The point of the testimonio is not to provide clear answers, but rather to speak beyond generational differences and sectarian debates to deeper resources of what Dalton calls "the elements of democratic culture produced by the exploited strata and classes within the 'national culture' in general" (pp. 27–28). Written over left schisms, poised between the heritage of the "classical period" of the CP represented by Mármol, the emergence of the armed struggle vanguards represented by Dalton himself, and the still uncertain future of the Salvadoran revolution, *Miguel Mármol*—the story in Eduardo Galeano's words of a "maestro in the art of resurrection"—is the germinal Central American testimonio of left activism.

The later 1970s produce two major testimonios in El Salvador, both by leaders of the armed struggle: *Secuestro y capucha en un país del "mundo libre"* (1979) by the late Salvador Cayetano Carpio and *Las cárceles clandestinas de El Salvador* (1979) by Ana Guadalupe Martínez. Both of these are prison testimonios without any particular literary pretense or elaboration.

Cayetano Carpio was, of course, one of the principal strategists and leaders of the Salvadoran armed struggle, the man who led the split in the Communist party that gave rise to the first guerrilla organizations at the end of the 1960s. *Secuestro y capucha* is not, however, a memoir of that experience. Published by EDUCA in 1979, it was undoubtedly written and perhaps circulated in another form much earlier. It is a modest, very simply and effectively narrated text dealing with Carpio's experiences as a political prisoner in the 1950s during the Osorio dictatorship, reflecting in its political line the idea of struggle for general democratic reforms and rights that prevailed in the orthodox Communist parties prior to the Cuban revolution.[12]

Las cárceles (1979), on the other hand, is very much a product of the new revolutionary left that emerged in the 1970s. Martínez had served as a military leader of the same organization Dalton became involved with, the Ejército Revolucionario del Pueblo (ERP). In 1976 she was captured, tortured, and imprisoned by the army. A year later she was released in exchange for a wealthy businessman kidnapped by the ERP. Her testimonio tells of her own experiences in the revolutionary movement and as a prisoner, and of the situation of the "disappeared" and political prisoners in general in El Salvador (a series of chapters present the "relatos" of other prisoners), framed by selections from news stories covering the major events of the period.

Martínez notes pointedly that *Las cárceles* "is the result of a collective and militant effort and has no intellectual or literary pretensions; it is a contribution to the ideological development and the formation of cadres on the basis of concrete experience that should be discussed and analyzed by those who are consistently immersed in the making of the revolution" (p. 14). The resulting tendency to constantly draw the appropriate lessons from the experiences narrated gives the book a somewhat didactic and sectarian character, putting it closer to what we called in our introduction "cadre literature" than more broadly conceived testimonios of left militancy such as *Miguel Mármol* or *La montaña*—but then Martínez would probably classify these as precisely too "literary."[13]

In both its disavowal of literary pretensions and its emphasis on the effectiveness of armed propaganda actions like the kidnapping, *Las cárceles* seems in a sense to have been written *against* both Dalton's literary model of collage-narrative and his political perspective on armed struggle. As we noted in our discussion of his poetry, at the time of his murder in 1975 Dalton had been arguing against what he had come to regard as military adventurism or *militarismo*, the need to shift to building mass organizations. We assume then that Martínez was associated with the faction of the ERP that Dalton opposed, and that the way *Las cárceles* is articulated has something to do with the internal debate in that organization. While she criticizes his execution as an "error," she also characterizes his ideas and writing as "petit bourgeois." The occasional dogmatism and factionalism of her testimonio, which makes it so different from Dalton's, is symptomatic of a courageous and militant revolutionary movement that has also been deeply marked (and perhaps held back) by sectarianism.

Dalton's own *Pobrecito poeta que era yo* (published just after his death in 1976 by EDUCA), is a coming-of-age novel set in the early and mid 1960s in San Salvador. It covers some of the same ground as *Las cárceles*—experiences of radicalization, sectarian debate, life in the underground, imprisonment—but is written in a highly ironic, self-conscious, experimental style as a combination of personal diary, Joycean *bildungsroman*, and testimonio. *Pobrecito poeta* is a sort of prehistory, from an extremely subjective point of view, of how a young petit bourgeois intellectual becomes a revolutionary; *Las cárceles* is more the chronicle of an already committed revolutionary activism.

The increase in repression after 1979 on the part of the army and the death squads projects testimonial forms deep into Salvadoran political and cultural life, now closely linked with the defense of human rights. They appear, as we noted in chapter 5, in the poetry of Manlio Argueta, Alfonso Hernández (*León de piedra*), Mercedes Durand, and Claribel Alegría (particularly her poem *La mujer del río Sumpul* and the anthology of Salvadoran combat poetry she edited with Darwin Flakoll); in the music of groups of the popular song movement like Cutumay Camones and Yolocamba Ita; and in the documentary films and videos made by the FMLN Film Institute.[14] Most significant, however, has been testimonio's impact on the novel: Argueta's *Un día en la vida* (1980), perhaps the best known work internationally of modern Salvadoran literature, is a prime instance.

Argueta, like Ramírez and Chávez Alfaro in Nicaragua, was trying for a polyphonic novel form without the narrative axis of a central hero: as in testimonio, characters would be "voices," representing as if from direct experience, in the vernacular, different aspects of Salvadoran national-popular. Argueta had incorporated a number of quasi-testimonial sections in his early novels *En el valle de las hamacas* and *Caperucita en las zona roja*, both of which have sections narrating personal experiences in the guerrilla). *Un día* has the form of a day-long interior monologue in the voice of a middle-aged peasant woman, Guadalupe Fuentes, who has been caught up in the struggle raging in the countryside after 1979. We learn from her monologue that her son-in-law has been "disappeared"; her granddaughter has been involved in demonstrations for agrarian reform, including an occupation of the cathedral of San Salvador, and is being sought by the Guardia; her husband has joined a peasant federation and supports the rebels fighting against the government; often he must hide in the hills above their house from the soldiers prowling the countryside The action of the novel centers on a moment when the narrator is forced by a death squad to identify a body that has been found nearby. It is in fact her husband, but knowing the consequences of admitting this she denies ever having seen the man.

The "day" of the novel has several levels of reference: it is the repeated cycle of work and rest of the daily life of the peasantry; the story of Lupe's own family; a microcosm of the political convulsion sweeping the countryside after 1979. It is also, through the threads of memory in Guadalupe's monologue, a reconstruction of the historical context of rural history in El Salvador: the Matanza of 1932, the formation of ORDEN and related death squads in the 1960s, the new and old church, the emergence of the peasant union FECCAS and armed resistance in the 1970s. Interpolated into Guadalupe's monologue are other testimonial voices: those of her granddaughter and her political *compañeros*; of her husband; of a Liberation Theology priest; of one of the soldiers.

In narrating *Un día* in the voice of a woman, Argueta was exploiting both the affinity of testimonio for women's narrative and the fact that, as the novel documents, by driving men underground, the repression had forced new responsibilities on women. In Lupe's act of denial and assertion, we see something that is fairly common in testimonio and that is related to the feminization of the Central American literary system we have noted in other contexts: women taking on new roles in the course of social struggle and the appearance of new bonds of affiliation between men and women.

Argueta's latest novel, *Cuzcatlán donde bate la Mar del Sur* (1986), focuses on several generations of a peasant family, shifting voices, perspective, and story back and forth from the 1930s to the present. It starts very much like an actual guerrilla testimonio (the speaker is a young woman involved in one of the revolutionary organizations):

> My alias is Beatriz. Ticha is my nickname. Age: twenty four.
> Peasant background . . .

Cuzcatlán extends Argueta's project of portraying peasant beliefs and customs as repositories of elements of precolonial culture that have survived the cycles of colonization and exploitation the rural population has lived through. These elements—the symbol of the *metate* and of corn, the millenarian image of a preconquest Cuzacatlán (the Indian name for El Salvador) itself, elements of Mayan cosmology and mythology—form a sort of underlying mosaic in the text, inserted more by the author than the characters themselves, who are also fictional constructs (compare Rigoberta Menchú's references, which we discuss below, to the same elements as part of her direct experience of community). Argueta is involved in a quest for international attention to and understanding of the Salvadoran struggle. The use of testimonial forms clearly serves this aim. But for all their testimonial echoes and closeness to the experience of peasants and rural workers (which make them very different from the urban milieu of Ramírez's *¿Te dió miedo?*), *Cuzcatlán* and *Un día* remain novels. As fictional constructions of the life-world of a rural proletariat, they are richer and more complex than testimonios, but they also lack the testimonio's immediacy and urgency.

Claribel Alegría's *No me agarrán viva. La mujer salvadoreña en la lucha* (1983) is a variation on the usual first-person form of testimonio by one of El Salvador's most versatile modern writers (see our remarks on her poetry in chap. 5). It narrates the life of a guerrilla comandante, Eugenia, who is killed in action, through a collage of oral testimonies by her friends and comrades. Like Alegría herself, Eugenia comes to revolutionary activism from an upper-class background, so her story is about personal and ideological transformation, changing from one form of social identification to another.

Alegría had published with her husband Darwin Flakoll in 1966 a partly autobiographical novel about the identity crisis of an upper-class woman who returns to El Salvador from abroad to attend her mother's funeral: *Cenizas de Izalco*. Through the daughter's recollections, the story of the mother's tragic affair with a visiting North American emerges, set against the events of the 1932 rebellion and massacre, and involving issues of love, loyalty, betrayal, and women's social roles. *No me agarrán* is in a sense a response both at the level of form (testimonio) and content (revolutionary activism) to the personal and historical impasse represented by the earlier novel. As George Yúdice has noted, the way Eugenia's story is told through the voices of her adopted class also embodies the struggle of women in and through the revolution for a new kind of subjectivity: "As in the gospel, [Eugenia] exists through the speech acts of her *compañeros*. Having worked as an organizer, an incorporator of cadres, she continues to 'embody' that function in death as the symbol of their collective self-representation" (Yúdice 1985a).

Alegría's *Luisa in Realityland* (1987a) is a multigeneric combination of childhood fable (like *Alice in Wonderland*, to which the title alludes), testimonio, autobiographical memoir, and poetry anthology. As such, it represents perhaps a feminized appropriation of or alternative to the collage metahistorical narrative form of Roque Dalton's *Las historias prohibidas del pulgarcito*. Where Dalton was trying for something akin to the objectivism and impersonalism of Cardenal's exteriorism, Alegría's book is deeply personal, extending to the most minor details and anecdotes of her private and family life. But there is no question that her project is parallel to Dalton's: to give some sense, through a montage of different literary forms, of the overall historical and political process Central America has gone through from the 1930s to the present, in her case presented, however, from within the intimate world of a particular woman's memories and experience. *Luisa* is not testimonio, but like *Las historias* it is representative of a range of new postfictional, quasi-testimonial narrative forms that have appeared in the context of the Central American revolutionary struggle. It is an effect, in other words, of the pressure of testimonio on the established genres and forms of the literary system.

By contrast, the final Salvadoran narrative we want to mention is very much in the utilitarian vein of cadre testimonio, even in its means of production and distribution. It is the extraordinary autobiographical story of the involvement of a Belgian woman, Karin Lievens (*nom de guerre* Laura) in the FMLN's eastern front between 1982 and 1985: *El quinto piso de la alegría. Tres años con la guerrilla* (1988).[15] The book narrates her work in cultural development and literacy training with peasants in the liberated areas; details of life in the FMLN guerrilla camps, including discussions about strategy and tactics; the situation of women in the FMLN; the death in combat of her *compañero* and fellow *internacionalista*, Sebastián; above all, the evolution of the war in these years seen from the perspective of her own participation. Like *Secuestro y capucha* and *Las cárceles clandestinas* (and unlike the Nicaraguan neo-testimonios we discuss above), it is written with absolutely no literary pretensions, incorporating in fact, a good deal of historical and descriptive material on the situation of the guerrilla that goes against even the testimonial convention of direct narrative. But these are precisely the sorts of materials someone in the guerrilla is constantly having to think about and deal with; to leave them out in the name of stylistic consistency would be to risk making the testimonio a new kind of literary *costumbrismo*, as we suggested happens in the case of Cabezas's sequel to *La montaña*.

There are few books that give as direct and contemporary a sense of what it means to be part of the process of armed struggle as *El quinto piso*. This is a politically significant achievement, given the present difficulties and uncertainties facing the Salvadoran revolutionary movement. The decision of the FMLN to bring out Lievens's testimonio under its own imprimatur is no doubt related to the fact that the text can be seen as a reaffirmation of its ability to survive and maneuver as a military-political organization even under the conditions of extreme repression it has experienced in recent years. It is a way of saying that the FMLN is not ready to be counted out of the picture.

Guatemalan Testimonio

As we observed in our account of Guatemalan poetry in chapter 6, the novel has been since colonial times both more important and more extensively cultivated in that country's literary system than in either Nicaragua or El Salvador. Perhaps because of the years of violence and repression in the 1960s and early 1970s, however, only gradually did Guatemalan novelists begin to elaborate equivalents to the sort of boom narrative that had become hegemonic elsewhere in Latin America. In the late 1960s, Augusto "Tito" Monterroso developed a prose style characterized by whimsy, irony, and allegory reminiscent of Borges, Cortázar, or Arreola, and Carlos Solórzano's first novels, *Los falsos demonios* (1966) and *Las celdas* (1971), showed an effort to introduce experimental techniques into Guatemalan narrative while keeping faith with the older commitment to use fiction as a means of probing national realities. But the dominant figures in the novel continued to be Asturias (who had anticipated some aspects of boom narrative in *El señor presidente*) and Monteforte Toledo, both working basically in social realist modes modified by their contrasting attempts to come to grips with the mythic and magical dimensions of Indian culture.

Beginning in the mid 1970s, however, Guatemala experienced an upsurge of prose narrative corresponding to the developing national crisis. A group of formally innovative novels appeared centered on the dialectic of military oppression, resistance, and armed struggle that has dominated the nation's life since the 1954 coup. They included *La semilla de fuego* (1976) and its sequel *El fuego interado* (1978), and the recent documentary novel on the last days of the Arbenz regime, *Operación Iscariote* (1989) by Miguel Angel Vázquez; *Los compañeros* (1976) by Marco Antonio Flores, on the *foquista* guerrilla experience of the 1960s;

El sendero de los bécares (1977) and *Violencia* (1978) by Carlos Cojulén Bedoya (1978); *Los demonios salvajes* (1978) by Mario Roberto Morales; *El pueblo y los atentados* (1979) by Edwin Cifuentes; *Después de las bombas* (1979) and *Itzan na* (1981) by Arturo Arias; finally, paralleling the emergence of an indigenous literary voice in the poetry of Luis Sam Colop and Rigoberta Menchú's testimonio, *El tiempo principia en Xibalba* (1985, but written earlier), by the Indian writer Luis de Lión. (One of the few oppositional writers to remain in Guatemala, Lión was subsequently "disappeared" in the early 1980s.)

In the new literary-political conjuncture represented by the emergence of RIN-78 and the Cerezo "opening" we described in chapter 6, collections of short fiction strongly marked by testimonial features begin to predominate over the novel. Writers like Ligia Escribá (*Cuentos*, 1985), Francisco Nájera (*Los cómplices*, 1988), or Franz Galich (*La princesa de onix*, 1989) began developing an experimental style in which the social horrors of the early 1980s became part of an intertextual, postmodern narrative grid. Others persisted in writing fiction with strongly testimonial and political tendencies. *Panzos y otras historias* by José Barnoya and *Cuentos para contar corriendo* (1984) by Catarino Mateo are fictional reconstructions of the massacres by the army in the highlands. *Cuando se vaya Liz* (1982) by Amilcar Zea presents a group of neopicaresque stories about the life of shoeshine boys in Guatemala City. *Recuento de cuentos y descuentos* by Marco Antonio Sagastume Gemmell traces a symbolic history of the nation, with erupting volcanoes, oppressive eagles and plumed serpents. Luis de Lión's last stories, written in 1984, explore the processes of alienation and deformation produced by the land seizures and military massacres under Ríos Montt and Mejía Victores. Carlos Menkos-Deka's ¡*Abre, abre, solarc-diez el baúl de los gigantes!* and *Grito, susurro y llanto* (1985) by physician Armando Bendaña offer highly politicized and dramatic testimonial vignettes of Guatemala City in the years of violence.

The novels of the 1980s likewise register the intense political pressure of these years. José Luis Perdomo's *El tren no llega* (1984), William Lemus's *Vida en un pueblo muerto* (1984)—among many other novels on the theme—explore the transformations of Guatemalan village life under the effects of modernization and militarization. Their urban counterparts are Francisco Albizúrez Palma's *Ida y vuelta* (1983), Fernando González Davison's *En los sueños no todo es reposo* (1988), and Mario Alberto Carrera's politically centrist coming-of-age trilogy *Hogar dulce hogar* (1982), *Don Camaleán* (1985), and *Diario de un tiempo escendido* (1988). Carlos René García Escobar's *La llama del retorno* (1984) and Roberto Quezada's *El filo de la locura* (1988) both deal with the problems of Guatemalan immigrants (in *La llama*, a political exile) living in

Southern California. U.S.-based Jewish writer Víctor Perera's autobiographical memoir, *Rites: A Guatemalan Boyhood* (1986), presents
glimpses of Guatemalan history from the tumultuous days of Ubico's
presidency to the armed struggle of the 1960s based primarily on visits
by the author (Perera is said to be collecting material in Guatemala for
a testimonial reconstruction of the social history of the last several
years). In *El esplendor de la pirámide* (1986), Mario Roberto Morales
takes up the question of armed struggle as it unfolds during the period
from 1980 to 1982. Edwin Cifuentes's second novel, *La nueva Esmer-
alda: la novela de Paris* (1987) deals with a revolutionary activist who
decides to leave Paris to collaborate with revolutionary groups in Central
America. In *Bajo la fuente: la historia no contada de un controversial
affair* (1986), Manuel Corleto writes a "dictator novel," chronicling in
quasi-testimonial form the years of Ríos Montt, the role of fundamentalist evangelism, the pope's trip to Guatemala, the maneuvers of the CIA,
the efforts of Amnesty International, and the terrible repression in the
Indian communities of the country. Adolfo Méndez Vides's *Las cata-
cumbas* (1987) is a short experimental "antinovel" portraying the
contradictions of Guatemalan society through the microcosm of a bar in
Mazatenango. Luis Alfredo Arango's *Después del tango vienen los moros*
(1988) focuses on the situation of poor Indian and ladina women. Arturo
Arias's *Itzan na* (1981) dealt with the problems of upper-middle-class
Guatemalan life through stories of teenagers trying to escape familial
and personal conflicts through drugs. Arias has recently published an
ambitious picaresque "ramble"—somewhat on the order of Roque
Dalton's metahistorical *Las historias prohibidas del pulgarcito*—through
some five hundred years of Guatemalan history and culture, whose
irreverent narrators are a pair of Sephardic Jews who survive the whole
process: *El jaguar en llamas* (1989).[16]

The overlapping tensions and splits evident in this production between committed and apolitical stances, militancy and disillusion,
realist and experimental literary techniques, ladino and Indian ethnic
worlds bespeak the ideological divisions of the ladino intelligentsia and
middle sectors in the face of the alternatives posed by dictatorship and
armed struggle. But, however interesting and significant this ongoing
work in fiction has been, the crucial narrative genre in recent Guatemalan literature in terms of revolutionary politics has been the testimonio,
to which we now turn.

There was a strong testimonial component in the work of Asturias and
many of the writers and artists emerging before and during the October
Revolution. But the first book that could be classified as a testimonio as
such is Manuel Galich's reconstruction of the struggles against the
Ubico dictatorship in the late 1930s and early 1940s, *Del pánico al ataque,*

first published in article form in 1946–1947 (1949; current edition 1985). The book, which has become something of a classic of modern Guatemalan literature, is somewhere between a historical essay and testimonio. Narrated mainly in the first-person from Galich's own standpoint as a participant observer in these struggles, it mixes in accounts from other actors and considerable historical description and documentation (Galich himself called the book a "testimonio estudiantil").[17]

The 1954 coup and its aftermath produced another wave of memoirs and testimonios. Perhaps the most representative example of these is *Guaridas infernales* by Rubén Barreda Avila, published and circulated clandestinely in Guatemala around 1960. Barreda had been a supporter of Arbenz and was arrested, tortured, and imprisoned for some three years under the Castillo Armas dictatorship. The book tells of this experience, which implicitly becomes an indictment of the regime itself. As such, *Guaridas* appears to have been much used in progressive and revolutionary circles in the early 1960s as a political education primer.

Guerrilla Testimonio

Mixing testimonio and political journalism, Uruguayan Eduardo Galeano incorporated first-person accounts by leaders of the major guerrilla groups active in the 1960s in his *Guatemala: País ocupado* (1969), which with its linkage of dependency and *foco* theory was an influential text at the time. The first major testimonio of the revolutionary process, Mario Payeras's *Días de la selva* (1980), is based, however, on a subsequent stage of the Guatemalan armed struggle. Its immediate context is the crisis of the revolutionary left in the early 1970s. The primarily ladino guerrilla leaders and organizations of the 1960s described by Galeano— never numbering more than some five hundred—had been almost obliterated, their strategy discredited.[18]

Días tells the story of the early days of Guatemala's Guerrilla Army of the Poor (EGP) when a small group crossed the border from Mexico to attempt to reinitiate guerrilla activity in the northwest highlands—the scenario of the most intense class and ethnic violence in recent Guatemalan history and therefore of most of the major testimonial literature related to the armed struggle and military repression. Payeras was one of the EGP's founders, and *Días*, like Cabezas's *La montaña*, is a graphic, sometimes humorous, sometimes poetic evocation of the effort to survive in the difficult conditions of a jungle region inhabited almost exclusively by indigenous peoples over a period of some five years. Payeras is concerned with the way in which actual experience tests and modifies abstract revolutionary theory. He tells of the first miserable and confused days in the jungle, the initial contacts with villagers, the problems of overcoming their suspicions and learning to communicate with them, of undoing the mistakes of earlier guerrilla groups, of settling into the life of the jungle, expanding and maintaining contacts, of small military actions undertaken to assert the group's position.

The book closes on one of those remarkable and terrible episodes that seem a constant feature of guerrilla narratives: the story of the confession and execution of a *guerrillero*, Fonseca, who had betrayed the group after being captured by the army. Payeras makes this small tragedy a symbol of the ability of the guerrilla to overcome its own limitations:

> At the moment of his execution, one of the women guerrillas could not hold back her tears. He told her not to weep because his death would keep others from making the same mistake. In his grave were placed the thirty-three centavos his sisters had sent from his village to accompany him in death. . . . We thought about what it means to be a revolutionary. We recalled a faraway bridge back in the highlands where we had once gone to pick up supplies. It was an immensely long and slender tree trunk laid across a dizzying torrent. The endless rain and the turbulent current drenched the trunk, making it glassy-smooth and slippery. . . . Halfway across, advancing slowly, trying to keep a foothold, the ceaseless flow of the water would suddenly make us feel dizzy. Whoever hesitated at midpoint would become paralyzed, unable to go back or forward. The secret was to cross slowly but without hesitation. We could not have imagined such perils on that night, five years earlier, when we had floated on the gentle current of the Río Lancantún under the January stars, beginning our days of the jungle. (P. 94)

Implicitly, Payeras constructs *Días* in reference to Che Guevara's *Episodios de la guerra revolucionaria cubana*, which had been the model testimonio of *foco* theory, in effect the empirical counterpart to Guevara's handbook *Guerrilla Warfare* and Debray's elaboration of this in *Revolution in the Revolution?* Juan Duchesne (1986) has noted that the concept of seeding and implantation is basic to the narrative structure of *Días*. Where Guevara emphasizes action, mobility, improvisation, and concatenation, and ends with the triumph of the revolutionary army, Payeras stresses adjustment, rootedness, repetition, and slow accumulation. What is involved is not only a question of contrasting narrative styles. Payeras intended *Días* as an intervention in the strategic reorientation of the Guatemalan armed struggle after the defeats of the *foco*-based groups of the 1960s. The model *Días* suggests is that of a rural-based "long war"—as in the concept of *guerra popular prolongada* shared by many Central American guerrilla groups—rather than the audacious and mobile unit of *foco* theory, the "small motor" that sets in motion the "large motor" of the revolution on a national or regional level. Such a war might take up to twenty years to develop (the narrative unit of *Días* represents in fact its initial or "implantation" phase). Those who enter the jungle do so to build a network of peasant support and in the process reeducate themselves. This requires something that *foco* strategy posited in theory but found difficult to achieve in practice: a close and real fusion between a mainly urban, ladino, Marxist vanguard group and the non-Spanish-speaking Indian peoples of the highlands with their own religious and cultural-political forms. Perhaps in anticipation of the impact of Liberation Theology and the sort of activism represented by a Rigoberta Menchú, the EGP showed a greater sensitivity to and acceptance of religion and superstition than the earlier groups that come out of the positivist and Jacobin heritage of the left.[19] In Duchesne's view, *Días* is a political version of that narrative trope in Latin American fiction—for example, in Alejo Carpentier's *Los pasos perdidos*—which is a cultural-ideological rebirth by a "return to origins." He writes:

> The protagonists [in *Días*] cross a socio-geographical space fragmented in an unevenly developed history, in search for a zone of vital reinauguration. The guerrilla column crosses the jungle painfully discovering symbolic ruins of Mayan civilization devoured by the vegetation. (1986: 111–112)

In spite its lack of action on a grand scale and its inconclusive ending, *Días* is epic in character in the sense that it shows how its protagonists are subjected to great tests of their capacities for survival, adaptation, and transformation. Above all, it articulates the growth of a sense of collectivity among the guerrillas themselves and between them and the people of the highlands. Rather than a campaign history like Che's *Episodios*, Payeras's narrative constructs the EGP guerrilla component as a school, a learning experience based, as in Paolo Freire's notions of a pedagogy of liberation, on shared experience and the interaction between educators and educated. Its textual strategy is to present an image of the "days" that involves the readers and has them share the process of initiation to the point where they feel a lived solidarity with it, which will be productive for future stages of development of what the text assumes implicitly will be a long process of struggle.

Rigoberta Menchú

Its literary value aside, *Días* has special significance because it gives expression to a process that was extending and deepening in Guatemala in the years subsequent to the experience it narrates. As we have noted, the period from the late 1970s through 1985 was a time of crisis in which military-backed land-development projects clashed with the interests of the indigenous communities, producing in response the situation *Días* suggests only as a tentative possibility: the linkage between at least a significant number of these communities, the Marxist guerrilla groups, and the mass organizations developed by ladino union and religious activists.

Because of the involvement of social scientists and local and international human rights organizations, the counterinsurgency war in the northern highlands generated an unusually large number of personal or collective testimonios.[20] *Me llamo Rigoberta Menchú, y así me nació la conciencia*—first published in 1983 when its eponymous narrator was twenty-three years old—is undoubtedly the most famous of these. Compiled and introduced by Venezuelan social scientist Elisabeth Burgos, this perhaps most celebrated Central American testimonio of all narrates the crisis of the traditional Indian family and community networks in the late 1970s and the parallel personal transformation of the narrator into an activist and organizer on behalf of her community. Rigoberta Menchú speaks through her narrative directly of the pain of her people and their modes of internalization and resistance: of the corn-centered culture of the villages of the Guatemalan *altiplano*; her family's struggle to keep and survive off of its *minifundio*; the rites of birth, marriage, and death; the death of siblings from malnutrition; the oppressive experience of seasonal work on the coastal cotton plantations; migration to the city to seek work as a maid; *machismo* and problems of women's oppression in both ladino and Indian cultures; the efforts to build self-defense organizations and the responding massacres by the army; the emergence of the CUC, the major mass organization of Indian-ladino peasant solidarity; the torture and murder of one of her brothers and her mother by soldiers; her own exile. Her personal history ties her to most of the major events of the Indian resistance movement: Panzós, Cajul, the occupation of the Spanish embassy (in which her father was killed), the creation of the CUC and the 1980 strike and march on Guatemala City, the counterinsurgency campaigns of the early 1980s.

The special appeal of *Me llamo Rigoberta Menchú* has to do with its matching of form and content, the textual characteristics of testimonio we have outlined and the sense of life and community it narrates. Testimonio is, first of all, a written transmission of voice and memory. For Menchú, testimonio is embedded in the life of the Quiché community itself, just as the "I" that speaks speaks in the name of a "we." The act of narration involves a love of and an identification with the people; it is a ceremonial form of representation in which the relations between spirit and body, individual and community, human beings and nature are defined and affirmed. These relations are depicted early in the text as Menchú speaks of the ceremonies that accompany birth and the progressive initiation of the child into the history of the group, its ancestors, its own special *nahual* or spirit double, the meaning of corn, the value of ceremony and ritual. Mayan cosmology as presented by Menchú sees humankind as integral to nature, composed of the same substance. "Man is part of the natural world," she comments. "There is not one world for man and one for animals, they are part of the same one and lead parallel lives" (p. 19).

This is the basis of the concept of the *nahual*, which runs throughout the text. Menchú explains that the *nahual* is like a sort of second self, "representative of earth, the animal world, the sun and water." But she cautions that she "can only tell very general things" about it because it is one of the secrets her people must keep hidden to protect their identity and culture. The narrator who says her name is Rigoberta and who speaks to the reader in Spanish has another name and identity that she will not reveal. The book concludes with these words, directed to her interlocutor and by extension her readers: ". . . I'm still keeping my Indian identity a secret. I'm still keeping secret what I think no-one should know. Not even anthropologists or intellectuals, no matter how many books they have, can find out all our secrets" (p. 247).

If the *nahual* is the true expression of one's identity—that which fuses in a utopian harmony self, family, land, community, nature, and cosmos—and if keeping secrets is crucial to the future the narrator seeks by telling the story of her people, then the sense of truth itself as something independent of collective human activity is problematized by this testimonio, which is told literally under the lethal gaze of a genocidal counterinsurgency campaign.

Yúdice has drawn out the relation between the religious and political aspects of Menchú's narrative. He points out that the concept of the *nahual* is part of a culture based on a "dialogical relationship with earth and nature":

> Land, [which] provides material sustenance and embodies *Dios Mundo* (earth god), cannot be owned or exploited instrumentally. The child undergoes certain rites to purify his hands so that he may never rob (i.e., take from the community, the social body). . . . The Indian analysis of existential and social strife, then, begins with the condemnation of private or state ownership of the land. (1985a: 12)

Yúdice's point enables us to see Rigoberta Menchú's testimonio as part of a practice, at once political and shamanistic, in which the community's broken relationship with the land is to be restored. It may be argued that she understates a number of problems of Quiché culture—ecological problems with land use, particularly the practice of wood burning, alcoholism, distrust of outsiders, confining traditional role models. But her program is not simply a defense of or return to a utopian Indian status quo ante; the production of the testimonio itself involves what her interlocutor calls a process of "disassociative acculturation: an attempt to revive the past by using techniques borrowed from the very culture one wishes to reject and free oneself from" (p. xvii). She has to give up the communally sanctioned roles of wife and mother. She learns Spanish to be able to communicate with potential allies among the ladino population (and not incidentally to narrate her testimonio). She is a Christian as well as a Mayan, in the spirit of the practical communal use of religion developed in Liberation Theology. Despite her general rejection of ladino and European culture, she considers herself a Marxist. These things are for her cultural forms that can be appropriated as what Yúdice calls "popular weapons" of survival and resistance.

Her testimonio models and enacts a strategy of selective and creative adaptation at a moment of crisis and profound danger of spiritual and physical annihilation. To maintain the group's identity, its members must transform themselves, move from passivity to rebellion, become part of a national and international movement for change. There is finally something playful in Menchú's strategies of resistance, something joyful in this story filled with scenes of incredible pain and hardship. She recounts that her father once told her: "Don't be afraid. Because this is our life, and if we didn't feel this pain, perhaps our life would be different, perhaps we wouldn't think of it as life. This is our life: we must suffer it but we must also enjoy it" (p. 193). It is by embodying this lesson that *Me llamo Rigoberta Menchú* comes to represent, even in the very difficult circumstances of the present, the deepest revolutionary possibilities and hope for Guatemala.[21]

Recent Guatemalan Testimonios

Politically, *Me llamo Rigoberta Menchú* represents the other side of the proposal of a revolutionary Indian/ladino alliance suggested in *Días de la selva*. What haunts a reading today of both these texts is the recognition that this project—Guatemala's third attempt at revolution in less than half a century—has been, if not totally destroyed, at least halted and contained by the brutal counterinsurgency campaigns. By 1983, the western highlands once again come under military control. The testimonios emerging since then express the experience of these more recent and desperate stages of urban and rural struggle. We will look briefly at three of the most important, all published in 1987: Víctor

Montejo's *Testimony: Death of a Guatemalan Village*, translated by Víctor Perera (we are not aware of an edition in Spanish); Payeras's *El trueno en la ciudad: episodios de la lucha armada urbana de 1981 en Guatemala*; and Miguel Angel Albizúres's history of Coca Cola workers' strike in Guatemala City, *Tiempo de sudor y lucha*.

Although its title seems to co-opt the genre as such, *Testimony* is not exactly a testimonio in the sense we have described. Montejo writes from a position intermediate between that of the popular narrator and the interlocutor in testimonio. As a schoolteacher working in a village in the northern highlands, he represents a westernized middle sector of the Mayan population. *Testimony* is his firsthand account of the virtual destruction of the village by the army in 1982. The incident is unleashed when some young men of the town who have been forced by the army to serve in civil defense units fire on an army patrol, mistaking it for the guerrillas. Montejo's story of the reprisals, which include his own arrest and interrogation, also allow him to describe in the fashion of *Me llamo Rigoberta Menchú* aspects of the daily life and customs of the village, Tzalalá. But where *Me llamo* ends on a note of difficult hope, *Testimony*, which is dedicated "to the memory of the many thousand Guatemalans who were killed or disappeared," is in effect a sort of elegy or requiem for the communities of the highlands. It ends with the narrator abandoning the village to pick up his life elsewhere.[22]

Like *Testimony*, Payeras's *El trueno* is a narrative of defeat and disappointment. It is a sequel to the story of the EGP guerrilla begun in *Días*, but now in the context of the urban underground. Written during the Ríos Montt years, it covers the events of the "fifth year" of the EGP's campaign in 1981, when it sought to extend its activities from the highlands into the cities. Partly as a result of the implantation work Payeras describes in *Días*, the EGP had become the largest guerrilla group in the late 1970s, and this was a crucial turning point for it and for the Guatemalan armed struggle as a whole. Payeras came to realize in the course of implementing the new strategy that the organization was operating on a completely mistaken understanding of what was happening in the country—particularly the nature and extent of the counterinsurgency offensive that the army was preparing in the highlands (and which the EGP failed to counter effectively). The consequences, which Payeras describes vividly, are the death of many *compañeros*, the deterioration of the organization, and ultimately the separation of Payeras and other members from the EGP. *Trueno* is a narrative of *desengaño* or disillusion, conceived to create a polemic in the Guatemalan left about why the armed struggle which had seemed to have the possibility of victory at least in sight in the early 1980s allowed the initiative to pass to the army.

Less interesting as a literary document than either *Testimony* or *Trueno* but suggesting a slightly more optimistic sense of possibilities of struggle is trade union organizer Albizúres's story of the Coca Cola strike, *Tiempo de sudor*. Told generally as an impersonal chronicle of dates and events, the text at first glance seems more like labor history than testimonio. But there are moments of direct narration that are informal, personal, lyrical in the fashion of Cabezas or Mármol. The strike itself, despite its inconclusive aftermath, was one of the great epics of modern Central American labor history, a limited victory in the midst of the very difficult circumstances of the early 1980s. It crisscrossed in a way Albizúres is careful to register many of the actions described in the rural testimonios (e.g., the demonstration at the Spanish embassy in which Rigoberta Menchú's father was killed), suggesting the linkage of the cause of urban, ladino trade unionists working directly for transnational capital with the movement of rural workers, peasant and Indian communities represented by a movement like the CUC. In this sense, in a modest and limited way *Tiempo de sudor* points to the new kinds of unity which will be required if the Guatemalan revolutionary movement is to renew itself.

Conclusion

We conclude this discussion of testimonio and this book very much in the middle of things as far as both the future of the form and of the Central American revolutionary process itself are concerned. The Soviet literary critic Mikhail Bakhtin defined what he called "prose art" (by which he meant the art of the novel and the chronicle) as involving a deliberate attention to the concreteness and relativity of living discourse, "a feeling for its participation in historical becoming and social struggle." Such a discourse, he concluded, "is still warm from that struggle and hostility, as yet unresolved and still fraught with hostile intentions and accents." (We are obliged to Barbara Harlow for bringing this passage from Bakhtin's essay "Discourse in the Novel" to our attention.)

These words capture perhaps best the sense of testimonio we have tried to convey here. Testimonios continue to be produced and to be of great importance in understanding the nature of social struggles in Central America and in projecting their future patterns and possibilities. As we have argued, they serve not only to reflect the praxis of emerging subaltern social and ethnic sectors in the region, but also to generate it, addressing various publics that are both internal and external to the popular movements themselves as records of human experiences that might otherwise remain anonymous, vehicles for local and international solidarity, models of new forms of personal and collective subjectivity, places to test and evaluate experience and strategy.

In this sense, testimonio remains one of the most important ideological weapons of the Central America revolutions. But if testimonio has been in Central America and elsewhere the literary form of the stages of both revolutionary mobilization and consolidation, paradoxically and against the expectations of its original protagonists—as both the previous Cuban experience with the form and recent Nicaraguan narrative suggest—it does not seem particularly well adapted to be the primary narrative form of an elaborated postrevolutionary society, perhaps because its dynamics depend precisely on the conditions of social and cultural inequality and direct oppression that fuel the revolutionary impulse in the first place. Like its ancestor, the picaresque novel, testimonio is a transitional literary form appropriate to the dynamics of a period of global social and historical transition, but also destined to give way to new forms of cultural representation as that transition moves to new stages and the human collectivities that are its agents come into possession of new forms of power and knowledge.

We return, therefore, in closing to the paradox that has been with us from the beginning of this book: literature has been a means of national-popular mobilization in the Central American revolutionary process, but that process also elaborates or points to forms of cultural democratization that will necessarily question or displace the role of literature as a hegemonic cultural institution.

Notes

1. See Barnet's 1969 essay—a sort of manifesto of the genre—"La novela-testimonio: socioliteratura." (reprinted in Vidal and Jara 1986).

2. In cases where testimonios are more directly part of political or social activism—for example, in the use of testimonio in the sanctuary movement for refugees or as a cadre literature by revolutionary groups—these editorial functions are often handled directly by the organization or party in question, constituting then not only a new literary form but also new, noncommodified forms of literary production and distribution.

3. Testimonio in this sense is uniquely situated to represent the components of what Sandinista theoreticians Roger Burbach and Orlando Núñez have called the "Third Force"—intellectuals, sectors of the petite bourgeoisie, the "marginal" unemployed or underemployed population, and the "new social movements" (religious *comunidades de base*, ethnic liberation movements, feminist groups, ecology organizations, human rights groups, and the like)—in relation or possible relation with working-class issues and movements (1987: 63–79).

4. This seems, for example, the implication of Roberto González Echevarría's (1985) influential discussion of Miguel Barnet's *Autobiography of a Runaway Slave* and Cuban testimonio.

5. Randall conducted a series of workshops to train literacy campaign and cultural brigade workers to encourage their students to collect their own experience and to begin building a popular history narrated by themselves. She is the author of a handbook on how to make a testimonio, which combines, as she puts it, "insights from the writings of Walter Benjamin as well as basic instructions on how to use and care for a tape recorder": *Testimonios* (1983b), recently translated as *Testimonies: A Guide to Oral History* (1985a). Her own testimonial work available in English includes *Cuban Women Now* (1974); *Doris Tijerino: Inside the Nicaraguan Revolution* (1978); *Sandino's Daughters* (1981); *Christians in the Nicaraguan Revolution* (1983a); and *Risking a Somersault in the Air: Conversations with Nicaraguan Writers* (1985).

6. For a useful summary of this tradition, including descriptions of some of the major novels, see Osses (1986) and Acevedo (1982: 273–445).

7. The book has a curious history. Written in 1933, it was not actually published until after the 1979 Sandinista victory. Though Román himself went into exile in the United States in the 1930s, the decision to withhold publication may have had something to do with the vanguardists' initial enthusiasm for Somoza after Sandino's death, which we noted in chapter 3. Parts of the book appeared in newspapers of the time, and the manuscript probably circulated privately among the vanguardists. The first edition (1979) was by Pablo Antonio Cuadra's publishing house, El Pez y la Serpiente. A second edition—related to Cuadra's and *La Prensa*'s escalating campaign against the Sandinista leadership—appeared in 1983.

8. See M. Cuadra (1982). A fascinating complement to Cuadra's work and another example of Nicaraguan proto-testimonio are the memoirs of Abelardo Cuadra edited from his papers after his death by Sergio Ramírez as *Hombre del Caribe* (1981). Abelardo had been involved in Somoza's plot against Sandino as a Guard officer. Later, he turned against Somoza, went into exile, and eventually ended up in the quixotic attempt of Arévalo's Caribbean Legion to overthrow Trujillo in 1947, a forerunner of Fidel Castro's *Granma* expedition.

9. *Bananos* was originally published by Tipografía la Patria, presumably in Managua, although the edition gives no particulars. In later editions, the subtitle appears as *La vida de los peones en la Yunai*, referring to the plantations of the United Fruit Company. Quintana also wrote a second, less-well-known "proletarian" novel, *Agustín Rivera: esbozo para una novela* (1953).

10. See Guadamuz's comments in Randall (1984: 73–75). Two postrevolutionary editions of the text exist: one in *Nicaráuac* 6 (1981), 21–50; and another in book form by Editorial Nueva Nicaragua (Managua, 1982), both with a series of drawings of prison scenes by painter Leonel Vanegas.

11. For other FSLN cadre testimonios, see Pilar Arias, *Nicaragua: Revolución. Relatos de combatientes del Frente Sandinista* (1980); William Agudelo, *El asalto a San Carlos: testimonios de Solentiname* (1982); *Nicaráuac* 10 (1984): 11–70; Argueles Morales, *Con el corazón en el disparador* (1986); and Margaret Randall's *Sandino's Daughters* (1981) and *Christians in the Nicaraguan Revolution* (1983a). See also Jaime Wheelock's reconstruction of the 1974 Castillo hostage taking by the FSLN, *Diciembre victorioso* (1979), and the recent posthumous collection of memoirs of the FSLN guerrilla written by comandante Germán Pomares in 1975, *El Danto* (1989). Under the sponsorship of Borge and

the Ministry of the Interior, a huge mass of oral histories of the revolution was gathered by literacy campaign and cultural brigade workers in the early 1980s, which is waiting a moment less urgent than the present one in Nicaragua to be turned into testimonial literature.

12. Carpio writes in the prologue to *Secuestro y capucha*: "El valor que podrán tener estas letras es mostrar con realismo tales procedimientos antidemocráticos, a fin de estimular la lucha de los sectores progresistas por su total abolición y por la puesta en práctica de los derechos democráticos y humanos" (the value that these writings can have is to show with realism the nature of these undemocratic procedures, so as to stimulate the struggle of the progressive sectors for their total abolition and for the implementation of democratic and human rights).

13. The prologue by ERP collaborator René Cruz notes along these lines: "There is considerable concrete experience which has been lost by not being processed and transmitted by militants and another large part has been deformed in its essence by being elaborated by leftist intellectual intermediaries who adjust what they are relating not in relation to revolutionary needs but in relation to the needs of fiction and bourgeois revolutionary theorizing" (p. 12).

14. See, for example, the powerful 1983 film *El Salvador: el pueblo vencerá*, which ends (in a scene some have claimed was contrived) with a young boy narrating the death of his father at the hands of the army. For a general orientation to testimonial forms in Salvadoran song, theater, and film see Calderón (1982) and Kirk (1985).

15. First published in Flemish in Holland (1986). The recent edition in Spanish was produced as a bound volume of mimeographed or Xeroxed typed text by Ediciones Sistema Radio Venceremos, the FMLN media collective.

16. For other examples of fiction published by writers in or close to Grupo RIN-78 see the anthologies by Lucrecia Méndez de Penedo, ed., *Joven narrativa guatemalteca* (1981), and Luis Alfredo Arango and Rolando Castellanos, eds., *De Francisco a Francisco. 50 años de narrativa guatemalteca* (1985). Also see Luis Aceituno, *Una ventana al cielo* (1983); Francisco Albizúrez Palma, *Casa de curas y otras locuras* (1982); Max Araújo, *Cuentos, fábulas y anti-fábulas* (1981); Franz Galich, *Ficcionario inédito* (1979); Dante Liano, *Jornadas y otros cuentos* (1978); Adolfo Méndez Vides, *Escritores famosos y otros desgraciados* (1980); Víctor Muñoz, *Atelor, su mamá y sus desgracias personales* (1980), *Lo que yo quiero es que se detenga el tren* (1984), and *Breve relato . . .* (1988); Marco Augusto Quiroa, *Semana mayor* (1984); and Francisco José Solares, *Cuentos e indiferencias* (1982) and *La orientación de la mirada* (1985).

17. There are a number of other more or less testimonial memoirs of the Ubico–October Revolution–1954 coup period that we should mention: José Zamora Alvarez, *Las memorias de Andrés. Relato de un soldado ex-combatiente del 20 de octubre de 1944* (1975; published, it's interesting to note, by the editorial house of the Guatemalan army); Carlos Samayoa Chinchilla, *El dictador y yo. Un relato sobre la vida del General Ubico* (1950; current edition 1967); the three-volume memoirs published between 1977 and 1989 of César Augusto Silva—an ex-colonel who remained loyal to Arbenz in 1954 (*La batalla de Gualín; 12 horas de combate; Cuando gobiernan las armas*); Guillermo Contreras, *El calvario del pueblo de Guatemala* (1985); and what is at least in

content the Guatemalan counterpart to Roque Dalton's *Miguel Mármol*, the memoirs of Guatemalan Communist party leader Antonio Obando Sánchez, *Memorias. La historia del movimiento obrero* (1978).

18. On the crisis of Guatemalan *foquismo*, see the testimonio of FAR commander Pablo Monsato in an interview with Marta Harnecker, "De las armas a las masas para ganar la guerra," a portion of which is translated along with a number of other short testimonios of the armed struggle in Fried et al. (1983).

19. On this point, see the translation of the manifesto of the EGP, "The Indian People and the Guatemalan Revolution," in Fried et al. (1983: 278–284).

20. Apart from numerous journalistic accounts, there are available in English, for example, *Voices of the Survivors: The Massacre at the Finca San Francisco* (1983); *Testimonies from Peasants of El Petén* (1981); Shelton Davis and Julie Hodson, *Witnesses to Political Violence in Guatemala: The Suppression of a Rural Development Movement* (1982), *Witnesses to Genocide: The Present Situation of Indians in Guatemala* (1983), and *We Continue Forever: Sorrow and Strength of Guatemalan Women* (1984), and *Granddaughters of the Corn* (1989).

21. In the wake of *Me llamo*, several quasi-testimonial texts on Indian life have appeared: Valentín Solórzano's *El relato de Juan Tayín* (1985)—a semifictional reconstruction of "conversations" the author had in his childhood with the eponymous Indian narrator, dealing with plantation life in the early twentieth century; Albertina Saravia's *El ladino me jodió: vida de un indígena* (1983), which reconstructs the legal case of an Indian, Julián Tzul, in the 1960s (Saravia is a lawyer who specializes in Indian rights cases). We should also mention here a book that is very much in the spirit of Rigoberta Menchú's narrative, but told from the point of view of a Catholic, ladino peasant community: the testimonio of the Honduran peasant organizer, Elvia Alvarado, *Don't Be Afraid, Gringo: A Honduran Woman Speaks from the Heart* (1987).

Though they belong more in the tradition of the ethnographic life history than of the radical testimonio we are sketching here, two books by anthropologist James Sexton based on the oral accounts of Ignacio Bizarro Ujpán should be mentioned as counterparts of *Me llamo Rigoberta Menchú: Son of Tecún Umán: A Maya Indian Tells His Life Story* (1981), and *Campesino: The Diary of a Guatemalan Indian* (1985). They cover more or less the same time period and topics as Menchú—the intense years of Indian uprisings and military reprisals in the 1970s and early 1980s—but with a very different tone and orientation. For example, where Menchú mentions the problems of Indian alcoholism only in passing, Bizarro Ujpán devotes pages and pages to his drinking bouts. Where Menchú describes land takeovers and Indians organizing and fighting against the government as in the great CUC strike of 1980, Bizarro Ujpán recalls fondly his own years in the army and complains that the same strike cost him $400. Where Menchú wants to see a preservation of Mayan identity within the context of a revolutionary Indian/ladino alliance, Bizarro Ujpán considers his Indian heritage a weakness and seems to be for assimilation to a modernizing capitalist and ladino-dominated system represented (for him) by the Ríos Montt regime. Finally, where Menchú's testimonio is conceived as a particular instance and instrumentality of a collective experience, Bizarro Ujpán's two books, for all the efforts of his interlocutor to see him as representative of the contemporary Maya in Guatemala, seem rather to represent that fraction of ladinized Indians broken away (often by service in the army) from their communities and integrated in relatively privileged ways into the dominant system.

22. Under threat from death squads, Montejo and his family eventually left Guatemala altogether. He was invited to teach at Bucknell and as of this writing is a graduate student in anthropology at the University of Connecticut.

Bibliography

Acevedo, Ramón Luis. 1982. *La novela centroamericana*. Río Piedras: Universidad de Puerto Rico.

Acevedo, Ramón Luis, Mario Roberto Morales, and Ileana Rodríguez. 1989. *Literatura y crisis en Centro América*. San José: CSUCA.

Achugar, Hugo. 1984/1985. "Poesía política e interpelación populista: el caso de la poesía salvadoreña." In Hernán Vidal, ed. *Literature and Contemporary Revolutionary Culture, I*. Minneapolis: Society for the Study of Contemporary Hispanic and Lusophone Revolutionary Literatures, 313–332.

———.1985. *Poesía y sociedad (Uruguay 1880–1911)*. Montevideo: Arca.

———. 1988. "The Book of Poems as a Social Act: Notes toward an Interpretation of Contemporary Hispanic American Poetry." In Cary Nelson and Lawrence Grossberg, eds. *Marxism and the Interpretation of Culture*. Chicago-Urbana: University of Illinois Press, 651–662.

Adams, Richard. 1956. *La ladinización en Guatemala*. Guatemala: SISG.

Agudelo, William, ed. 1982. *El asalto a San Carlos. Testimonios de Solentiname*. Managua: Editorial La Ocarina/Ministerio de Cultura.

Aguilar, Rosario. 1976. *Primavera sonámbula* (anthology). San José: EDUCA.

———. 1986. *Siete relatos sobre el amor y la guerra*. San José: EDUCA.

Aguilera, Julio Fausto. 1973. *Antología de poetas revolucionarios*. Guatemala: Asociación de Estudiantes El Derecho.

Albizures, Miguel Angel. 1987. *Tiempo de sudor y lucha*. Mexico: Praxis Editores.

Albizúrez Palma, Francisco. 1983. *Grandes momentos de la literatura guatemalteca*. Guatemala: Editorial José de Pineda Ibarra.

Albizurez Palma, Francisco, and Catalina Barrios. 1986. *Historia de la literatura guatemalteca*, vols. 2 and 3. Guatemala: Editorial Universitaria.

Alegría, Claribel, ed. 1981. *Homenaje a El Salvador*. Madrid: Visor.

———. 1982a. *Flowers from the Volcano*. Translated by Carolyn Forché. Pittsburgh: University of Pittsburgh Press.

———. 1982b. *Album familiar*. San José: EDUCA.

———. 1982c. *Nicaragua, la revolución sandinista. Una crónica política, 1855–1979*. Mexico: Era.

———. 1983. *No me agarrán viva. La mujer salvadoreña en la lucha*. Mexico: Era.

———. 1984. *Para romper el silencio: Resistencia y lucha en las cárceles salvadoreñas.* Mexico: Era.

————. 1987a. *Luisa in Realityland.* Translated by Claribel Alegría and Darwin J. Flakoll. Willimantic, Conn.: Curbstone.

————. 1987b. *They Won't Take Me Alive.* Translated by Amanda Hopkinson. London: Women's Press.

————. 1988a. *Y este poema rio* (anthology). Managua: Editorial Nueva Nicaragua.

————. 1988b. *Woman of Sumpul and Other Poems.* Translated by Darwin J. Flakoll. Pittsburgh: University of Pittsburgh Press.

Alegría, Claribel, and Darwin J. Flakoll. 1966. *Cenizas de Izalco.* Barcelona: Seix Barral.

————, eds. 1984. *El Salvador en armas.* Havana: Casa de las Américas.

————. 1989a. *Ashes of Izalco.* Translated by Darwin J. Flakoll. Willimantic, Conn.: Curbstone.

————, eds. 1989b. *On the Front Line. Guerrilla Poetry of El Salvador.* Willimantic, Conn.: Curbstone.

Alegría, Fernando. 1978. "Antiliteratura." In César Fernández Moreno, ed. *América Latina en su literatura.* Mexico: Siglo XXI, 243–258.

Althusser, Louis. 1970. *For Marx.* Translated by Ben Brewster. New York: Vintage.

————. 1971. *Lenin and Philosophy and Other Essays.* Translated by Ben Brewster. New York: Monthly Review Press.

Alvarado, Elvia. 1987. *Don't Be Afraid, Gringo. A Honduran Woman Speaks from the Heart.* San Francisco: Institute for Food and Development Policy.

Alvarado, Humberto. 1947. *Mesa redonda sobre el artista y los problemas de nuestro tiempo.* Guatemala: Ediciones Saker-ti.

————. 1953. *Por un arte nacional democrático y realista.* Guatemala: Ediciones Saker-ti.

————. 1967. *Preocupaciones.* Guatemala: Ediciones Vanguardia.

Anderson, Benedict. 1983. *Imagined Communities. Reflections on the Origin and Spread of Nationalism.* London: Verso.

Anderson, Marilyn, and Jonathan Garlock. 1989. *Granddaughters of the Corn.* Willimantic, Conn.: Curbstone.

Anderson, Thomas. 1971. *Matanza: El Salvador's Communist Revolt of 1932.* Lincoln: University of Nebraska Press.

Anglesey, Zoë, ed. 1987. *Ixok Amar-Go: Central American Women's Poetry for Peace.* Penobscott, Maine: Granite Press.

Arango, Luis Alfredo, and Rolando Castellanos. 1985. *De Francisco a Francisco. 50 años de narrativa guatemalteca.* Guatemala: Grupo Literario RIN-78.

Arellano, Jorge Eduardo. 1969. *El movimiento de vanguardia de Nicaragua: Gérmenes, desarrollo, significado 1927–1932.* 2d ed. Managua: Colección Revista Conservadora de Pensamiento Centroamericano.

————. 1977. *Panorama de la literatura nicaragüense.* 3d ed. Managua: Ediciones Nacionales.

————. 1982. *Panorama de la literatura nicaragüense.* 4th ed. Managua: Editorial Nueva Nicaragua.

Argueta, Manlio. 1977. *Caperucita en la zona roja.* Havana: Casa de las Américas.

————. 1980. *Un día en la vida.* San José: EDUCA.

————. 1982. *El valle de las hamacas.* 2d ed. San José: EDUCA.

————. 1983a. *One Day of Life.* Translated by Bill Brow. New York: Vintage Books.

————, ed. 1983b. *Poesía de El Salvador.* San José: EDUCA.

————. 1986. *Cuzcatlán donde bate la mar del sur.* Mexico: Editorial Guayamuras.

————. 1987. *Cuzcatlán: Where the Southern Sea Beats.* Translated by Clark Hansen. New York: Vintage Books.

Arias, Arturo. 1979a. *Después de las bombas.* Mexico: J. Mortiz.

————. 1979b. *Ideologías, literatura y sociedad durante la revolución guatemalteca.* Havana: Casa de las Américas.

————. 1981. *Itznamna.* Havana: Casa de las Américas.

————. 1989. *Jaguar en llamas.* Guatemala: Editorial Cultura.

————. 1990. *After the Bombs.* Translated by Aza Katz. Willimantic, Conn.: Curbstone.

Arias, Pilar. 1980. *Nicaragua: Revolución. Relatos de combatientes del Frente Sandinista.* Mexico: Siglo XXI.

Armijo, Roberto, and Rigoberto Paredes, eds. 1983. *Poesía contemporánea de Centro América.* Barcelona: Los Libros de la Frontera.

Arranz, María del Rosario. 1984. *El Nuevo Signo: historia de un grupo literario en Guatemala.* Guatemala: RIN-78.

Arrién, Juan Batista, ed. 1982. *Nicaragua: revolución y proyecto educativo.* Managua: Ministerio de Educación.

Asís Fernández, Francisco de, ed. 1979. *Poesía política nicaragüense.* Mexico: UNAM (2d ed., Managua: Ministerio de Cultura, 1981).

Asturias, Miguel Angel. 1950. *Viento fuerte.* Buenos Aires: Losada.

————. 1954. *El papa verde.* Buenos Aires: Losada.

————. 1960. *Los ojos de los enterrados.* Buenos Aires: Losada.

————. 1977. *Leyendas de Guatemala.* Buenos Aires: Losada (1st ed. 1930).

————. 1984a. *El señor presidente.* San José: EDUCA (1st ed. 1946).

————. 1984b. *Hombres de maíz.* San José: EDUCA (1st ed. 1949).

————. trilogy

Balcárcel, José Luis. 1981. "Literatura y liberación nacional en Guatemala." *Casa de las Américas* 126 (May–June 1981): 17–26.

Baltadono, Charlotte. 1988. *No se rompía el silencio.* Managua: n.p.

Barreda Avila, Rubén. 1960. *Guaridas infernales.* Guatemala: n.p.

Barrientos Tecúm, Dante. 1989. *La situación social del escritor en Guatemala.* Guatemala: Editorial Esfuerzo.

Belli, Gioconda. 1974. *Sobre la grama.* Managua: El Pez y la Serpiente.

————. 1978. *Línea de fuego.* Havana: Casa de las Américas.

————. 1982. *Truenos y arco iris.* Managua: Editorial Nueva Nicaragua.

————. 1984. *Amor insurrecto* (anthology). Managua: Editorial Nueva Nicaragua.

————. 1987. *De la costilla de Eva.* Managua: Editorial Nueva Nicaragua.

————. 1988. *La mujer habitada.* Managua: Editorial Vanguardia.

————. 1989a. *From Eve's Rib.* Translated by Steven White. Willimantic, Conn.: Curbstone.

————. 1989b. *Poesía reunida.* Mexico: Diana.

Benedetti, Mario. 1977. *Poesía trunca.* Havana: Casa de las Américas.

Bennett, Tony. 1979. *Formalism and Marxism.* London: Methuen.

———, ed. 1984. *Formations of Nations and People.* London: Routledge & Kegan Paul.

———. 1985. "Texts in History: The Determinations of Readings and Their Texts." *Journal of the Midwest Modern Language Association* 18:1 (Fall 1985): 1–16.

Berrigan, Daniel. 1979. "Conversation between Brothers." *Movement* (Dublin) 35 (1978): 3–4.

Beverley, John. 1985. "Poetry and Revolution in Central America." In *The Year Left: An American Socialist Yearbook,* I. Edited by Mike Davis, Fred Pfeil, and Michael Sprinker. London: Verso, 155–180. Reprinted in *Metamorphosis* 5–6 (1984/1985): 52–58; and Vidal 1984/85: 295–312.

———. 1987. *Del Lazarillo al Sandinismo: Estudios sobre la función ideológica de la literatura española e hispanoamericana.* Minneapolis: Institute for the Study of Ideologies and Literature /Prisma Institute.

———. 1989. "The Margin at the Center: On *Testimonio." Modern Fiction Studies* 35: 1 (Spring 1989): 11–28.

Blanco, Yolanda. 1977. *Cerámica Sol.* Managua: Editorial Universitaria de la UNAN.

———. 1985. *Aposentos.* Caracas: Ediciones con Textos.

Blandón, Chuncho. 1988. *Cuartel general.* Managua: Editorial Nueva Nicaragua.

Bogantes, Claudio, and Ursula Kuhlmann. 1983. "El surgimiento del realismo social en Centroamérica: 1930–1970." *Revista de Crítica Literaria Latinoamericana* 17 (1983): 39–64.

Borge Martínez, Tomás. 1980. *Carlos, el amanecer ya no es una tentación.* Managua: Editorial Nueva Nicaragua.

———. 1984. *Carlos, the Dawn Is No Longer beyond Our Reach.* Translated by Margaret Randall. Vancouver, B.C.: New Star Books.

———. 1985. "Encontrar a Ernesto Cardenal" *Nuevo Amanecer Cultural* V, 241 (January 20, 1985): 1–3.

———. 1989a. *Have You Seen a Red Curtain in My Weary Chamber?* (anthology). Translated by Russell Bartley, Kent Johnson, and Sylvia Yoneda. Willimantic, Conn.: Curbstone.

———. 1989b. *La paciente impaciencia.* Managua: Editorial Vanguardia.

———. 1990 (forthcoming). *The Patient Impatience.* Translated by Darwin J. Flakoll. Willimantic, Conn.: Curbstone.

Borgeson, Paul. 1984. *Hacia el hombre nuevo: poesía y pensamiento en Ernesto Cardenal.* London: Tamesis.

———. 1987. "Nicaragua" and "El Salvador." In David William Foster, ed. *Handbook of Latin American Literature.* New York: Garland, 405–414, 517–528.

Botherstone, Gordon, and Edward Dorn, eds. 1968. *Our Word: Guerrilla Poems from Latin America.* London: Cape Goliard Press.

Brett, Guy. 1987. *Through Our Own Eyes. Popular Art and Modern History.* Philadelphia: New Society Publishers.

Burbach, Roger, and Orlando Núñez. 1987. *Fire in the Americas. Forging a*

Revolutionary Agenda. London: Verso.

Bürger, Peter. 1984. *Theory of the Avant-Garde.* Translated by Michael Shaw. Minneapolis: University of Minnesota Press.

Cabezas, Omar. 1982. *La montaña es algo más que una inmensa estepa verde.* Havana: Casa de las Américas.

———. 1985. *Fire from the Mountain: The Making of a Sandinista.* Translated by Kathleen Weaver. New York: Crown.

———. 1988. *Canción de amor para los hombres.* Managua: Editorial Nueva Nicaragua.

Caistor, Nick, ed. n.d. *El Salvador: Poems of Rebellion.* London: El Salvador Solidarity Committee.

Calderón, Manuel, ed. 1982. *El Salvador: Comunicación en la revolución.* Mexico: Editorial Integración Latinoamericana.

Camacho, Daniel, and Rafael Menjívar, eds. 1985. *Movimientos populares en Centroamérica.* San José: EDUCA.

Cardenal, Ernesto. 1960a. *Gethsemani, Ky.* Mexico: Ediciones Ecuador.

———. 1960b. *Hora 0.* In *Antología.* San José: EDUCA, 1982 (originally published in parts in *Revista Mexicana de Literatura* between 1957 and 1960).

———. 1964. *Psalmos.* Medellín: Universidad de Antioquia.

———. 1966. *El estrecho dudoso.* Madrid: Ediciones Cultura Hispánica.

———. 1969. *Homenaje a los indios americanos.* León, Nicaragua: Editorial Universitaria.

———. 1970. *En Cuba.* Havana: Casa de las Américas.

———. 1971. *Psalms of Struggle and Liberation.* Translated by Emile McAnany. New York: Herder and Herder.

———. 1972. *To Live Is to Love.* Translated by Kurt Reinhardt. New York: Herder and Herder.

———. 1973a. *Canto nacional.* Mexico: Siglo XXI (1st ed. 1972).

———. 1973b. *Oráculo sobre Managua.* Managua: Editorial José Martí.

———, ed. 1973c. *Poesía nicaragüense.* Havana: Casa de las Américas.

———. 1974a. *Homage to the American Indians.* Translated by Monique and Carlos Altschul. Baltimore: Johns Hopkins University Press.

———. 1974b. *In Cuba.* Translated by Donald Walsh. New York: New Directions.

———. 1975. *El evangelio de Solentiname,* vol. 1. Salamanca: Ediciones Sígueme.

———. 1976. *La santidad de la revolución.* Salamanca: Ediciones Sígueme.

———. 1977a. *Apocalypse and Other Poems.* Translated by Robert Pring-Mill, Donald Walsh, et al. New York: New Directions.

———. 1977b. "Lo que fue Solentiname." *El Nacional* (Caracas), November 27, 1977.

———. 1979. *The Gospel in Solentiname.* Translated by Donald Walsh. Maryknoll, N.Y.: Orbis Books.

———. 1980. *Zero Hour and Other Documentary Poems.* Translated by Donald D. Walsh et al. New York: New Directions.

———. 1981a. "Con Ernesto Cardenal." *Amanecer: reflexión cristiana en la Nueva Nicaragua* 3 (1981): 15–16.

———. 1981b. "Talleres de poesía: socialización de los medios de producción poéticos." In Daisy Zamora, ed. *Hacia una política cultural de la revolución popular sandinista.* Managua: Ministerio de Cultura, 225–232.

———. 1981c. "Algunas reglas para escribir poesía." Managua: Ministerio de Cultura (mimeo).

———. 1982a. *Antología.* San José: EDUCA.

———. 1982b. *La democratización de la cultura.* Managua: Ministerio de Cultura.

———. 1983. "Socialización de los medios de producción poéticos." In Mayra Jiménez, ed. *Poesía de la nueva Nicaragua: talleres populares de poesía.* Mexico: Siglo XXI, 9–17.

———. 1985a. *Flights of Victory/Vuelos de Victoria.* Translated by Marc Zimmerman et al. Maryknoll, N.Y.: Orbis Books. New edition, Willimantic, Conn.: Curbstone, 1988.

———. 1985b. "Interview." In Kent Johnson, ed. *A Nation of Poets: Writings from the Poetry Workshops.* Los Angeles: West End Press, 7–24.

———. 1985c. *With Walker in Nicaragua and Other Early Poems, 1949–1954.* Translated by Jonathan Cohen. Middletown, Conn.: Wesleyan University Press.

———. 1986. "Quetzalcoatl." *Nicaráuac* 12 (April 1986): 75–97.

———. 1987. *From Nicaragua with Love: Poems, 1979–1986.* Translated by Jonathan Cohen. San Francisco: City Lights Books.

———. 1988. *Nicaraguan New Time.* Translated by Dinah Livingstone. London and New York: Journeyman/Kampman.

———. 1989. *Canto cósmico.* Managua: Editorial Nueva Nicaragua.

Cardenal, Ernesto, and Ernesto Mejía Sánchez, eds. 1962. *Poesía revolucionaria nicaragüense.* Mexico: Ediciones Patria y Libertad.

Cardoso, Ciro. 1972. "Severo Martínez Peláez y el carácter del régimen colonial." *ESC* 1 (January–April 1972).

Cardoso, Fernando Enrique, and Enzo Faletto. 1979. *Dependency and Development in Latin America.* Translated by Marjorie Mattingly. Berkeley: University of California Press.

Cardoza y Aragón, Luis. 1976. *Guatemala, las líneas de su mano.* Mexico: Fondo de Cultura Económica (1st ed. 1955).

Carmack, Robert. 1988. *Harvest of Violence: Guatemala's Indians in the Counterinsurgency War.* Norman: University of Oklahoma Press.

Carmona, Fernando, ed. 1980. *Nicaragua: la estrategia de la victoria.* Mexico: Editorial Nuestro Tiempo.

Carpio, Iván. 1989. *A lo que el viento dijera. Los náufragos de Masachapa.* Guatemala: Editorial Impacto.

Carrera, Margarita. 1984. *Toda la poesía de Margarita Carrera* (anthology). Guatemala: Colección Guatemala.

———. 1986. *Signo XX.* Guatemala: Editorial Serviprensa Centroamericana.

Carrera, Mario Alberto. 1983. *Panorama de la poesía femenina guatemalteca del siglo XX.* Guatemala: Editorial Universitaria de Guatemala.

Carter, Brenda, et al. eds. 1989. *A Dream Compels Us. Voices of Salvadoran Women.* Boston: South End Press.

Castillo, Otto René. 1965. *Vámonos patria a caminar.* Guatemala: Editorial Vanguardia.

———. 1971. *Poemas* (anthology). Havana: Casa de las Américas.

———. 1982. *Informe de una injusticia (antología poética).* San José: EDUCA.

————. 1989. *Let's Go!* Translated by Margaret Randall. Willimantic, Conn.: Curbstone.

Castro, Fidel. 1964. *The Second Declaration of Havana.* New York: Pathfinder.

Castro, Nils. 1979. *Cultura nacional y liberación.* San José: Editorial Universitaria de Costa Rica.

Cayetano Carpio, Salvador. 1979. *Secuestro y capucha en un país del "Mundo Libre."* San José: EDUCA.

Cea, José Roberto, ed. 1971. *Antología general de la poesía de El Salvador.* San Salvador: Editorial Universitaria.

————. 1985. *Los pies sobre la tierra.* San José: EDUCA.

————. 1986a. *Corral no, corral de desplazados.* San Salvador: Cuadernos Universitarios No. 3.

————. 1986b. *Pocos y buenos* (anthology). San Salvador: Canoa Editores.

————. 1989a. *De la guanaxia irredenta.* San Salvador: Canoa Editores.

————. 1989b. *Los herederos de Farabundo.* San Salvador: Editorial Universitaria (1st ed. Managua, 1981).

Chamorro Cardenal, Jaime. 1988. *La Prensa: The Republic of Paper.* Lanham, Md.: Freedom House.

Chase, Alfonso. 1982. "Temas en la poesía de Otto René Castillo." In Otto René Castillo, *Informe de una injusticia.* San José: EDUCA.

————, ed. 1985. *Las armas de la luz. Antología de la poesía contemporánea de la América Central.* San José: Departamento Ecuménico de Investigaciones.

Chatterjee, Partha. 1986. *Nationalist Thought and the Colonial World—A Derivative Discourse.* London: Zed Books.

Chávez Alfaro, Lizandro. 1963. *Los monos de San Telmo.* Havana: Casa de las Américas.

————. 1969. *Trágame tierra.* Mexico: Editorial Diógenes.

Concha, Jaime. 1974. "La literatura colonial hispanoamericana: problemas e hipótesis." *Neohelicon* 4, 1–2: 31–50.

Conti, Mario. 1984. "La cultura en El Salvador: una peristente lucha y visión universal." In *Centroamérica en la Mira* 8 (September–October 1984).

Cornejo Polar, Antonio. 1989. "Los sistemas literarios como categorías históricas. Elementos para una discusión latinoamericana." *Revista de Crítica Literaria Latinoamericana* 29: 19–25; 39–58.

Coronel Urtecho, José. 1979. "Prefacio." Edwin Castro, *Y si no.* San José: EDUCA.

————. 1982. "Anotaciones y exageraciones sobre *La montaña es algo más...*" *Nicaráuac* 7 (June 1982): 39–42.

Craven, David. 1989. *The New Concept of Art and Popular Culture in Nicaragua since the Revolution of 1979.* Lewiston, N.Y.: Edwin Mellen Press.

Cuadra, Abelardo, with Sergio Ramírez. 1981. *Hombre del Caribe.* San José: EDUCA.

Cuadra, Manolo. 1982. *Solo en la compañía* (anthology). Managua: Editorial Nueva Nicaragua.

Cuadra, Pablo Antonio. 1974. *El Nicaragüense.* San José: EDUCA.

————. 1986. *Torres de Dios: memorias del movimiento de vanguardia.* Managua: El Pez y la Serpiente.

————. 1988. *The Birth of the Sun* (anthology). Translated by Steven White.

Greensboro, N.C.: Unicorn Press.

Cueva, Agustín. 1977. *El desarrollo del capitalismo en América Latina.* Mexico: Siglo XXI.

Dalton, Roque. 1963. "Poesía y militancia en América Latina." Havana: Casa de las Américas 20–21 (1963): 15–23.

———. 1969. *Taberna y otros lugares.* Havana: Casa de las Américas.

———. 1970. *¡Revolución en la revolución! y la crítica de derecha.* Havana: Casa de las Américas.

———. 1971. "Prológo." In Otto René Castillo, *Poemas e informe de una injusticia.* Havana: Casa de las Américas.

———. 1974. *Las historias prohibidas del pulgarcito.* Mexico: Siglo XXI.

———. 1976. *Pobrecito poeta que era yo.* San José: EDUCA.

———. 1980. *Poemas clandestinos.* San José: EDUCA.

———. 1981. *Poetry and Militancy in Latin America.* Translated by James Scully. Willimantic, Conn.: Curbstone.

———. 1982a. *Miguel Mármol. Los sucesos de 1932 en El Salvador.* San José: EDUCA.

———. 1982b. "Poems." Translated by Edward Baker. *Social Text* 5 (Spring 1982): 74–85.

———. 1983. *Poesía escogida.* San José: EDUCA.

———. 1984a. *Poemas clandestinos/Clandestine Poems.* Translated by Jack Hirschman and edited by Barbara Paschke and Eric Weaver. San Francisco: Solidarity.

———. 1984b. *Poems.* Translated by Richard Schaaf. Willimantic, Conn.: Curbstone.

———. 1986. *Un libro rojo para Lenin.* Managua: Editorial Nueva Nicaragua (1st ed. 1973).

———. 1987. *Miguel Mármol.* Translated by Kathleen Ross and Richard Schaaf. Willimantic, Conn.: Curbstone.

Dalton, Roque, et al. 1969. *El intelectual y la sociedad.* Mexico: Siglo XXI.

Darío, Rubén. 1977. *Rubén Darío, Poesía.* Caracas: Biblioteca Ayacucho.

Davis, Shelton, and Julie Hodson. 1982. *Witnesses to Political Violence in Guatemala: The Suppression of a Rural Development Movement.* Boston: Oxfam America.

———. 1983. *Witnesses to Genocide: The Present Situation of Indians in Guatemala.* London: Survival International.

———. 1984. *We Continue Forever: Sorrow and Strength of Guatemalan Women.* New York: Women's International Resource Exchange.

Dawes, Gregory. 1990. *Contemporary Nicaraguan Poetry: Aesthetic Commitment in an Age of Postmodernism.* Unpublished PhD diss., University of Washington.

Debray, Régis. 1967. *Revolution in the Revolution?* Translated by Bobbye Ortiz. New York: Grove Press.

———. 1975. *Las pruebas de fuego. La crítica de las armas/2.* Translated by Félix Blanco. Mexico: Siglo XXI.

Diskin, Martin, ed. 1984. *Trouble in Our Backyard: Central America and the United States in the Eighties.* New York: Pantheon.

Di Tella, Torcuato. 1965. "Populism and Reform in Latin America," in Claudio

Veliz, ed., *Obstacles to Change in Latin America.* London: Oxford University Press.

Dore, Elizabeth. 1985. "Culture." In Thomas Walker, ed. *Nicaragua: The First Five Years.* New York: Praeger, 413–422.

Doyle, Judith, and Jorge Lozano, eds. 1984. *Culture of Nicaragua.* Special issue of *Impulse* 11: 1 (Summer 1984).

Duchesne, Juan. 1986. "Las narraciones guerrilleras: configuración de un sujeto épico de nuevo tipo." In Hernán Vidal and René Jara, eds. *Testimonio y literatura.* Minneapolis: Institute for the Study of Ideologies and Literature, 185–197.

Dunkerley, James. 1982. *The Long War. Dictatorship and Revolution in El Salvador.* London: Junction/Verso.

———. 1986. "Central American Impasse." *Bulletin of Latin American Research* 5 (1986): 105–119.

———. 1988. *Power in the Isthmus.* London: Verso.

Eagleton, Terry, Fredric Jameson, and Edward Said. 1990. *Nationalism, Colonialism, and Literature.* Minnesota: University of Minnesota Press.

Ellis, Keith. 1986. "Rubén Darío y la idea del progreso." *Nicaráuac* 12 (1986): 133–141.

Ellner, Steve. 1989. "The Latin American Left since Allende: Perspectives and New Directions." *Latin American Research Review* XXIV, 2 (1989): 143–167.

Escobar, Ticio. 1988. "Posmodernismo/precapitalismo." *Casa de las Américas* 168 (1988): 13–19.

Esquivel, Julia. 1981. *El Padre Nuestro desde Guatemala y otros poemas.* San José, Costa Rica: Departamento Ecumenico de Investigaciones.

———. 1982. *Threatened with Resurrection/Prayers and Poems from an Exiled Guatemalan.* Elgin, Ill.: Brethren Press.

Fernández Moreno, César, ed. 1978. *América Latina en su literatura.* Mexico: Siglo XXI.

Fernández Retamar, Roberto. 1984. *Para una teoría de la literatura hispanoamericana.* Havana: Editorial Pueblo y Educación.

Flakoll, Darwin J. 1990. *A Guerrilla History of Central America.* Willimantic, Conn.: Curbstone.

Flora, Jan. 1987. *Roots of Insurgency in Central America.* Latin American Issues Monographs 5. Meadville, Penn.: Allegheny College/University of Akron.

Flora, Jan, and Edelberto Torres Rivas, eds. 1989. *Central America.* New York: Monthly Review Press.

Flores, Marco Antonio. 1968. *Muros de luz.* Mexico: Siglo XXI.

———. 1976. *Los compañeros.* Mexico: Joaquín Mortiz.

Flores Alvarado, Humberto. 1973. *El adamscismo y la sociedad guatemalteca.* Guatemala: Editorial Piedra Santa (1st ed. 1968).

FMLN. 1982. *Sandinistas Speak.* New York: Pathfinder Press.

Fonseca Amador, Carlos. 1980. *Ideario político de Augusto César Sandino.* Managua: Departamento de Propaganda y Educación Pública del FSLN.

———. 1984. *Obras.* Caracas, Venezuela: Editorial Nueva Nicaragua/Ediciones Centauro (one-volume facsimile of the original two-volume edition: Managua: Editorial Nueva Nicaragua, 1981, 1982).

Foppa, Alaíde. 1970. *Elogio de mi cuerpo*. México, D.F.: n.p.
———. 1979. *Las palabras y el tiempo* (Words and time). Flushing, N.Y.: La Vida Press.
———. 1982. *Poesías*. Guatemala: Serviprensa.
Forgacs, David. 1984. "National-Popular: Genealogy of a Concept." In Tony Bennett, ed., *Formations of Nations and People*. London: Routledge & Kegan Paul, 83–97.
Foster, David William, ed. 1987. *Handbook of Latin American Literature*. New York: Garland.
Franco, Jean. 1977. "The Crisis of the Liberal Imagination and the Utopia of Writing." *Ideologies and Literature* 1 (1976–1977): 6–24.
———. 1986. "Apuntes sobre la crítica feminista y la literatura hispanoamericana." *Hispamérica* 45 (1986): 31–43.
———. 1988. "Beyond Ethnocentrism: Gender, Power, and the Third World Intelligentsia." In Cary Nelson and Lawrence Grossberg, eds. *Marxism and the Interpretation of Culture*. Chicago-Urbana: University of Illinois Press, 503–515.
———. 1989. *Plotting Women. Gender and Representation in Mexico*. New York: Columbia University Press.
Fried, Jonathan, Marvin Gettleman, Deborah Levenson, and Nancy Peckenham, eds. 1983. *Guatemala in Rebellion: Unfinished History*. New York: Grove Press.
Galeano, Eduardo. 1969. *Guatemala: Occupied Country*. Translated by Cedric Belfrage. New York: Monthly Review Press.
Galich, Manuel. 1985. *Del pánico al ataque*. Guatemala: Editorial Universitaria (1st ed. 1949).
García Canclini, Néstor. 1981. *Las culturas populares en el capitalismo*. Havana: Casa de las Américas.
García Laviana, Gaspar. 1979. *Cantos de amor y guerra*. Managua: Ministerio de Cultura.
García Márquez, Gabriel. 1967. *Cien años de soledad*. Buenos Aires: Editorial Sudamérica.
———, et al. 1979. *Los sandinistas. Documentos, reportajes*. Bogotá: La Oveja Negra.
Germani, Gino. 1971. *Política y sociedad en una época de transición*. Buenos Aires: Editorial Paidos.
Gibbons, Reginald. 1987. "Political Poetry and the Example of Ernesto Cardenal." *Critical Inquiry* 13:3 (Spring), 648–671.
Girardi, Gilio. 1983. *Fe en la revolución: revolución en la cultura*. Managua: Editorial Nueva Nicaragua.
González, Otto Raúl. 1948. *Poetas de Guatemala*. San Salvador: Revista Bibliográfica Nacional.
González, Paulino. 1985. "Las luchas estudiantiles en Centroamérica; 1970–1983." In Daniel Camacho and Rafael Menjívar, eds. *Movimientos populares en Centroamérica*. San José: EDUCA, 238–292.
González Casanova, Pablo ed., 1984. *América Latina: historia de medio siglo. 2. México, Centroamérica y el Caribe*. Mexico: Siglo XXI.
González Echevarría, Roberto. 1985. *The Voice of the Masters: Writing and*

Authority in Modern Latin American Literature. Austin: University of Texas Press (ILAS).

Gramsci, Antonio. 1985. *Selections from the Cultural Writings.* Edited and translated by David Forgacs and Geoffrey Nowell-Smith. London: Lawrence and Wishart.

Guadamuz, Carlos José. 1982. *Y . . . "Las casas quedaron llenas de humo."* Managua: Editorial Nueva Nicaragua.

Guevara, Che. 1961. *Guerrilla Warfare.* New York: Monthly Review Press.

———. 1968a. *El diario de campaña del Che Guevara en Bolivia.* Havana: Instituto Cubano del Libro.

———. 1968b. *Reminiscences of the Cuban Revolutionary War.* Translated by Victoria Ortiz. New York: Monthly Review Press.

Guevara, Otoniel. 1988. *El violento hormiguero.* San Salvador: Ediciones la Flor Rojinegra.

Gullete, David, ed. 1988. *Nicaraguan Peasant Poetry from Solentiname.* Albuquerque, N.M.: West End Press.

Guzmán, José Luis, and Roberto Herrera. 1987. "Sobre el papel del trabajador del arte y la cultura en el momento actual salvadoreño." *Taller de Letras* (Universidad Centroamericana José Simeón Canas) 5:114 (April 1987): 51–58.

Guzmán Böckler, Carlos. 1975. *Colonialismo y revolución.* Mexico: Siglo XXI.

———. 1986. *Donde enmudecen las conciencias: crepúsculo y aurora en Guatemala.* Mexico: SEP/CIESAS.

Guzmán Böckler, Carlos, and Jean-Loup Herbert. 1970. *Guatemala: una interpretación histórico-social.* Mexico: Siglo XXI.

Halperin Donghi, Tulio. 1980. "Nueva narrativa y ciencias sociales hispanoamericanas en la década del sesenta." *Hispamérica* 27 (1980): 3–18.

Hamilton, Russell. 1982. "A Country Built of Poems: Nationalism and Angolan Literature." *Research in African Literature* 13:3 (Fall 1982): 315–325.

———. 1985. "Posturing with Resolve: Poetry and Revolution in Mozambique and Angola." In Hernán Vidal, ed. *Literature and Contemporary Revolutionary Culture, I.* Minneapolis: Society for the Study of Contemporary Hispanic and Lusophone Revolutionary Literatures, 158–173.

Harlow, Barbara. 1987. *Resistance Literature.* New York: Methuen.

Harnecker, Marta, ed. 1984. *Pueblos en armas: Guatemala, El Salvador, Nicaragua.* Mexico: Era.

Heijningen, Hans Van, ed. 1987. *¡Que se convierta este dolor en fuerza para seguir luchando! Relato del asesinato del dirigente campesino Alfonso Núñez y seis comalapeños más.* Managua: UNAG.

Hernández, Alfonso. 1981. *León de piedra: testimonios de la lucha de clases en El Salvador.* n.p.

Hernández Aguirre, Mario. 1961. "La nueva poesía salvadoreña: la Generación Comprometida." *Cultura* (San Salvador) 20: 77–99.

Hirshon, Sheryl, with Judy Butler. 1983. *And Also Teach Them to Read.* Westport, Conn.: Lawrence Hill.

Hodges, Donald. 1986. *Intellectual Foundations of the Nicaraguan Revolution.* Austin: University of Texas Press.

Iffland, James. 1985. "Hacia una teoría de la función del humor en la poesía revolucionaria (a propósito de Roque Dalton)." In Hernán Vidal, ed. *Literature and Contemporary Revolutionary Culture, I.* Minneapolis: Society for the Study of Contemporary Hispanic and Lusophone Revolutionary Literatures, 112–157.

―――. 1989. "Ideologías de la muerte en la poesía de Otto René Castillo." *Ideologies and Literature* 4:1 (Spring 1989):95–148.

Ilce, Ana. 1975. *Las ceremonias del silencio.* Managua: El Pez y la Serpiente.

Ipola, Emilio de. 1983. *Ideología y discurso populista.* Buenos Aires: Folios Ediciones.

Jailer, Todd. 1988. "Nicaragua: Poetry and War." *Zeta Magazine* (April 1988): 60–66.

Jameson, Fredric. 1972. *The Prison House of Language: A Critical Acount of Structuralism and Russian Formalism.* Princeton, N.J.: Princeton University Press.

―――. 1981. *The Political Unconscious: Narrative as a Socially Symbolic Act.* Ithaca, N.Y.: Cornell University Press.

―――. 1984. "Postmodernism, or the Cultural Logic of Late Capitalism." *New Left Review* 146: 53–92.

―――. 1986. "Third-World Literature in the Era of Multinational Capitalism." *Social Text* 15 (Fall 1986): 69–80.

Jiménez, Mayra, ed. 1980. *Poesía campesina de Solentiname.* Managua: Ministerio de Cultura.

―――. 1983. *Poesía de la nueva Nicaragua: talleres populares de poesía.* Mexico: Siglo XXI.

―――. 1985a. *Fogata en la oscuridad. Los talleres de poesía en la alfabetización.* Managua: Editorial Nueva Nicaragua.

―――. 1985b. *Poesia de las fuerzas armadas.* Managua: Ministerio de Cultura.

Jitrik, Noé. 1978. "Destrucción y forma en las narraciones." In César Fernández Moreno, ed. *América Latina en su literatura.* Mexico: Siglo XXI, 259–271.

Johnson, Kent, ed. 1985. *A Nation of Poets: Writings from the Poetry Workshops.* Los Angeles: West End Press.

Kaplan, Marcos. 1969. *Formación del estado nacional en América Latina.* Santiago de Chile: Editorial Universitaria.

Kirk, John. 1985. "Revolutionary Music, Salvadoran Style: 'Yolacamba Ita.'" In Hernán Vidal, ed. *Literature and Contemporary Revolutionary Culture, I.* Minneapolis: Society for the Study of Contemporary Hispanic and Lusophone Revolutionary Literatures, 338–352.

Labastida, Julio, ed. 1985. *Hegemonía y alternativas políticas en América Latina.* Mexico: Siglo XXI.

Lacan, Jacques. 1977. *Ecrits. A Selection.* Translated by Alan Sheridan. New York: Norton.

Laclau, Ernesto. 1977. *Politics and Ideology in Marxist Theory.* London: New Left Books.

Laclau, Ernesto, and Chantal Mouffe. 1985. *Hegemony and Socialist Strategy: Towards a Radical Democratic Politics.* Translated by Winston Moore and Paul Cammack. London: Verso.

―――. 1988. "Politics and the Limits of Modernity." In *Universal Abandon. The Politics of Postmodernism*, edited by Andrew Ross. Minneapolis:

University of Minnesota Press.

Lancaster, Roger N. 1988. *Thanks to God and the Revolution: Popular Religion and Class Consciousness in the New Nicaragua.* New York: Columbia University Press.

Lars, Claudia. 1975. *Poesía última.* San Salvador: Ministerio de Educación.

Lascaris, Constantino. 1970. *Historia de las ideas en Centroamérica.* San José: EDUCA.

Lenin, V. I. 1971. "Party Literature and Party Organization." In *Where to Begin?* Moscow: Progress Publishers. (Originally published, 1905.)

Leonard, Irving A. 1966. *Baroque Times in Old Mexico.* Ann Arbor: University of Michigan Press (1st ed. 1959).

Leyva, Roberto José. 1983. "Hacia un arte más bello . . ." *Ventana* (July 9, 1983).

Liano, Dante. 1984. *La palabra en el sueño: literatura y sociedad en Guatemala.* Rome: Bulzoni Editore.

————, ed. 1986. *Poeti di Guatemala (1954–1986).* Rome: Bulzoni Editore.

Lievens, Karin. 1988. *El quinto piso de la alegría. Tres años con la guerrilla.* N.p.: Ediciones Sistema Radio Venceremos.

Lorand de Olazagasti, Adelaide. 1968. *El indio en la narrativa guatemalteca.* Río Piedras: Editorial Universitaria de la Universidad de Puerto Rico.

Losada, Alejandro. 1979. "El surgimiento del realismo social en la literatura de América Latina." *Ideologies and Literature* 11 (1979): 20–55.

————. 1981. *La literatura en la sociedad de América Latina.* Aarhus, Denmark: Romansk Institut Aarhus Universitet.

Lovell, Terry. 1983. *Pictures of Reality. Aesthetics, Politics and Pleasure.* London: British Film Institute.

Lovell, W. George. 1988. "Surviving Conquest: The Maya of Guatemala in Historical Perspective." *Latin American Research Review* XXIII, 2 (1988): 25–57.

Lyons, John, ed. 1983. *Poems of Love and Revolution from the Nicaraguan Poetry Workshops.* London: Nicaraguan Solidarity Committee.

Lyotard, Jean-François. 1984. *The Postmodern Condition: A Report on Knowledge.* Translated by Geoff Bennington and Brian Massumi. Minneapolis: University of Minnesota Press.

McLean, George F. , Raul Molina, and Timothy Ready, eds. 1989. *Culture, Human Rights and Peace in Central America.* Lanham, Md.: University Presses of America.

MacLeod, Murdo. 1973. *Spanish Central America: A Socioeconomic History, 1520–1720.* Berkeley: University of California Press.

Marcuse, Herbert. 1978. *The Aesthetic Dimension. Toward a Critique of Marxist Aesthetics.* Boston: Beacon Press.

Mariátegui, José Carlos. 1928. *Siete ensayos sobre la realidad peruana.* Lima: Amauta.

Márquez, Roberto, ed. 1974. *Latin American Revolutionary Poetry.* New York: Monthly Review Press.

Martin, Randy. 1988. "Nicaragua: Theater and State Without Walls." *Social Text* 18 (Winter 1987/88): 83–94.

Martínez, Ana Guadalupe. 1979. *Las cárceles clandestinas de El Salvador.* Mexico: Casa El Salvador.

Martínez Peláez, Severo. 1983. *La patria del criollo*. San José: EDUCA (1st ed. 1971).

Mattelhart, Armand, ed. 1986. *Communicating in Popular Nicaragua*. New York: International General.

Mejía, José, ed. 1970. *Las plumas del serpiente* (anthology). Guatemala: Editorial Nuevo Signo.

————. n.d. *Introducción a Nuevo Signo: piedra de sacrificios*. Guatemala: n.p.

Mejía Godoy, Carlos, and Pablo Martínez. 1981. *La misa campesina nicaragüense*. Managua: Ministerio de Cultura.

Menchú, Rigoberta. 1984. *I, Rigoberta Menchú: An Indian Woman in Guatemala*. Translated by Ann Wright. London: Verso.

Menchú, Rigoberta, with Elisabeth Burgos. 1983. *Me llamo Rigoberta Menchú, y así me nació la conciencia*. Havana: Casa de las Américas.

Méndez, Luz. 1985. *Las voces silenciadas (poemas feministas)*. Guatemala: RIN-78.

————, ed. 1986. *La poesía del grupo RIN-78*. Guatemala: RIN-78.

Méndez de la Vega, Luz, ed. n.d. *Poetisas desmitificadoras guatemaltecas*. Guatemala: Colección Guatemala.

————. 1986. *La poesía del Grupo RIN-78*. Guatemala: Editorial RIN-78.

Meneses, Vidaluz. 1975. *Llama guardada*. Managua: n.p.

————. 1982. *El aire que me llama*. 2d ed. Managua: Unión de Escritores de Nicaragua.

Menjívar Ochoa, Rafael. 1985. *Historia del traidor de nunca jámas*. San José: EDUCA.

Menton, Seymour. 1985. *Historia crítica de la novela guatemalteca*. Guatemala: Editorial Universitaria.

Ministerio de Cultura (Nicaragua). 1982. *Reseña de la nueva canción en Nicaragua. Antecedentes, desarrollo y actualidad. Avances de investigación*, documento no. 4: Dirección de Investigaciones Culturales.

Molloy, Sylvia. 1984. "At Face Value: Autobiographical Writing in Spanish America." *Dispositio: Revista Hispánica de Semiótica Literaria* 24–26: 1–18.

Molyneux, Maxine. 1985. "Women." In Thomas Walker, ed. *Nicaragua: The First Five Years*. New York: Praeger, 163–182.

Monsiváis, Carlos. 1985. "De las relaciones literarias entre 'alta cultura' y 'cultura popular.'" *Texto Crítico* 33 (1985): 46–61.

Monteforte Toledo, Mario. 1972. *Centro América: subdesarrollo y dependencia*. Mexico: UNAM.

Montejo, Víctor. 1987. *Testimony: Death of a Guatemalan Village*. Translated by Víctor Perera. Willimantic, Conn.: Curbstone.

Morales, Arqueles. 1986. *Con el corazón en el disparador. Entrevistas testimoniales de la insurreción sandinista*. Managua: Editorial Vanguardia.

Morales, Beltrán. 1975. *Sin páginas amarillas*. Managua: Ediciones Nacionales.

Morales, Mario Roberto. 1990. *El vuelo del quetzal*. San José: CSUCA (forthcoming).

Morales Avilés, Ricardo. 1981. *Obras*. Managua: Editorial Nueva Nicaragua.

Moraña, Mabel. 1984. *Literatura y cultura nacional en Hispanoamérica (1910–1940)*. Minneapolis: Institute for the Study of Ideologies and Literature.

Murguía, Alejandro, and Barbara Paschke, eds. 1983. *Volcán. Poems from Central America.* San Francisco: City Lights Books.

Murillo, Rosario. 1981. *Un deber de cantar.* Managua: Ministerio de Cultura.

———. 1982. *Amar es combatir: selecciones de Gualtayan y sube a nacer conmigo.* Managua: Editorial Nueva Nicaragua.

———. 1985. *En las espléndidas ciudades.* Managua: Editorial Nueva Nicaragua.

Najlis, Michele. 1969. *El viento armado.* Guatemala: Editorial Universitaria.

———. 1981. *Augurios.* San José: Editorial Costa Rica.

———. 1988. *Ars combinatoria* (anthology). Managua: Editorial Nueva Nicaragua.

Nelson, Cary, and Lawrence Grossberg, eds. 1988. *Marxism and the Interpretation of Culture.* Urbana: University of Illinois Press.

Nolan, David. 1984. *The Ideology of the Sandinistas and the Nicaraguan Revolution.* Coral Gables, Fla.: University of Miami Institute of Interamerican Studies.

Obando Sánchez, Antonio. 1978. *Memorias: la historia del movimiento obrero.* Guatemala: Editorial Universitaria.

Obregón, Roberto. 1973. *Poesía de barro.* Guatemala: Editorial Universitaria.

Olazagasti, Adelaida Lorand de. 1968. *El indio en la narrativa guatemalteca.* Río Piedras: Universidad de Puerto Rico.

Osorio, Nelson. 1985. *La formación de la vanguardia literaria en Venezuela.* Caracas: Biblioteca de la Real Academia Nacional de la Historia.

Osses, Esther María. 1986. *La novela del imperialismo en Centroamérica.* Maracaibo: Editorial de la Universidad de Zulia.

Paige, Jeffrey. 1975. *Agrarian Revolution: Social Movements and Export Agriculture in the Underdeveloped World.* New York: Free Press.

Pailler, Claire. 1989. *Mitos primordiales y poesía fundadora en América Central.* Paris: Editions de la CNRS.

Partnoy, Alicia, ed. 1988. *You Can't Drown the Fire: Latin American Women Writing in Exile.* Pittsburgh/San Francisco: Cleis Press.

Paschke, Barbara, and David Volpendista, eds. 1989. *A Clamor of Innocence: Stories from Central America.* San Francisco: City Lights Books.

Payeras, Mario. 1980. *Los días de la selva.* Havana: Casa de las Américas.

———. 1983. *Days of the Jungle: The Testimony of a Guatemalan Guerrillero, 1972–1976.* Introduction by George Black. New York: Monthly Review Press.

———. 1987. *El trueno en la ciudad: episodios de la lucha armada urbana de 1981 en Guatemala.* Mexico: Juan Pablos Editores.

Pearce, Jenny. 1986. *Promised Land. Peasant Rebellion in Chaltenango.* London: Latin American Bureau.

Perera, Víctor. 1986. *Rites: A Guatemalan Boyhood.* San Diego: Harcourt, Brace, Jovanovich.

Perus, Françoise. 1976. *Literatura y sociedad en América Latina: el modernismo.* Mexico: Siglo XXI.

———. 1982. *Historia y crítica literaria: el realismo social y la crisis de la dominación oligárquica.* Havana: Casa de las Américas.

Pomares, Germán. 1989. *El Danto.* Managua: Editorial Nueva Nicaragua.

Pring-Mill, Robert. 1970. "Both in Sorrow and Anger: Spanish American Protest Poetry." *Cambridge Review* 91 (February 1970): 112–122.

———. 1980. "The Redemption of Reality through Documentary Poetry." In Ernesto Cardenal, *Zero Hour and Other Documentary Poems.* New York: New Directions, ix–xxi.

Quintana, Emilio. N.d. *Bananos. La vida de los peones en la Yunai.* N.p.

Rama, Angel. 1970. *Rubén Darío y el modernismo.* Caracas: Universidad Central de Venezuela.

———. 1982. *Transculturación narrativa en América Latina.* Mexico City: Siglo XXI.

———. 1984. *La ciudad letrada.* Hanover, N.H.: Ediciones del Norte.

Ramírez Mercado, Sergio, ed. 1974. *El pensamiento vivo de Sandino.* San José: EDUCA.

———, ed. 1982a. *Antología del cuento centroamericano.* San José: EDUCA.

———. 1982b. "La Revolución: el hecho cultural más importante de nuestra historia." In Daisy Zamora, ed. *Hacia una política cultural de la revolución popular sandinista.* Managua: Ministerio de Cultura.

———. 1983a. *Balcanes y volcanes.* Managua: Editorial Nueva Nicaragua.

———. 1983b. *¡Te dió miedo la sangre!* Barcelona: Argos Vergara (1st ed. Caracas, 1977).

———. 1984a. "El escritor centroamericano." *Texto Crítico* (1984): 66–74.

———. 1984b. *To Bury Our Fathers.* Translated by Nick Caistor. London & New York: Readers International.

———. 1986. *Stories.* Translated by Nick Caistor. London and New York: Readers International.

———. 1988. *Castigo divino.* Managua: Editorial Nueva Nicaragua.

———. 1989. *La marca del Zorro. Hazañas del comandante Francisco Rivera Quintero.* Managua: Editorial Nueva Nicaragua.

———. 1990 (forthcoming). *You Are in Nicaragua.* Translated by Darwin J. Flakoll. Willimantic, Conn.: Curbstone.

Ramos, Julio. 1989. *Desencuentros de la modernidad en América Latina. Literatura y política en el siglo XIX.* Mexico: Fondo de Cultura Económica.

Randall, Margaret. 1974. *Cuban Women Now.* New York: Women's Press.

———. 1978. *No se puede hacer la revolución sin nosotras.* Havana: Casa de las Américas.

———. 1981. *Sandino's Daughters. Testimonies of Nicaraguan Women in Struggle.* Vancouver, B.C.: New Star Books.

———. 1983a. *Christians in the Nicaraguan Revolution.* Vancouver, B.C.: New Star Books.

———. 1983b. *Testimonios.* San José: Alforja.

———. 1984. *Risking a Somersault in the Air: Conversations with Nicaraguan Writers.* San Francisco: Solidarity Publications.

———. 1985a. *Testimonies: A Guide to Oral History.* Toronto: Participatory Research Group.

———, ed. 1985b. *Women Brave in the Face of Danger.* Trumansberg, N.Y.: Crossing Press.

Rincón, Carlos. 1978. *El cambio en la noción de la literatura.* Bogotá: Instituto Colombiano de Cultura.

Rincón, Carlos, and Dieter Eich. 1985. *The Contras. Interviews with Anti-Sandinistas.* San Francisco: Synthesis Publications.

Rivas, Lucinda. 1967. *Cantar para vivir.* Guatemala: Editorial Istmo.

Rivero, Eliana. 1985. "Testimonios y conversaciones como discurso literario: Cuba y Nicaragua." In Hernán Vidal, ed. *Literature and Contemporary Revolutionary Culture, I.* Minneapolis: Society for the Study of Contemporary Hispanic and Lusophone Revolutionary Literatures, 218–228.

Rodas, Ana María. 1973. *Poemas de la izquierda erótica.* Guatemala: Editorial Testimonio del Absurdo Diario.

Rodríguez, Ileana. 1981. "El texto literario como expresión mestizo-criollo: *in memoriam.*" *Casa de las Américas* 126 (1981): 52–62.

———. 1982. "Organizaciones populares y literatura testimonial: los años treinta en Nicaragua y El Salvador." In Rose Minc, ed., *Literatures in Transition: The Many Voices of the Caribbean Area.* Gaithersburg, Md.: Montclair State College/Hispamérica, 85–96.

Rodríguez Mojón, María Luisa. 1973. *Poesía revolucionaria guatemalteca.* Bilbao: Máximo Aguirre Zero.

Román, José. 1979. *Maldito país.* Managua: El Pez y la Serpiente.

Rugama, Leonel. 1981. *Poemas.* Managua: Departamento de Propaganda y Educación Pública del FSLN.

———. 1985. *The Earth Is a Satellite of the Moon.* Translated by Sara Miles, Richard Schaaf, and Nancy Weisberg. Willimantic, Conn.: Curbstone.

Rushdie, Salman. 1987. *A Jaguar Smile.* New York: Pantheon.

Salgado, María A. 1987. "Guatemala." In David W. Foster, ed. *Handbook of Latin American Literature.* New York: Garland, 1987, 291–306.

Sam Colop, Luis. 1978. *Versos sin refugio.* Guatemala: Editorial San Antonio.

———. 1979. *La copa y la raíz.* Guatemala: Grupo Editorial RIN-78.

Santos, Rosario ed. 1989. *And We Sold the Rain: Contemporary Fiction from Central America.* New York: Four Winds.

Saravia Enríquez, Albertina. 1983. *El ladino me jodió: Vida de un indígena.* Guatemala: Editorial "José de Pineda Ibarra."

Schaefer-Rodríguez, Claudia. 1985. "Peace, Poetry, and Popular Culture: Ernesto Cardenal and the Nicaraguan Revolution." *Latin American Theatre Review* (July–December 1985): 7–15.

Schneider, Michael. 1985. "Central American Poetry: An Introductory Essay." Unpublished MA paper, University of Pittsburgh.

Scully, James. 1981. "Afterword." In Roque Dalton, *Poetry and Militancy in Latin America.* Willimantic, Conn.: Curbstone.

Selser, Gregorio. 1978. *Sandino, general de hombres libres.* Mexico: Editorial Diógenes. (1st ed. 1957.)

Sexton, James, and Ignacio Bizarro Ujpan. 1981. *Son of Tecún Umán: A Maya Indian Tells His Life Story.* Tucson: University of Arizona Press.

———. 1985. *Campesino: The Diary of a Guatemalan Indian.* Tucson: University of Arizona Press.

Sierra, Luis. 1975. "Introducción." José Luis Villatoro, *Pedro a secas.* Guatemala: Editorial José de Pineda Ibarra.

Smith, Carol. 1987. "Culture and Community: The Language of Class in Guatemala." In Mike Davis et al., eds., *The Year Left 2.* London: Verso, 197–217.

Smith, Carol, and Jeff Boyer. 1987. "Central America since 1979." *Annual Review of Anthropology* 16 (1987): 197–221.

Solá, Roser, and María Pau Trayner. 1988. *Ser madre en Nicaragua. Testimonios de una historia no escrita.* Barcelona: Icaria.

Solórzano, Valentín. 1985. *El relato de Juan Tayín: la vida de un indio guatemalteco.* Mexico: Costa-Amic Editores.

Spivak, Gayatri. 1988. "Can the Subaltern Speak?" In Cary Nelson and Lawrence Grossberg, eds. *Marxism and the Interpretation of Culture.* Urbana: University of Illinois Press, 271–313.

Taussig, Michael. 1987. *Shamanism, Colonialism, and the Wild Man. A Study in Terror and Healing.* Chicago and London: University of Chicago Press.

Testimonies from the Peasants of El Petén. 1981. Detroit: Latin American Task Force.

Tijerino, Doris María. 1975. *Somos millones.* n.p.

Tijerino, Doris María, with Margaret Randall. 1977. *"Somos millones . . ." La vida de Doris María, combatiente nicaragüense.* Mexico: Editorial Extemporáneos.

Tijerino, Doris María, with Margaret Randall. 1978. *Doris Tijerino. Inside the Nicaraguan Revolution.* Translated by Elinor Randall. Vancouver, B.C.: New Star Books.

Torres-Rivas, Edelberto. 1968. *Interpretación del desarrollo social latinoamericano: procesos y estructuras de una sociedad dependiente.* San José: EDUCA.

———. 1981. *Crisis del poder en Centroamérica.* San José: EDUCA.

———. 1984. "Central America Today: A Study in Regional Dependency." In M. Diskin, ed., *Trouble in Our Backyard.* New York: Pantheon, 1–34.

———. 1985. "El estado contra la sociedad: Las raíces de la revolución nicaragüense." In J. Labastida, ed., *Hegemonía y alternativas políticas en América Latina.* Mexico: Siglo XXI, 425–443.

Toruño, Juan Felipe. 1958. *Desarrollo literario de El Salvador.* San Salvador: Ministerio de Cultura.

Tünnerman, Carlos. 1980. *Pensamiento universitario centroamericano.* San José: EDUCA.

Urdanivia Bertarelli, Eduardo. 1984. *La poesía de Ernesto Cardenal: Cristianismo y revolución.* Lima: Latinoamérica Editores.

Uriarte, Iván. 1980. *La poesía de Ernesto Cardenal en el contexto histórico-social centroamericano.* Unpublished PhD diss., University of Pittsburgh.

Urtecho, Alvaro. 1983 "El humanismo erótico de Gioconda Belli." *Ventana* III, 104 (February 12).

Valdés, Jorge. 1983. "The Evolution of Cardenal's Prophetic Poetry." *Latin American Literary Review* 23 (Fall–Winter): 25–40.

Valle, Rafael Heliodoro. 1960. *Historia de las ideas contemporáneas en Centro América.* Mexico: Fondo de Cultura Económica.

Valle-Castillo, Julio, ed. 1979. *Los modernistas nicaragüenses.* Caracas: Biblioteca Ayacucho.

———, ed. 1981–1986. *Poesía libre.* 18 vols. Managua: Ministerio de Cultura.

———. 1986. *Materia jubilosa* (anthology). Managua: Editorial Nueva Nicaragua.

Vidal, Hernán. 1976. *Literatura hispanoamericana e ideología liberal: surgimiento y crisis.* Buenos Aires: Hispamérica.

Vidal, Hernán, and René Jara, eds. 1986. *Testimonio y literatura.* Minneapolis: Institute for the Study of Ideologies and Literature.

Vidal, Hernán, with Ronald Sousa and Marc Zimmerman, eds. 1984/85. *Literature and Contemporary Revolutionary Culture, I.* Minneapolis: Society for the Study of Contemporary Hispanic and Lusophone Revolutionary Literatures.

————. 1985. *Socio-historia de la literatura colonial hispanoamericana.* Minneapolis: Institute for the Study of Ideologies and Literature.

Vilas, Carlos. 1986. *The Sandinista Revolution. National Liberation and Social Transformation in Central America.* Translated by Judy Butler. New York: Monthly Review Press.

————. 1989. "Revolutionary Unevenness in Central America." *New Left Review* 175: 111–125.

Vilas, Carlos, and Richard Harris, eds. 1985. *Nicaragua: A Revolution under Siege.* London: Zed Books.

Villatoro, José Luis. 1968. *Pedro a secas.* Guatemala: Nuevo Signo.

Voices of the Survivors: The Massacre at the Finca San Francisco. 1983. Cambridge, Mass.: Cultural Survival and Anthropology Resource Center.

Walker, Thomas, ed. 1985. *Nicaragua: The First Five Years.* New York: Praeger.

Wellings, Klaus W. 1989. *Nueva cultura nicaragüense (debate sobre el realismo).* Buenos Aires: Libros de Utopias del Sur.

Wheelock, Jaime. 1979. *Diciembre victorioso.* Managua: Secretaría Nacional de Propaganda y Educación Política del FSLN.

Whisnant, David. 1988. "Sandinista Cultural Policy: Notes towards an Analysis in Historical Context." In Ralph Lee Woodward, ed. *Central America: Historical Perspectives on the Contemporary Crisis.* Westport, Conn.: Greenwood Press, 169–191.

————. 1989. "La vida nos ha enseñado: Rigoberta Menchú y la dialéctica de la cultura tradicional." *Ideologies and Literature* 4:1 (Spring): 317–344.

White, Steven, ed. 1982. *Poets of Nicaragua. A Bilingual Anthology, 1918–1979.* Greensboro, N.C.: Unicorn Press.

————. 1986. *Culture and Politics: Testimonies of Poets and Writers.* New York: Lumen Press.

Williams, Robert. 1986. *Export Agriculture and the Crisis in Central America.* Chapel Hill: University of North Carolina Press.

Witnesses to Genocide: The Present Situation of Indians in Guatemala. 1983. London: Survival International.

Woodward, Ralph Lee, ed. 1988. *Central America: Historical Perspectives on the Contemporary Crisis.* Westport, Conn.: Greenwood.

Yanes, Gabriela, Manuel Sorto, Horacio Castellanos Moya, and Lyn Sorto, eds. 1985. *Mirrors of War. Literature and Revolution in El Salvador.* Translated by Keith Ellis. New York: Monthly Review Press.

Yúdice, George. 1985a. "Central American Testimonial." Unpublished manuscript. (Forthcoming in *Latin American Perspectives.*)

————. 1985b. "Letras de emergencia: Claribel Alegría." *Revista Iberoamericana* 51: 53–64.

————. 1988. "¿Se puede hablar de posmodernidad en América Latina?" *Revista de Crítica Literaria Latinoamericana*: 105–128.

Zamora, Daisy. 1981. "La mujer nicaragüense en la literatura." *Plural* (September): 19–25.

————, ed. 1982. *Hacia una política cultural de la revolución popular sandinista*. Managua: Ministerio de Cultura.

————. 1983. *La espuma violenta*. Managua: Editorial Nueva Nicaragua.

————. 1988. *En limpio se escribe la vida*. Managua: Editorial Nueva Nicaragua.

————. 1989. *La mujer nicaragüense en la poesía (antología)*. Unpublished manuscript.

Zepeda, Eraclio. 1988. "Casi un prólogo." In Roque Dalton, *Taberna y otros lugares*. Mexico: La Letra Editores.

Zimmerman, Marc. 1980. "Pablo Antonio Cuadra y Leonel Rugama: dos poetas, dos poéticas, dos políticas." *Taller* 16 (1980): 27–39.

————. 1982. "Françoise Perus and the Interventions of Althusser in Latin America." *Praxis* 6 (1982): 156–176.

————. 1983. "The Unity of Caribbean Literature." In I. Rodríguez and M. Zimmerman, eds., *Process of Unity in Caribbean Society, Ideologies and Literatures*. Minneapolis: Institute for the Study of Ideologies and Literature: 28–56.

————, ed. 1985. *Nicaragua in Reconstruction and at War: The People Speak*. Minneapolis: MEP.

————, ed. 1988a. *El Salvador at War: A Collage Epic*. Minneapolis: MEP.

————. 1988b. "Introduction." Ernesto Cardenal, *Flights of Victory/Vuelos de Victoria*. Willimantic, Conn.: Curbstone.

Zimmerman, Marc, with Bridget Aldaraca, Edward Baker, and Ileana Rodríguez, eds. 1980. *Nicaragua in Revolution: The Poets Speak*. Minneapolis: MEP.

Index